# 8 ESSENTIALS FOR EMPOWERED TEACHING & LEARNING K–8

*To Mom, Dad, Lynn, Alan, Jeff, Ari, Jordy, and
all the family, friends, teachers, and students
whose support, expertise, and encouragement made this book possible*

# 8 ESSENTIALS FOR

# EMPOWERED

# TEACHING & LEARNING

## K–8

BRINGING OUT THE
**BEST**
IN YOUR STUDENTS

# STEVE REIFMAN

Skyhorse Publishing, Inc.

Copyright © 2008 by Corwin Press.
First Skyhorse Publishing edition 2018

Skyhorse Publishing books may be purchased in bulk at special discounts
for sales promotion, corporate gifts, fund-raising, or educational purposes.
Special  editions can also be created to specifications. For details, contact
the Special Sales Department, Sky Pony Press, 307 West 36th Street, 11th
Floor, New York, NY 10018 or info@skyhorsepublishing.com.

Skyhorse® and Skyhorse Publishing® are registered trademark of Skyhorse
Publishing, Inc.®, a Delaware corporation.

Visit our website at www.skyhorsepublishing.com.

10 9 8 7 6 5 4 3 2 1

Library of Congress Cataloging-in-Publication Data is available on file.

Cover design by Scott Van Atta

Print ISBN: 978-1-51073-695-5
Ebook ISBN: 978-1-51073-701-3

Printed in the United States of America

# CONTENTS

# LIST OF FIGURES

# ESSENTIAL 4

# ESSENTIAL 5

# ESSENTIAL 6

## ESSENTIAL 7

## ESSENTIAL 8

# ACKNOWLEDGMENTS

 am extremely grateful for the time, effort, energy, and assistance that so many have given to make this book a reality.

- To Carol Collins, Brett Ory, Gem Rabanera, Faye Zucker, Veronica Stapleton, Tina Hardy, and everyone else at Corwin Press who contributed to the production of this book.

- To Shanie Fink, Andy Hecht, and Mike Travers, the three original readers of this book, who provided invaluable feedback.

- To Dr. David Sands, who, while sitting next to me on a flight from Cancun, Mexico, to Los Angeles, California, saw my manuscript, picked it up, and read it from cover to cover in one sitting. Your interest in and support of my project mean a great deal to me.

- To Mervat Fam, Judith Estanislao, and the rest of the Education Department at UCLA Extension for supporting the course that enabled me to field test the ideas that comprise the foundation of this book.

- To all the dedicated professionals in my extension classes at UCLA, whose creativity and feedback helped me strengthen the ideas that would become the Eight Essentials for Empowered Teaching and Learning.

- To Amy Argento, Viola Callanen, Jillian Esby, and Darlene Fish for their support of this project and for their classroom vignettes.

- To Larry Greene, whose encouragement and expertise made the publication of this book possible.

- To Jim Braley for going above and beyond the call of duty on numerous occasions in providing technical support for this project.

- To Lorie Alexander for her ideas, enthusiasm, and friendship.

- To Eric Meyerowitz, whose efforts and architectural skills helped bring the Tower of Opportunity to life.

- To W. Edwards Deming, Stephen Covey, Theodore Sizer, Howard Gardner, William Glasser, Lee Jenkins, Alfie Kohn, and the many other experts cited in this book for inspiring me to be the best teacher I can be.

- To Paul Kingston, my professor at the University of Virginia, who taught the "Sociology of Education" course during my final semester that sparked my interest in becoming a teacher.

- Finally, to all of my former teachers who had such a strong influence on my development as a student and as a person.

Corwin Press thanks the following reviewers for their contribution to this book:

C. M. Charles
Emeritus Professor
San Diego State University
San Diego, CA

Julie Duford
5th Grade Teacher
Polson Middle School
Polson, MT

Launa Ellison
5th/6th Grade Teacher
Clara Barton School
Minneapolis, MN

Debbie Halcomb
4th Grade Teacher
Robert W. Combs Elementary School
Cornettsville, KY

Joanna Hicks
Humanities Teacher
Liberty Charter High School
Melba, ID

Karen Kersey
2nd Grade Teacher
Albans Elementary School
St. Albans, WV

Kate Kinnan
6th Grade Teacher
Junction City Middle School
Manhattan, KS

Laurie McDonald
Teacher
Duval County School District
Jacksonville Beach, FL

Wendy Miner
Assistant Professor of Education
Truman State University
Kirksville, MO

Cathy Sasaki-White
Elementary School Teacher
Thomas Jefferson Charter School
Caldwell, ID

Gary Willhite
KDP Co-counselor
Reading and Language Studies
Southern Illinois University
Carbondale, IL

# ABOUT THE AUTHOR

**Steve Reifman** has been an elementary school teacher for the past 14 years. During that time he has earned National Board Certification, traveled to Japan as a Fulbright Memorial Fund Scholar, and completed two master's degrees. He has experience working with students in all of the elementary grade levels, and he has taught in both public and private schools. Currently, Steve teaches third grade at Roosevelt Elementary School in Santa Monica, California.

Ever since reading William Glasser's *The Quality School* (1990) at the beginning of his career, his primary interest has been the field of quality control. Steve has read extensively in this area, created and led numerous professional development courses, and attended many conferences and workshops. Specifically, the focus of his work in the classroom has involved defining quality in student-friendly terms, measuring it, and creating the conditions where all students are empowered to reach their full potential and appreciate the joy of learning. The author can be reached at sreifman@verizon.net.

# INTRODUCTION

F ollowing the devastation of World War II, the people of Japan faced an uncertain economic future. The tiny island nation, already hampered by a lack of natural resources and an international reputation for producing shoddy goods, now had to overcome the destruction of its industrial base. Prospects for a strong recovery looked bleak: survival was the immediate goal. In the years to come, however, the Japanese people would do more than just survive; they would achieve perhaps the greatest economic turnaround in modern history.

Ironically, the individual widely credited with initiating the Japanese postwar transformation was an American. His name was W. Edwards Deming. Born in 1900, Deming was trained in mathematics, physics, and engineering, earning his PhD from Yale University in 1928. While working as a statistician for the U.S. Census Bureau in the 1930s, he first received notoriety pioneering the use of sampling techniques in the gathering of data. Under Deming's leadership, the bureau won recognition for its ability to provide accurate information on a broad range of areas at a cost that no other organization, public or private, could match. Deming's successes earned him an invitation to Japan in the summer of 1950 to meet with top business leaders who were determined to revitalize their nation.

On arriving in Japan, Deming insisted that producing high quality goods was the key to the nation's future. Improving quality, as the chain reaction that follows illustrates, leads to greater productivity due to a decrease in costs and a better use of machine time and materials.[1] With the resulting higher quality, lower priced goods, companies capture the market, enabling them to stay in business and employ more people. As the chain reaction reverberates throughout society, the number of jobs grows and the entire standard of living rises. Citizens live more comfortably, and workers take more pride in their efforts. In this situation, according to Deming, everybody wins.

Deming contended that if business leaders followed his teachings, Japanese products would become the envy of the world. His declaration that Japanese industry could shed its poor manufacturing reputation and achieve economic prosperity within five years shocked his audiences. Although the leaders dared not to believe such rapid progress was possible, they were receptive to Deming's hopeful message. They listened intently, spending the next few years learning and implementing his theory. Ultimately, though, Deming's prediction proved to be inaccurate. It didn't take five years for the Japanese to turn out top quality goods. It took four.[2]

Deming's teachings would later become known as the "Fourteen Points of Quality," a set of integrated principles that provides a comprehensive framework for reform. The Fourteen Points constitute a broad prescription for quality improvement, not a rigid series of steps or a prepackaged recipe for success. Each Japanese company, therefore, implemented Deming's

**Figure 0.1** The Deming Chain Reaction

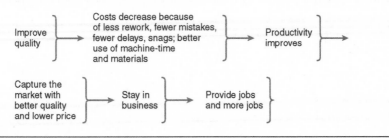

SOURCE: W. Edwards Deming.

teachings somewhat differently, adapting the points to address unique needs. Although each organization launched its own distinct improvement effort, none operated in isolation. Deming urged cooperation among Japanese businesses, including competitors, so that they could learn from and assist one another. He explained that for national prosperity to occur, all of Japan must work together to implement his teachings, not just one group of companies. "This movement must be a prairie fire," he proclaimed, blazing through the entire nation.[3]

A similar prairie fire must now blaze through the educational landscape in the United States. It must engulf all our schools, not just some. For too long, education in America has carried the same unfavorable reputation that plagued Japanese manufacturing prior to Deming's arrival. But, as history has proven, a reputation for poor quality does not have to be permanent.

A prairie fire of our own will set off a new chain reaction. The chain, as the following figure indicates, begins with a focus on producing quality work. Focusing on quality enables students to develop and internalize effective habits of mind and habits of character, patterns of behavior that are essential to success in school and beyond. Students who commit to this cause will mature into adults who are able to care for themselves and those around them and who are able to look outward and make meaningful contributions to society. Focusing on quality during their school years will ultimately empower future generations with the knowledge, skills, and habits to lead quality lives and help others. Again, everybody wins.

Deming's work with the Japanese shows that stunning progress is possible if leaders focus attention in the right places. In Japan, business leaders did not revitalize industry by pressing for a longer workday, tougher and more frequent evaluations of employees, and smaller factory sizes. They did not look to place blame. Instead, they focused on a holistic set of principles designed to help managers and workers perform their jobs better.

In America, the time has come for educational leaders to focus attention on helping teachers and students perform their jobs better. Until we establish a set of principles to guide teachers in their interactions with students, it will not matter how long children attend school each day, how often or how rigorously they are tested, or how many classmates they have. The principles responsible for revitalizing Japanese industry following World War II hold the same promise for improving America's schools at the start of the 21st century.

**Figure 0.2**   The Educational Chain Reaction

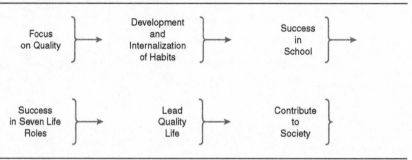

Make no mistake, however, this book is not an argument that schools should be transformed into businesses. Schools are not businesses. Schools do not manufacture products, students are not "workers," and the objective of education is not to earn a profit. Rather, this is a book about a set of principles. They are not *business* principles, but *quality* principles that have been successfully applied to business and that have only recently begun finding their way into our schools. Leaders of any organization where people work together cooperatively in the pursuit of quality will benefit from Deming's ideas, whether they be Little League coaches, orchestra conductors, or classroom teachers.

*Eight Essentials for Empowered Teaching and Learning, K–8,* an educational application of the Fourteen Points, offers teachers an introduction to Dr. Deming's philosophy. While it also draws from the work of other important minds, this book, above all, embraces the substance and spirit of Deming's teachings. The focus is on the classroom setting, where teachers and students work together on a daily basis to prepare for the future. The chapters include dozens of classroom examples, illustrating how to bring these principles to life for the betterment of children. Deming, a long-time teacher himself at Columbia and New York University, cared deeply about education. This book is meant to honor him and to contribute, in some small way, to what will hopefully be the next great quality revolution, American education.

# Essential 1 ESTABLISHING A SENSE OF PURPOSE

At the age of seven, I began my Little League baseball career as a member of the Yankees. (Our green shirts had no pinstripes, but they called us the Yankees nonetheless.) My teammates and I practiced one afternoon a week to prepare for the Saturday morning games. We spent our practice time working on the skills that would help us play better in the games. We ran around the bases, hit balls off the batting tee, and caught pop flies. Even though we were young, my teammates and I quickly grasped the purpose and importance of every practice activity. A clear connection existed between what we did in practice and what we would need to do in a game. The coach didn't have to take much time explaining these connections because we could figure them out for ourselves.

Think about other organized activities in which children participate. At band practice, for example, musicians understand why they need to rehearse. They know that rehearsing is important because at a later date the group will perform its songs to a live audience. Again, the connection between today's preparation and tomorrow's performance is straightforward. Young actors in a drama club are also aware of this relationship.

Curiously, the organized activity that occupies more of a child's waking hours than any other, school, is the one where the purposes of attending each day are the least well understood by its participants. What are the purposes of attending school? Most students answer that they come to school to learn. But when pressed further, they are often unable to articulate compelling reasons why learning is important. Some students mention that they need to learn "to get a good job" or "to get into a good college." Rarely, though, does a child express that learning adds quality to our lives, that it enables us to contribute to the lives of others, that it maximizes our options later in life, and that the development of the mind is a joy and benefit in and of itself.

The larger purposes of education are not as obvious as those of Little League, band, or drama club. As a result, children have greater difficulty discovering on their own what these purposes are.

As teachers, it is our responsibility to establish a sense of purpose with our students so they know why it's important to come to school every day and so they understand how learning can benefit them now and in the future. Raising this issue helps children connect what they learn in the classroom to their own lives. When educators neglect to discuss the worthwhile purposes of attending school, students frequently fail to see meaning in their work and lack the motivation to persevere when challenged. There is no more important, no more fundamental question a teacher can pose to students than, "Why are we here?" We can't assume that they already know.

Establishing a sense of purpose is a process that requires an investment of time and energy. The process must start during the first few days of a new school year because what occurs in our classrooms at this time sets the tone for the months ahead. Taking the time to establish purpose promotes the creation of a productive work environment, a necessary precondition of quality learning. But students can only work with a sense of purpose when their teachers have established a sense of purpose.

## THE OVERALL AIM

The process of establishing purpose begins on a general level with the introduction of the classroom aim. The aim is the overall objective you and your students work to accomplish. The first brick in the foundation of a quality classroom, the aim begins to answer the question, "Why are we here?" Once introduced, the aim pervades every aspect of class functioning, driving decisions and determining goals.

Following the 1994–1995 school year, the Enterprise School District in Redding, California, became one of the first districts in the nation to adopt an aim. Many factors led to this decision. During the three years preceding adoption of the aim, Enterprise had conducted a yearly attitude survey, in which students, K–8, expressed their feelings about each subject they studied. A happy face meant students liked a subject, a neutral face meant ambivalence, and a sad face meant the students disliked a subject.

The data shown in Figure 1.1 enabled district staff to compare the percentage of happy faces by grade level for each year of the survey.[1] In his book *Improving Student Learning*, Enterprise Superintendent Lee Jenkins (1997) comments that "the data clearly show that each grade level contributed to the loss of enthusiasm. The loss is gradual, slow, and continual."[2] To heighten awareness of this decline, Jenkins makes the point that if 30 kindergartners enter school together, and 2 children per year lose their enthusiasm for learning, then only a handful would still be enthusiastic as they finish high school.[3]

Jenkins believes that teachers are responsible for both learning and enthusiasm. He considers student enthusiasm to be an invaluable asset that educators must cherish. Students who have lost their enthusiasm for learning are less motivated to learn, less likely to put their learning to use in creative ways, and more likely to cause discipline problems. Jenkins contends that typical kindergartners have enough enthusiasm to last a lifetime, but they don't have all the knowledge. Educators, he stresses, must guard this enthusiasm, must protect it throughout a child's academic career. It is a school's most precious resource.

Dr. Deming's proposed aim for education also influenced the Enterprise School District's decision. In 1992 Deming suggested that the overall aim for education be the following: "Increase the positives and decrease the negatives so that all students keep their yearning for learning." He believed that if educators preserved students' love of learning by removing the practices that decrease enthusiasm and spread those that foster it, more students would succeed in school.[4]

In response to both the survey data and Deming's proposal, the staff of the Enterprise School District wrote and adopted the following aim: "Maintain enthusiasm while increasing learning." Jenkins remarks, "Orchestrating classrooms so that all students progress in learning and maintain their enthusiasm for learning is an incredible challenge. It is, however, the responsibility of educators to maintain enthusiasm while increasing learning. We must not allow ourselves to stray from this path."[5]

After learning of the pioneering work done by the Enterprise District, I decided to adopt a classroom aim for the 1997–1998 school year. Rather than adopt Enterprise's aim verbatim, however, I chose to modify it. I felt the word *maintain* was ineffective for three reasons. First,

**Figure 1.1**   Enterprise School District 1992–1995 Attitude Survey Results

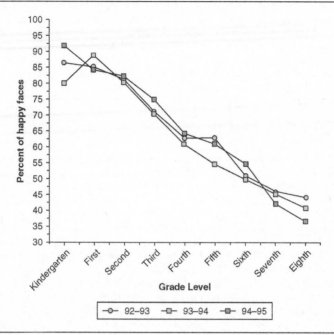

SOURCE: Reprinted with permission from *Improving Student Learning,* ASQ Quality Press © 1997 American Society for Quality.

once students lose enthusiasm for a subject, there is nothing left to maintain, and the term no longer applies. In this situation, restoring enthusiasm becomes the goal. Second, if students already enjoy a subject, there's no reason why they can't enjoy it more. I wished to achieve more than maintenance. At the end of the year, I wanted students to like each subject more than they did at the beginning. Third, the pursuit of quality demands a commitment to continuous improvement. It is not enough simply to maintain *anything*. Successful teachers constantly look for ways to make every aspect of classroom life better. Nothing is already at such a high level that we can settle for maintenance. Because of these reasons, I needed a stronger, more aggressive word than maintain. Therefore, I adopted the following aim: "Increasing learning while increasing enthusiasm." I have maintained this aim ever since.

An aim provides focus and direction. It states what you consider to be your very highest priorities. In my case, the aim declares that learning and enthusiasm are inseparable entities and that our success as a classroom community depends on increasing both. Furthermore, our aim is brief, making it easy for students to memorize and, ultimately, internalize. Students will even become eager to contribute toward the realization of this aim because they will appreciate being in a class where the teacher truly wants them to enjoy the learning process. In addition, the aim helps students discover two reasons why they attend school: (1) to learn and (2) to *love* learning. Dr. Deming once said that a successful teacher is one whose students are more interested in learning about a subject at the end of the year than they were at the beginning. With an aim in place to guide us, we create an opportunity for ourselves to meet this challenge.

An aim doesn't have to focus exclusively on the concepts of learning and enthusiasm. You may find that your highest priorities include other emphases. For example, prior to the 1998–1999 school year, a group of teachers at Anderson School in Lawndale, California, decided to incorporate the idea of service into their aim to highlight the importance of helping others. They adopted the following aim: "Increasing learning while increasing enthusiasm and service." Whichever concepts you choose to include in your aim, limit yourself to the two or three with the broadest application and the greatest strength. You don't want your aim to be a laundry list that nobody can remember. Less is more.

## CLASS MISSION STATEMENT

Developing an aim is only the beginning of the journey to establish a sense of purpose with students. Jenkins describes the aim as the "bull's-eye of the organizational target."[6] If the aim represents the center of the target, then the ring surrounding the bull's-eye is the class mission statement.

A mission statement is an organization's formal statement of purpose. According to Stephen Covey, author of *The Seven Habits of Highly Effective People* (1989) and *First Things First* (1994), mission statements "capture what you want to be and what you want to do . . . and the principles upon which being and doing are based."[7] Alan Blankstein, author of *Failure is Not an Option*, adds, "The mission of an organization is essential to its success. A mission statement should be created and published as a means of giving those involved with the organization a clear understanding of its purpose for existence." (p. 66) A class mission statement picks up where the aim leaves off, further developing your high priority ideas and supplementing them with others that identify yours as a unique group. The document enables students to see themselves not just as individuals, but also as "contributing parts to a greater whole."[8] Developing the mission statement provides individuals with an opportunity "to envision ways their combined talents and energies can make a difference."[9]

Begin the process of creating your class mission statement by discussing the word *mission*. I have found that kids more easily understand the term when I introduce it as part of the phrase "on a mission." I tell them that when people are on a mission, they are determined to accomplish something important. I accompany my definition with examples of historical figures, athletes, and other well-known individuals who were determined to accomplish important things, names such as Martin Luther King, Jr.; Susan B. Anthony; and Michael Jordan. Next, I ask students to share personal stories of when they have been on a mission. I then explain that when groups of people come together to work as a team, they frequently create something called a mission statement to express the important things that they want to accomplish.

Once the students know that they will compose a class mission statement, ask them to answer the following questions:

Who are we?

Why is it important to come to school to learn?

What are we determined to accomplish together?

What kind of class do we want to be?

What do we have to do each day to make it happen?

The kids will later draw on their responses to these questions when they create the first draft of the class mission statement. Having the kids work in groups to answer these questions in class produces many rich conversations and wonderful ideas, but I prefer to use this as a homework activity so that the kids can discuss the project with their parents. Sending the questions home with the kids accomplishes the following: (1) It gets parents and children talking about fundamental issues that are too often left undiscussed, (2) it involves parents early in the school year in a meaningful project and shows them that you value their participation in the educational process, and (3) it greatly increases the likelihood that the kids will generate high quality, thoughtful responses.

After the kids have answered these questions, move on to the next step of the activity. Show the kids actual corporate and organizational mission statements to familiarize them with the format and substance of this type of writing. At the end of the chapter, I have included several examples for you to share. You can find others at local stores and restaurants. Emphasize to your kids that groups of people create these documents to describe who they are and what they want to become.

As you read through these examples with your class, chart or highlight the words and phrases that the kids think would be appropriate for a classroom mission statement. For example, take a look at the Noah's Bagels Mission Statement shown in Figure 1.2.

Analyzing mission statements to locate suitable words teaches students the power of language. From the Noah's Bagels example, the kids will likely suggest that you chart words such as fun, fair, honest, friendly, and supportive. The words your students choose and the way they phrase ideas will determine the overall effectiveness of the class statement. Look, for example, at the last stanza of the Noah's Bagels document. Notice that it doesn't say, "To be a pretty good bagel company." It reads, "To be the best bagel company in America!" The words used here carry high expectations. It is important for students to see that and to carry this spirit of high expectations to their own mission statement.

After charting words from each of the examples, you and your class now have a second source of ideas for the class mission statement. Now, it is time for the kids, working either alone or in small groups, to use both the charted words and the answers to the five homework questions to begin drafting the class mission statement. I give my students three choices as to how they wish to contribute to the drafting process. I believe it is appropriate

**Figure 1.2**    Noah's Bagels Mission Statement

Noah's Bagels strives in
all words and actions:
To create a fun, supportive,
and fair work environment;
To provide friendly, personal
service to our customers;
To ensure the highest standards
of product quality;
To be fair, honest, and considerate
in our relationships with our suppliers;
To be an active and
positive force
in the communities
where we do business; and
To be the best bagel
company in America!

to differentiate the process at this point due to variations in students' readiness and in their overall comfort level with this type of project.

Encourage your most ambitious students to try to write a complete class mission statement. These two- to three-paragraph efforts should address all five of the previously mentioned questions and include many of the words and phrases you charted. Kids who undertake this challenge, however, should also include thoughts and ideas of their own. Nobody should feel bound or constrained by these other two sets of ideas. Sometimes, the sentences that best convey the mission of the class are those that students create all by themselves.

Students who may not feel confident or comfortable enough to create an entire mission statement can still make an equally valuable contribution to the project by choosing one of the other two drafting alternatives. With both of these options, the students should still draw from their responses to the five questions, the charted words, and their own imaginations. Kids who choose the first option should list individual words that they want to see in the final class statement; those selecting the second should write individual phrases and sentences. The latter two options can also be combined, affording students the opportunity to write individual words and short phrases. A final possibility allows kids to begin by listing words and then follow up by connecting pairs of words to form short phrases. For example, if a child listed the words *achieve* and *quality,* she could then draw a line connecting them, thus creating the phrase *achieve quality.*

Regardless of which option the kids choose, the students should feel no pressure—there is no right or wrong. This time is simply an opportunity for each child to offer input as to how the final statement will read. Motivation will be high as the kids work seriously to craft a class statement. Your students will appreciate the chance to do something they view as "adult."

The last step in the missioning process requires you, the teacher, to read the drafts and combine them into a formal class statement. You will notice from the students' papers that several major themes recur. In the final draft include these commonly expressed ideas as well as any outstanding words, phrases, or sentences that appear only once or twice.

Creating the final draft is not an easy task. At first, you may find yourself with a mission statement that is 15 pages long because you didn't want to leave out anyone's input, or you may not know where to start because you see so many fine ideas spread out in front of you. Use the following criteria, offered by Covey, to guide you.[10]

Effective mission statements should

1. Be clear and understandable to all team members

2. Be brief enough to keep in mind (two to three paragraphs at most)

3. Be focused yet flexible

4. Excite people into action

5. Focus on worthwhile purposes

Enlarge and laminate the final statement so that it can occupy a prominent place on the front wall and front door of your classroom for the entire year. The first time you read it with the class, you will notice something special occur. Because you took the time to have the kids answer the same five questions, charted words from the same sample statements, and provided the opportunity for the students to incorporate these words into their own drafts, *every* single child will be able to look at some part of the final version and say, "I had that" or "That word came from mine" or "That sentence was from mine." This creates shared ownership. There is a realization that everyone contributed to the final draft. As Covey puts it, "The process changes us. It changes our relationships with others who are part of it."[11] "It bonds people together. It gives them a sense of unity and purpose that provides great strength in times of challenge."[12]

The class mission statements that my students and I created for both the 1996–1997 and 1997–1998 school years are shown in Figures 1.3 and 1.4, respectively. As you read through them, keep a few points in mind. First, we have maintained a tight connection with our overall aim. Our 1997–1998 mission statement, for example, emphasizes the importance of being "enthusiastic learners" as well as the importance of learning itself. The aim, once again, provides the main focus. The mission statement expands on the two concepts contained in the aim and expresses other worthwhile ambitions.

Second, both statements establish several purposes for coming to school. In the 1996–1997 statement, for example, our class declares, "We come to school every day determined to work for the highest quality education possible." In the following paragraph, we explain why putting forth this effort is important. "We learn because it makes our lives better. We understand that our education will go to good use in the future, helping us get good jobs, do well later in school, and reach our goals in life." These sentences establish the purposes that we are serving in school, but they also recognize the fact that all of us may have different purposes. We may all want different jobs, have different educational plans for the future, and have different goals in life. But we have articulated, as a group, a variety of reasons why we need to come to school for an education. This section of our statement is, as Covey recommends, focused yet flexible.

Finally, both mission statements emphasize the importance of a productive classroom environment. Teachers cannot force learning and enthusiasm to happen. With our students, however, we can create the conditions where these entities will thrive. Learning and enthusiasm will flourish in an atmosphere of teamwork, trust, respect, caring, and honesty. Students contribute to this cause by being attentive listeners, helpful team members, and effective decision makers. They further strengthen the learning environment by trying their best and never giving up, by committing themselves to continuous improvement, and by taking full responsibility for their actions. Thoroughly discussing these crucial ideas and codifying them in a mission statement ensures that they will occupy a prominent position in classroom conversations throughout the year.

**Figure 1.3**　　Class Mission Statement, 1996–1997

---

*We are Team 1011.[13] We have high hopes for our class. We create an environment of teamwork, honesty, trust, caring, and respect. We come to school every day determined to work for the highest quality education possible.*

*We learn because it makes our lives better. We understand that our education will go to good use in the future, helping us get good jobs, do well later in school, and reach our goals in life. We try our best and never give up. We recognize the importance of continuous improvement, taking pride in our work, and enjoying the learning process.*

*We are hard workers, attentive listeners, good decision-makers, and organized students. We are all teachers and all learners. We are bright kids who always use our best ideas and behavior. We deserve all the responsibility we can handle. We are good role models for the younger students. We keep our room sparkling clean.*

**Figure 1.4**    Class Mission Statement, 1997–1998

---

*We are Team 1011. Together we strive to be the best students we can be. We are an extraordinary class with high expectations. We create an environment of trust, caring, teamwork, respect, friendship, and honesty.*

*We are determined to achieve the highest quality education possible so that we can accomplish our goals in life, become better people, and help others. We are attentive listeners, enthusiastic learners, and hard workers. We are fantastic role models for both younger and older students. We will never stop learning and never stop teaching.*

*We are obsessed with continuous improvement. We commit ourselves to becoming organized, helpful, disciplined, and cooperative students. We take pride in our work. We try our best and never give up. We are responsible for all the actions we take. We take full responsibility for keeping our room sparkling clean.*

---

The missioning process produces a powerful founding document. The statement now "becomes the constitution, the criteria for decision making in the group."[14] Its words will guide us throughout the school year, helping to keep everyone focused on what it is we are here to accomplish. It is our map that shows us the way in times of trouble and uncertainty. Blankstein refers to the mission as the group's "polestar," and writes, "just as a ship sails toward but never actually reaches its guiding star, we too strive toward but never actually fulfill our mission." (p. 72) Our mission statement establishes our identity as a unique group of people with a unique sense of purpose. It reminds us of the combined actions we need to take if we are to live up to the high expectations we set for ourselves.

A mission statement represents an ideal. Your class will have to make a concerted, consistent effort to bring this ideal to life. None of your aspirations will happen automatically. Each student must do his or her part each day—quality is everyone's responsibility. The mission statement cannot just be words on a piece of paper. For a class to realize its mission, the ideas contained therein must live in the hearts and minds of all group members. As Covey notes, these lofty ideas must constantly be translated from the mission to the moment.[15]

In addition, your class mission statement provides students with something to say "Yes" to:

"Yes, I want to reach my goals in life."

"Yes, I want to do well later in school."

"Yes, I will try my best and never give up."

"Yes, I will be a good role model for younger students."

"Yes, I want to learn so I can help others."

According to Austrian psychologist Victor Frankl, a survivor of the concentration camps of Nazi Germany, this future-oriented vision, this compelling, deep-burning "Yes!" was the primary force that kept many prisoners alive despite the unbearable conditions they encountered.[16] "Empowering mission statements [that] focus on contribution, on worthwhile purposes . . . create [this] collective deep-burning 'Yes!'"[17] This point is especially significant for children whom we are constantly telling to say no: no to drugs, no to alcohol, no to cigarettes, and no to sex. Telling them to say no is not enough. Children will only find it satisfying to say no to these temptations when they have a powerful, positive, future-oriented vision in their lives that provides them with something to say yes *to*.

# THE SEVEN LIFE ROLES

With the classroom aim and mission statement firmly in place, it is now our responsibility to show students how the work they do each day contributes to the fulfillment of that mission. According to Dale Parnell, author of *Why Do I Have to Learn This?* "The major task of the teacher [is] to broaden students' perceptions so that meaning becomes visible and the purpose of learning immediately understandable. It is not enough to help students see the specific objectives of a lesson or even of an overall course. Instead, teachers must help students understand the larger meaning of a particular study—how it relates to real-life issues and actual life roles."[18]

By "life roles," Parnell means those experiences and sets of responsibilities that individuals have in common. Parnell believes that "no matter what our specific interests, talents, or backgrounds,"[19] humans all perform the following seven life roles throughout their lives:

1. Lifelong Learner

2. Citizen

3. Consumer

4. Producer (worker)

5. Individual (self)

6. Family Member

7. Leisure Participant

Parnell makes the point that teachers should not view these roles as responsibilities that students will occupy later in life, but as roles they already occupy today. It is necessary, therefore, for students to have a clear understanding of each one. (See Resource A for priorities associated with each role.) Because students will be able to relate to these human commonalities, Parnell believes that the life roles offer teachers a promising start in the quest to help kids find meaning in their work.[20] The life roles, then, can serve as a bridge, helping students connect their daily learning to the higher purposes embedded in the aim and class mission statement.

Examples of how we can integrate the life roles into our curricula are limitless. At the most basic level we can incorporate the life roles into individual lessons pertaining to any subject area. One simple example occurred in a first grade classroom during our study of subtraction. I invited a student volunteer, David, to the front of the room to participate in a role-play situation. We imagined we were in a candy store. I was the clerk. David was the consumer. He purchased a chocolate bar for $2, paying me with a $5 bill, which we represented with a stick of five unifix cubes. I turned around, pretending to put the bill in the cash register, and I intentionally gave him only $1 in change. At the end of the activity, I explained to the class that if David didn't understand how to subtract, he could easily fall victim to a dishonest clerk. While observing the demonstration, a classmate, who was fond of money, spontaneously responded, "Wow, subtraction *is* important!" The ability to subtract would, thus, empower students to be effective shoppers. With that brief demonstration, and the unexpected curricular validation that followed, I connected a math lesson on subtraction to the larger idea that we learn because it makes our lives better, a sentiment expressed in the 1996–1997 class mission statement, by highlighting the importance of being an intelligent consumer.

Beyond individual lessons, a higher form of incorporating the life roles into the curriculum involves the area of assessment. Traditionally, most assessment of student learning has taken the form of decontextualized, paper-and-pencil tests, most notably multiple choice, true-false, and short answer. While these evaluations can supply useful information about what our students know and are able to do, they lack any sense of authenticity. The life roles can add authenticity by providing an immediate, engaging context, one that requires students to demonstrate knowledge, apply skills, and grapple with meaningful, real-life problems.

Consider the following assessment example from geometry:[21]

*Congratulations! Your school has just hired you to be its new graphic designer. You will be responsible for creating new wallpaper for the auditorium. The design for the wallpaper must contain a pattern using one or more of the following regular polygons: triangle, square, pentagon, hexagon, and octagon. The pattern, however, can only include polygons that tessellate (cover a surface completely with no overlaps or gaps). Your task includes two parts. First, test each polygon to determine which ones tessellate and which do not. Second, submit a one-page design that you believe would make for the best wallpaper.*

Notice the advantages this type of assessment has over traditional testing. First, most kids will find the activity interesting, and, as a result, their enthusiasm for math will increase. Second, the task demands much more than basic recall of isolated facts. The kids need not only to know the definitions of the various polygons but also to understand the unique properties of each one and put this knowledge to use to create an original product. All the while, the kids are receiving legitimate experience in one of the life roles: worker. Using computer programs such as Clarisworks for this project only adds to its authenticity, interest, and effectiveness.

Grant Wiggins (1993), whose *Assessing Student Performance* is an absolute must-read for educators interested in authentic evaluations, offers the following list of other professional roles, beyond graphic designer, that we can use to structure student assessments.[22] Entitled "Professional Roles and Situations Through Which Students Can Perform With Knowledge," this list creates exciting possibilities for our kids to participate in a wide variety of engaging scenarios (see Figure 1.5).

**Figure 1.5** Professional Roles and Situations Through Which Students Can Perform With Knowledge

| | |
|---|---|
| Museum Curator | U.N. Representative |
| Engineering Designer | Characters in Historical Reenactments |
| Ad Agency Director | Tour Organizer |
| Cultural Exchange Facilitator | Psychologist/Sociologist |
| Bank Manager | Archaeologist |
| Essayist/Philosopher | Newspaper Writer/Editor |
| Historian | Product Designer |
| Job Applicant | Teacher |
| Expert Witness | Speaker-Listener |
| Debug Expert | Reviewer |
| Commercial Designer | |

As helpful as the preceding list can be for creating interesting assessment situations, these ideas, by themselves, only address one of the seven life roles. There's much more to life than work, and the assessment experiences we provide our students should reflect that fact. Furthermore, it would send an incomplete and inaccurate message about the purposes of education if the role of worker were the only to which we exposed our kids. Therefore, when planning authentic assessments, look for ways to involve the other six roles. Ask your kids to analyze a social studies topic from the perspective of a citizen, to discuss a novel as a leisure participant, or to solve a budgeting problem from the viewpoint of a consumer or family member. The more balance you are able to achieve in this regard, the more your students will understand the multiple purposes you are trying to promote as a teacher.

Beyond individual lessons and assessments, the highest form of incorporating Parnell's work into your curriculum involves basing an entire unit of study around one of the life roles. Consider the following example, also from the subject of geometry.

## The Olympics Project

(I distributed the information that follows to my students in the form of a handout in February 2002.)

*As you probably know, the 2002 Winter Olympics have just begun in Salt Lake City, Utah. What you may not know is that the next Winter Olympics will take place in 2006 in Turin, Italy. The International Olympic committee, the group that's in charge of organizing the Olympics, is already starting to plan for the 2006 Games. The committee has just hired you to be the official city planners for the 2006 Games.*

*As city planners, you will have the chance to decide where all the events will take place, and you will also build a model of the Olympic Village. The Games will include the following NINE events:*[23]

| | | |
|---|---|---|
| *ALPINE SKIING* | *BOBSLEDDING* | *CURLING* |
| *FIGURE SKATING* | *ICE HOCKEY* | *LUGE* |
| *SKI JUMPING* | *SNOW BOARDING* | *SPEED SKATING* |

*The project will consist of two phases. In the first phase we will be creating detailed maps of the Olympic Village. In the second phase we will build a three-dimensional model of all nine venues* (I gave my students information about the second phase verbally).

### Phase I: Creating the Map

- *You must place all nine venues somewhere on your map. Think about which venues would make sense next to one another and place them as logically as you can.*
- *You will be using a 21-by-15 inch sheet of graph paper to make your map. The paper will be organized in half-inch squares, so, it will be an array of 42 by 30 squares.*
- *Your map must meet the following specifications:*
  1. *You must have a border of at least 1 square on all four sides of the grid.*
  2. *There must be at least 1 square between venues for roads.*
  3. *Each venue will be represented by a different geometric shape. We will color in each shape on the map using a different color.*

     *(Ex. The snowboarding venue will be represented by a brown hexagon.)*

4. *The **perimeter** of each venue must be between 30 and 40 units.*

5. *The **area** of each venue must be between 50 and 100 square units.*

6. *All angles of each shape must be labeled as either acute, obtuse, or right.*

From the kids' perspective, beginning a new unit with a real-life scenario and authentic role builds immediate interest in the task at hand. In addition, it creates an instant demand for the knowledge and skills that will be required to successfully complete the culminating project. With the Olympics Project, for example, students, from the outset, will *want* to know the meaning of such terms as perimeter and area because they will *need* to know this information to design their maps successfully.

Furthermore, planning a unit this way allows us to bring a number of discrete skills together in a holistic manner. In other words, a cohesiveness results from the way these skills have been combined, and the overall structure makes sense to the kids. In a textbook, by contrast, lessons on perimeter, area, angles, and polygons appear one after the other with no clear connection between any of them. Certainly, we may choose to include lessons from the text as we teach these standards to our students, but the text will not drive our instruction because it cannot match the authenticity that the life roles provide.

However you choose to incorporate the life roles into your curriculum, a powerful visual metaphor called *the Tower of Opportunity* will greatly strengthen your implementation. The four-sided tower contains seven stories, one for each role. The role names occupy one side of the tower while specific examples of each role occupy the other three. Please see Figure 1.6 for photographs of two of the tower's four sides and Figure 1.7 for a template of

**Figure 1.6**  Photographs of the Tower of Opportunity

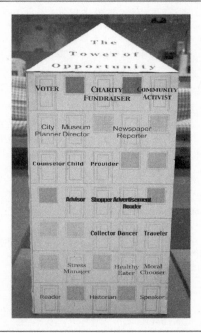

**Figure 1.7** Template of the Tower of Opportunity

| | Red Cross Volunteer | PTA Volunteer | Little League Coach | Voter | Charity Fundraiser | Community Activist | Museum Docent | Environmental Leader | Editorial Writer |
|---|---|---|---|---|---|---|---|---|---|
| Citizen | Red Cross Volunteer | PTA Volunteer | Little League Coach | Voter | Charity Fundraiser | Community Activist | Museum Docent | Environmental Leader | Editorial Writer |
| Worker | Candy Box Designer | Chef | Comic Book Writer | City Planner | Museum Director | Newspaper Reporter | Doctor | Engineer | Advertising Director |
| Family Member and Friend | Parent | Sibling | Supporter | Counselor | Child | Provider | Crisis Manager | Caregiver | Money Manager |
| Consumer | Money Manager | Quality Evaluator | Saver | Advisor | Shopper | Advertisement Reader | Critical Thinker | Mathematician | Investor |
| Leisure Participant | Athlete | Musician | Hobbyist | Collector | Dancer | Traveler | Enthusiast | Artist | Model Builder |
| Individual | Self-Manager | Problem Solver | Goal-Setter | Stress Manager | Healthy Eater | Moral Chooser | Effective Communicator | Self-Esteem Booster | Principled Decision-Maker |
| Lifelong Learner | Student | Listener | Scientist | Reader | Historian | Speaker | Teacher | Researcher | Writer |

13

the tower, from which you can make copies for your students, fold the sides into a free-standing replica, or design a larger model for your classroom. As the photos indicate, the examples of each role are printed on doors that include tiny doorknobs. The design of the tower allows us, as teachers, to convey the message that life is rich with opportunities, choices, and options, but that to take advantage of these opportunities, maximize our choices, and give ourselves the greatest number of options, we need an education. Put simply, education is the key that opens doors. The harder we work in school and the more we learn, the more doors we can open for ourselves.

An important aspect of the tower's design relates to the sequence of roles from bottom to top. The arrangement isn't random. Rather, it is an attempt to illustrate each role's potential for contributing to and impacting the larger society. While the potential certainly exists for people assuming any role to make a difference in the lives of others, the roles located on the bottom tend to focus primarily on individual needs, goals, and priorities while those higher on the tower tend to involve progressively larger numbers of people. I'm the first to concede that this order is rough at best, but I believe it benefits students to arrange the roles in this manner to highlight the idea of service. As long as we discuss the inexactness of the sequence with students so that they don't view the order as being overly rigid, there shouldn't be any problem.

The tower, like the class mission statement, is a significant reference point that students should revisit frequently. Whenever you begin a new unit or project, choose to discuss an item you heard on the news, want to capitalize on a teachable moment, or even decide to share a personal story, try connecting it to something on the tower. Every time you do, you remind your students of the numerous ways in which their learning can be put to use and the numerous reasons why learning matters. You expand their perspective and encourage them to think beyond their present reality. Furthermore, you provide them with a glimpse of what a productive, well-rounded life can look like.

To conclude, the life roles present opportunities for teachers to connect daily learning activities to higher purposes. Whether you choose to incorporate Parnell's work at the lesson, assessment, or unit level, these roles use real-life situations to help students find meaning in their work. This approach also adds interest and builds enthusiasm for students and teachers alike.

## PERSONAL MISSION STATEMENTS

Three rings of the organizational target are now complete. Recall Jenkins' assertion that the aim represents the bull's-eye of the target. The class mission statement occupies the next outer ring, and Parnell's seven life roles reside in the third. Moving from inside-out, the effort to establish purpose begins in general terms with the aim of increasing learning while increasing enthusiasm, and each new layer develops these ideas more fully and adds specificity. This pattern continues as we attach the fourth and final layer to our class target, personal mission statements (please see Figure 1.8).

Like the class compositions discussed earlier, personal mission statements express hopes, purposes, and guiding principles. The document, however, focuses on the individual student, not the group as a whole. Creating a personal mission statement empowers team members to chart their own directions, declaring who they are, who they want to become, and what they are determined to accomplish. This process demands careful reflection. For many students, it will be the first time they have thought about their lives on such a deep level.

**Figure 1.8**    Target for Establishing a Sense of Purpose

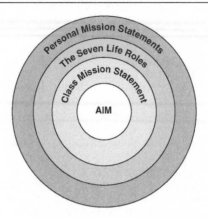

The personal missioning process offers students a chance to discover the deep-burning "Yes!" that can channel their energies in a positive direction. Covey comments that one of the unique characteristics of humans is that no matter our circumstances, we have "the creative imagination to envision a better way and the independent will to create change."[24] We can choose our attitude in any given set of circumstances, choose our own way.[25] Furthermore, he argues, developing a compelling vision of the future "is the best manifestation of creative imagination and the primary motivation of human action. It's the ability to see beyond our present reality, to create, to invent what does not yet exist, to become what we not yet are. It gives us capacity to live out of our imagination, instead of our memory."[26]

Asking students to chart their own directions also shows them that we value each as a unique and special person. Trusting students with this responsibility sends the message that we believe the work they do is important, that they are all valuable resources to their community, and that the world needs them to make it a better place. We express our faith that they have the potential to make a difference in the lives of people and that they have the ideas, energy, and ability to improve the quality of life of their communities. According to Covey, "Everyone has his specific vocation or mission in life; everyone must carry out a concrete assignment that demands fulfillment. Therein he cannot be replaced, nor can his life be repeated. Thus, everyone's task is unique as his specific opportunity to implement it."[27]

Unlike class mission statements, which must be done early in the year to maximize their effectiveness, there's no best time for your kids to create these personal constitutions. Students should begin defining their personal missions when you believe they are comfortable with the concept of a mission statement and understand how it can help them think about and shape their futures. Generally, I like my kids to start in January right after the winter break. That way, I can make a big deal about the project and take advantage of the fact that kids usually return from vacations more focused, more open to new ideas, and more ready for a challenge than usual.

The procedure for creating personal mission statements differs from the class missioning process described earlier. I recommend a four-step plan where everyone works on one

## An Idea From a Teacher: Putting Essential 1 Into Practice

Viola Callanen

*Corpus Christi School*
*Pacific Palisades, CA*
*2nd Grade Teacher*

"How can you expect a 2nd grader to write a personal mission statement when my son, who is a sophomore in high school, doesn't even know what a mission statement is?" This was the message that I was receiving all year long from parents who doubted that their seven-year-old children could understand, let alone articulate, who they were and how they were going to become responsible for their own learning. As a fourth year teacher, I must say it was a long process. But after months of patiently working on the Seven Life Roles, every one of my 29 2nd graders was able to write a heart-felt two-paragraph personal mission statement that wowed even the biggest doubters. One parent said, "I am so impressed with my son's journey this year. I never believed that he could verbalize so clearly who he is and where he wants to go!"

Here are some sample sentences from my students' mission statements.

I come to school to learn, be with my friends, have fun, and learn to be a teacher.

My goal this year is to go to third grade, be a leader, and to be a great writer.

In the future, I hope to be a good example for others, graduate, travel the world, and get a good job.

I believe family is number one and that education equals opportunity.

My goal this year is to be a better friend.

In the future, I hope to earn a scholarship to USC. (Author's Note: As a loyal, lifelong UCLA Bruin, I sincerely hope this youngster sets his educational sights a bit higher.)

SOURCE: Viola Callanen and 2nd grade students at Corpus Christi school.

step per week for homework. In Week 1 I ask the kids to complete the following imagination-stretching activity, a variation of one suggested by Covey:[28]

> Pretend that you have just turned 80 years old. To celebrate this milestone, your family, friends, and people from all walks of your life have organized a special dinner in your honor and will give speeches about the kind of person you have been in your life. Imagine the event in as much detail as you can—the setting, the people, the decorations. What would you like your guests to say about you? What personality characteristics would you like them to emphasize? What achievements, contributions, memories, and stories would you like them to share? Assume that you have accomplished everything that you ever dreamed of accomplishing and reached all

the goals you ever set for yourself. Finally, as you look around the room, think about the difference you have made in these people's lives.

For Week 2 the kids answer the following questions:

What are you determined to accomplish in the future?

What kind of person do you want to become?

What goals do you have in life?

What beliefs and ideas are truly important to you?

What kind of contribution to society would you like to make?

The tributes from Week 1 and the answers from Week 2 become the raw material from which the kids draft their personal mission statements in Week 3. At this stage, it is the responsibility of each child to shape these two sets of ideas into 10 sentences that begin with the phrase *I choose*. Starting each sentence with these words reinforces the point that it is the choices we make in life that will ultimately determine our success and happiness. Goals will not be reached and success will not be attained by accident or luck. Only when we make the choice to act a certain way or pursue a certain course will we give ourselves the best chance to fulfill our mission.

Following is a list of sentences that have appeared on students' personal mission statements:

"I choose to be a veterinarian."

"I choose to help save the environment."

"I choose to study foreign languages."

"I choose to go to college."

"I choose to help support my family."

"I choose to be responsible and respectful."

"I choose to be an excellent mother."

"I choose to be a basketball and soccer player."

In the final week of this process, the kids revise and edit their initial drafts and then produce a clean copy. Besides emphasizing correct grammar, punctuation, and spelling at this stage, I also use this final week to ensure that each mission statement contains a balanced set of priorities. By balanced, I mean that the 10 sentences address all five of the questions the kids answered during Week 2 and reflect a variety of life roles. For example, I will ask students who focused their statements exclusively on work and educational goals to add sentences about the contributions they would like to make or the type of people they would like to become.

You probably won't need to supervise the kids heavily during the four-week missioning process because of their experience crafting the class statement and referring to it throughout the year. Be sure, however, to remind everyone about the importance of word choice and phrasing. Also, you may want to share with your class the criteria of effective mission statements listed previously. Once the students complete the process, it is important that they have regular opportunities to revisit their personal statements to internalize the ideas they contain.

Culminate this process with a terrific art activity. Have the kids design their own personal mission boxes. (I have found that 9-inch by 9-inch white gift boxes work best.) The project calls for students to represent visually the ideas in their personal statements using photographs from home, pictures cut from magazines, and any other stickers, images, and available materials that they can attach to their boxes. Each side of the box features a specific aspect of the statements. These six areas follow:

1. Who I Am

2. Important People in My Life

3. My Contribution to Society

4. My Interests and Hobbies

5. My Goals for the Future

6. Ideas and Beliefs That Are Important to Me

Please see Figure 1.9 for photographs of sample student boxes.

Expressing these hopes and thoughts artistically, as well as verbally, both broadens and deepens students' understanding of what they want to accomplish. In addition, observing the kids trying to determine how best to communicate their ideas visually is fascinating. The

**Figure 1.9**   Photographs of Student Personal Mission Boxes

experience also has a wonderful effect on class cohesiveness and morale. It helps the kids learn more about one another and better appreciate one another's uniqueness.

Our organizational target is now complete. We have proceeded inside-out from the general to the specific, from the group level to the individual level. Each successive ring advances our cause to establish a sense of purpose in our classrooms. Establishing purpose requires that we commit ourselves to making a consistent effort to help students find meaning in their work. We achieve this objective by connecting classroom learning to higher, worthwhile purposes that kids value.

## KEY POINTS FROM ESSENTIAL 1

- Teachers must establish a sense of purpose with students so they know why it's important to come to school every day and so they understand how learning can benefit them now and in the future.
- Establishing a sense of purpose is a process that requires an investment of time and energy, and this process must start during the first few days of each new school year.
- The process of establishing a sense of purpose begins with the introduction of the overall aim, a short phrase that captures your highest priorities, provides focus and direction, and becomes the primary reference point for future decision making and goal setting.
- The class mission statement further develops the priorities included in the aim, supplements these ideas with others that identify your class as a unique group, and results from a creative process that brings students together and enables them to see one another as contributing parts to a greater whole.
- The seven life roles present opportunities for teachers to connect daily learning activities to the higher purposes set forth in the classroom aim and mission statement.
- Creating individual personal mission statements empowers students to chart their own courses, reflect on what matters most to them, and decide who and what they would like to become in the future.

### Reflection Questions

- What are the high priority ideas you will include in your classroom aim?
- As you prepare to begin for the class missioning process, what are some examples that you can share with students involving times where either you or someone else was on a mission to accomplish something important?
- How might you need to tailor the class missioning process and personal missioning process to suit your grade level?
- What are some ways you can incorporate the seven life roles into your daily lessons, assessments, and instructional units?
- How do you plan to build time into your schedule on a regular basis to review the aim, class mission statement, seven life roles, and personal mission statements so these reference points remain relevant and accessible to your students?

### Sample Organizational Mission Statements

#### See's Candies Mission Statement

*For over 65 years we have worked hard to maintain the tradition of quality which literally millions of faithful See's candy eaters have come to expect, year after year.*

*Our philosophy is quite simple: Be absolutely persistent in all attitudes regarding quality—buy only the best ingredients obtainable—offer the most delicious and interesting assortments of candies available in the United States—own and operate all See's sparkling white shops, while providing the highest level of customer service. At the same time we fully believe that we can always do a better job at what we try to do—ultimately make people happy.*

### Disney Mission Statement

*Disney's mission is to provide the highest quality family-oriented entertainment and education in all of its business segments around the world. This will be accomplished by the Disney Team by combining Disney values with modernism and innovation.*

### Cedars-Sinai Medical Center Mission Statement

*Cedars-Sinai Medical Center is committed to maintaining our leadership position in providing the highest quality care and service, delivered with empathy and compassion, to the community, our patients, their families and all others whom we serve.*

*We are committed to providing the most appropriate level of service to our patients, physicians and each other in the pursuit of that goal.*

*We will achieve this by continuously improving the quality, efficiency, and cost-effectiveness of our programs, and services, utilizing a multidisciplinary team approach.*

# Essential 2    DETERMINING GOALS

I n this chapter we determine our goals for the year. Specifically, I discuss four types of worthwhile goals, as well as a framework that unites these goals in a cohesive, user-friendly manner. Once in place, this framework will serve to guide our curricular and instructional planning for the year and act as yet another critical reference point for decision making. All four of the goals focus on year-end student outcomes.

## WHAT IS QUALITY?

Before introducing the classroom goals, I want to take a moment to focus on the concept of quality. Put simply, quality must always be our ultimate goal. As such, it is a cornerstone idea that we will revisit frequently as we generate the rest of our goals. But what is quality? Specifically, in an educational context, how can we define the term so that our kids understand its meaning? Defining quality can be a bit tricky because it's one of those words where if you asked 50 people to define it, you would likely get 50 different answers.

On one hand, quality is subjective. What I consider to be a quality car, for example, you may not. Imagine for a moment that you and I are walking down the street one summer afternoon discussing our goals for the upcoming school year when we both notice a school-bus-yellow, two-door, convertible sports car scream by us. Suddenly, your goals for the upcoming school year don't seem quite as important as your eyes grow wide with admiration. To you, that's a quality car. After all, you love sports cars, school-bus-yellow has been your favorite color since the first day of kindergarten, and riding in convertibles exhilarates you. Not me. I need something more practical. I need four doors and more space for the family. I abhor school-bus-yellow, and don't get me started on what riding in convertibles does to my hair. Because we are human and have our own tastes, preferences, and opinions, the subjective nature of quality will always exist.

If, however, quality is to become the driving force in our classrooms, we will need to find a way to acknowledge and respect the subjective, individual nature of quality while also working toward a more objective, shared definition. We need a shared definition to enable team members to speak the same language. Without a common definition, everyone will rely on his or her personal notion of quality, making communication more difficult and progress less likely. Combining the subjective and the objective in a manner that maintains the integrity of both may sound logically impossible, but it can be done.

In *The Quality School* (the book that first introduced me to Dr. Deming's work), noted author William Glasser introduces the concept of the "Quality World," and, in so doing, demonstrates how it is possible to create a shared, objective definition of a term that will always be subjective and personal.[1] According to Glasser, human beings are continuously attempting to satisfy five basic needs: survival, power, friendship, fun, and freedom. From birth, he claims, we learn and remember all the people, things, and situations that help us satisfy these needs. In fact, we store pictures and perceptions of all these need-satisfiers in a part of our memory that Glasser calls the Quality World. Thus, when defining quality, Glasser focuses on the mental pictures that all of us have stored in our Quality Worlds, whether they include school-bus-yellow sports cars that satisfy our need for freedom, the homes in which we grew up that satisfied our need for survival, or our favorite games that satisfy our need for fun. Glasser's would be a shared, objective definition of quality because it's based on five basic needs that we all share in common. Because each of us stores different mental pictures in our Quality Worlds, however, this objective definition also recognizes the subjective nature of quality.

Our definitional quest continues with the work of quality expert Philip Crosby. According to Crosby, the major problem with most definitions of quality stems from the fact that quality is usually defined in terms of "goodness." As a result, these definitions do nothing to advance a common understanding because we all have different ideas of what goodness means; what's good to one person isn't to another. Or, as Crosby puts it, when someone speaks of goodness, "nobody knows what that means except the speaker."[2]

As an alternative, Crosby argues that quality must be defined as *conformance to requirements.* Imagine, for example, I was in the market for a new pair of running shoes. I need my shoes to be gray, provide extra toe support, consist of waterproof material, and cost less than $100. Under this definition any shoes that conform to these requirements would be quality running shoes.

For several reasons conformance to requirements is the most effective definition of quality to use with students. First, it best resolves the difficulties associated with acknowledging the subjective while requiring the objective. Assume, for example, your students are set to begin work on a poster project summarizing their recently completed independent science investigations. You explain that you expect everyone to produce a quality poster. Were your instructions to end there, without a common definition, students would simply try their best to create posters that satisfied their own ideas of goodness, and the results would vary widely. As author Mary Walton puts it, though, "Trying your best isn't enough. You have to know what to do, *then* do your best."[3] So, you brainstorm with your students a list of criteria that would constitute quality work for this project. Likely, students would suggest a write-up of the various stages of the scientific method, perhaps a photograph of the materials used or some other visual aid, and maybe a few nuts-and-bolts items, such as the title of the project and their names. You may choose to add other criteria, such as neatness, or some suggestions regarding organization. After further discussion, you and your students will have cocreated a list containing a reasonable number of specific criteria that exemplify quality. The list will never be perfect, and although people will never completely agree on goodness, we can agree on requirements. Not everyone will get his or her way regarding every criterion, but you will reach agreement on a shared definition born from everyone's personal, subjective opinions.

The posters your students create using your quality criteria as a common reference point will be far better than those they would have created based solely on their individual notions of goodness, and any student's project that conforms to your class-generated requirements will deserve to be considered quality work. In addition, the brainstorming process itself, as with the class missioning process, builds teamwork, increases class cohesiveness, and provides students with genuine opportunities to contribute to the group. Another advantage of using Crosby's definition lies in its flexibility. The idea of defining quality as conformance to requirements can be applied with equal effectiveness to any type of work or endeavor for which quality is the goal, from creative writing to science investigations to behavior at an assembly.

Another example of this definition's flexibility can be found in the generic quality rubric shown in Figure 2.1. As the title implies, this rubric is not meant to apply to any specific subject or project, but to the idea of quality in general so that students may better understand the relationship between the work itself and the attitudes and ingredients needed to produce it. When students satisfy these six criteria, they will be far more likely to achieve quality.

Students should learn to define quality as conformance to requirements early in the school year. Discussing the generic quality rubric shown in Figure 2.1 or Glasser's Quality World construct are two possible ways of introducing Crosby's definition to your students. Another interesting approach involves choosing an object relevant to your students' lives and asking them what makes that object a *quality* object. Take, for example, the cupcake. Begin the exercise by holding up a cupcake in front of your class and asking, "Is this a quality cupcake?" (By the way, yes, I did just use the words "exercise" and "cupcake" in the same sentence.) Whether students answer yes or no doesn't matter; what matters are the reasons they give to support their opinions. Juan believes it is a quality cupcake because it has icing while Emily argues that it isn't because it's partially burnt. As the students offer their opinions, we are listing criteria on the board. At this point, we accept all contributions without judgment. Later, we'll comb through our list, combining overlapping ideas, filling gaps, and perhaps removing nonessential criteria. Thus far, we have two requirements: quality cupcakes have icing and aren't burnt. In a short time, you'll have a complete list of requirements. Again, not everyone will agree with each criterion, but the class will reach agreement on a quality cupcake definition that can be used as a reference point to evaluate future cupcakes.

Should you not wish to promote high-calorie desserts in your classroom, many other object possibilities exist for this exercise, including baseball cards, pencils, and backpacks, just to name a few. Any object will do. The crucial factor is that your students receive valuable practice defining quality in terms of specific criteria. Once the kids can carry out the task of defining quality cupcakes and pencils comfortably, they will be ready to define quality work for various subject areas, projects, and worthwhile endeavors that await them throughout the school year. One final note: because the phrase *conformance to requirements* can be difficult for students, particularly younger ones, to remember or to say, you may prefer a more kid-friendly definition: *quality means that something has what it's supposed to have.*

## DETERMINING STUDENT GOALS

With our definition in hand, we're ready to return to the primary purpose of this chapter: determining our goals for the school year. I will first describe four types of student goals and then tie everything together into a cohesive framework that will guide our planning and drive our curricular and instructional decision making throughout the year.

The aim introduced in the last chapter ("Increasing learning while increasing enthusiasm") provides the starting point for goal creation. Specifically, the second half of the aim leads directly to our first goal: *increasing student enthusiasm*. Ideally, every student will enjoy every subject you teach by the end of the year. That outcome represents the ultimate realization of our goal to increase student enthusiasm. Unfortunately, though, the goal of 100 percent happy faces will most likely be unattainable because students often enter our classrooms in September with strong negative feelings about certain subjects due to prior experiences, both in-school and

**Figure 2.1** How Do I Give Myself the Best Chance to Produce Quality Work?

---

### How Do I Give Myself the Best Chance to Produce Quality Work?

1. **Care Deeply**—"Quality = Caring." This simply means that to accomplish great things in any endeavor, individuals must care a great deal about the work they do.

2. **Very Best Effort**—Quality students give their very best effort, day in and day out.

3. **Take Pride in It**—When students produce quality work, you can see the pride in their faces and in the way they act.

4. **Improvement**—The idea of continuous improvement means that each piece of work represents, in some way, an improvement over the last one.

5. **Intrinsic Motivation**—For work to be considered quality, the effort, the desire, and the focus must come from within. Quality students do not need to be reminded to get started or to stay on task.

6. **Purpose**—Quality work is important work; it serves a purpose. Students should be able to understand how completing the activity will benefit them (and perhaps others), now and in the future.

---

out-of-school, and these feelings are resistant to change, particularly with older students. But remember, the goal emphasizes improvement, not perfection, and it serves a valuable purpose because it charts a direction in which we would like to move with our kids.

Suppose you administer the Fall Enthusiasm Survey and find that 12 out of 20 students enjoy math. You administer it again in December and find that now 14 students enjoy math. Even though you have not yet reached the point where every student enjoys math, your class has made genuine progress—exactly the type of progress you would like to foster throughout the year. Thus, when you administer the final Enthusiasm Survey at the end of the year, you probably won't have all happy faces. That's to be expected. Your goal is to have *more* total happy faces than you had in the beginning. If there are more happy faces in June than there were in September, then you are truly reaching our first goal of increasing student enthusiasm.

The first half of the aim leads to the remaining three student goals. Because the word *learning* is flexible, we can use the phrase *increasing learning* to encompass different types of student learning. As Figure 2.2 indicates, under the umbrella term *learning*, I include both academic learning and what I call *character learning*, the latter referring to issues of student behavior, attitudes, work habits, and social and moral development. I regard character learning to be as important as academic learning, if not more so. While our students may not all go on to become world-class scholars, they can all become world-class people. They can learn to work hard, relate well with others, act with honor and integrity, and contribute meaningfully to society.

The second student goal focuses on academic learning. Specifically, this goal focuses on the knowledge and skills contained in the content standards set forth by our state, district, or school. These standards establish what students in each grade level are expected to learn in each subject area. In the past decade or so, the standards movement has gained great momentum and today is probably the most influential reform initiative in the nation. In fact, standards have become such an integral part of our work that when we are asked by parents, students, administrators, or interested citizens about our curricular priorities, most of us would answer by first referencing our content standards. Consequently, our second student goal would read as follows: *for students to learn the content standards for the subject(s) and grade level(s) that we teach.*

For our next student goal we turn to noted educator Theodore Sizer, author of the widely respected *Horace* trilogy and one of the founders of the Coalition of Essential Schools. According to Sizer, the purpose of schooling involves helping students learn to use their minds well and develop enduring intellectual habits. As Sizer puts it, "Knowing stuff is nice. Being able to use that stuff makes sense. Being disposed to use it always, as a

**Figure 2.2** Defining Learning as Both Academic and Character Learning

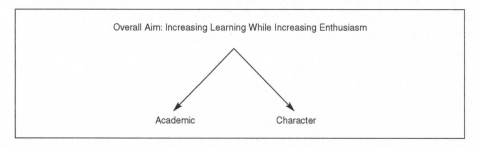

matter of habit, is the brass ring, the ultimate standard."[4] Sizer's work helps us recognize that even though learning content standards may be an important goal for children, such learning cannot serve as the only academic goal due to the fact that standards typically emphasize basic knowledge and skills and are designed to ensure only a minimal level of academic proficiency. In other words, standards offer a foundation and should be viewed as a floor, not a ceiling. Students who know how to use their minds well do, indeed, have a strong command of basic knowledge and skills, but they are set apart academically by their ability to think and act in certain ways. Sizer refers to these desired dispositions as "habits of mind." *Developing enduring habits of mind* is our third student goal.

In Figure 2.3 you will find a list of nine habits of mind along with descriptors. These habits transcend traditional subject-area boundaries and promise to enrich any topic you and your students study. Proceed with caution, however, as you decide which of these to use with your students. More is not necessarily better. Consider which ones are age-appropriate for your kids, and be careful not to overwhelm your students with too many. As you gain skill and confidence incorporating these habits into your curriculum, you can always add more at a later time.

The most effective way to introduce these habits to your students is simply by taking advantage of natural opportunities that present themselves on a daily basis. Incorporating the habits of mind into your repertoire should not feel like a burden for you or like another demand added to your already overcrowded plate. The habits fit nicely with what you are already doing. During read-aloud, for example, encourage your students to make **connections.** They may want to connect one aspect of the plot to another aspect that occurred several chapters earlier. Or, they may choose to connect the personality of the protagonist to that of a

## An Idea From a Teacher:
## Putting Essential 2 Into Practice

Amy Argento

*Seaside Elementary School*

*Torrance, CA*

*4th Grade Teacher*

In an effort to set goals and establish a plan to meet the California Content Standards through a quality approach, I created a table using the standards for both Reading and Writing. Each table is made up of three columns and anywhere from five to ten rows. One column, entitled *"Standard,"* gives the standards for a particular focus. Another, entitled *"Approach,"* outlines specific approaches that we use to meet each standard. The third column is blank with the heading *"Dates"* to record the date each approach was used. I have added asterisks to the boxes of standards to express test prevalence in STAR testing with a key at the bottom of the table explaining that one asterisk represents low test prevalence, two asterisks represent medium test prevalence and three asterisks represent high test prevalence. I have enlarged both tables to a 2 x 3 foot poster, one in blue and the other in yellow. The table offers a year-long plan for instruction, a model of quality in the classroom, and the direct participation of the students who record the dates each approach is used.

SOURCE: Amy Argento, Seaside Elementary School.

**Figure 2.3**    Habits of Mind

---

**Habits of Mind**

*Bias*

- Understanding how our preferences, experiences, and attitudes may hinder our ability to address issues objectively

*Connections*

- Understanding cause and effect
- Seeing the big picture (how people, places, and events fit together)

*Craftsmanship*

- Paying attention to detail
- Possessing a passion for excellence
- Displaying thoroughness

*Evidence*

- Maintaining a reasonable skepticism
- Articulating reasoned arguments
- Differentiating between fact and opinion

*Judgment*

- Weighing and evaluating evidence
- Choosing among alternatives
- Having a sense of the relative values of the various features of a complex situation

*Openness*

- Admitting mistakes freely
- Being willing to consider seriously the thoughts and ideas of others
- Being curious to learn new things and asking questions out of personal interest

*Relevance*

- Distinguishing between the important and unimportant

*Thoughtfulness*

- Thinking deeply in an informed, disciplined, and logical manner
- Taking time before answering questions and stating opinions
- Reflecting on past performance to improve future performance

*Viewpoint*

- Understanding events, issues, problems, and phenomena from multiple perspectives

---

character in a different book. Pretty soon, after guiding our kids to expand the types of connections they make, students will become comfortable raising their hands and saying, "I'd like to make a connection." Furthermore, they will become more competent with cause and effect, foreshadowing, and other literary features that require them to focus on the big picture. Soon, the kids will be making connections in other subjects, and you will have added a valuable thinking skill to their repertoires with only a modest expenditure of time and effort.

Opportunities to introduce other habits of mind are just as plentiful. I like to introduce *craftsmanship* before art projects or before the kids use rulers to create graphs for the first time during math. *Viewpoint* is a helpful habit to discuss when focusing on behavioral issues or when students are first learning to work in cooperative groups. As part of my overall effort to help students become more independent and less reliant on teacher assistance, we talk about the importance of developing and trusting our *judgment* to solve our own problems. *Evidence* becomes important during literature and social studies, when we need to refer to the text to find support for our assertions or conclusions.

Over time, these habits will become an indispensable part of your classroom vocabulary, and you will find that your students' development as thinkers far exceeds what it would have been had you focused exclusively on the standards. Finally, as you become more comfortable with the habits of mind, you will be ready to move beyond spontaneous use of them and begin incorporating them purposefully into your curricular and instructional planning.

Measuring student proficiency with the habits of mind is more difficult than measuring enthusiasm or assessing progress toward most content standards. Should you decide to assess student proficiency with the habits of mind formally, I recommend creating a checklist or rubric based on the descriptors mentioned earlier. On the other hand, you may decide that your students receive enough formal assessment throughout the year with respect to the content standards and don't need to be assessed formally with these habits. This is the choice I have made, and I don't believe my kids have received a less thorough treatment of the habits because of my decision.

We now turn our attention to character learning and our fourth student goal. Character education has become a hot topic in recent years, and schools have responded to society's concerns by adopting a variety of programs, hiring guest speakers, and scheduling special assemblies. Well-intentioned as these efforts may be, they are, by themselves, unlikely to bring about lasting results because they are only marginally related to daily classroom life. Program activities typically occur too infrequently for their lessons to remain in the minds of students, guest speakers leave, and assemblies end. For character education to be effective, it must be built into the core of a student's school experience.

Character development is most effectively achieved when teachers are able to incorporate meaningful "habits of character" into the standards-based curriculum on a daily basis. *Cooperation*, for example, is a great habit to discuss as the kids are learning to work in groups. We discuss *responsibility* the first time kids receive a homework packet that is due at the end of the week. *Perseverance* is a terrific topic to explore the first time we engage in a truly rigorous, challenging assignment where students might be tempted to quit when they encounter frustration. Soon, we reach the point where literally every academic activity has embedded within it a lesson about character. A multiplication game played in pairs, of course, is designed to improve everyone's multiplication skills, but its purpose is also to help us become kinder and more cooperative. Once we, as teachers, start analyzing our daily teaching for ways to incorporate lessons about character, it will be almost impossible to operate any other way.

Character education, then, is not an add-on. It should not be viewed as a topic that will take time away from the long list of standards that we are already being asked to teach. Rather, infusing our curriculum with habits of character will result in a mutually beneficial situation. Students will learn academic material better than they would have without the emphasis on character, and students will learn more about developing character than they would have had we broached it as a separate entity. After all, when is a better time to develop perseverance, at an assembly when a guest speaker talks about it or right in the middle of a difficult academic activity when students are tempted to stop?

In Figure 2.4 you will find a list of 13 habits of character that I use with my students. Originally, this list was created during a class meeting when my kids and I were discussing the question, "What does it mean to be a quality student?" We used this list to guide our character development work for the rest of the year. I liked this list so much that I have used it ever since, with only minor modifications.[5]

Sizer's earlier quote about the habits of mind is equally applicable to the habits of character. It's not enough for students to know what the words on this list mean or to display these traits occasionally. The ultimate standard is for students to think and act in these ways all the time, as a matter of habit. I will provide descriptors of each habit along with more information about how to assess student progress with these habits in Chapter 5. For now, it is sufficient to state that our fourth goal is for students to *develop enduring habits of character.*

Obviously, helping students work toward this last goal requires a tremendous amount of time and effort, but I believe it's the most satisfying work we can do, and it's the aspect of students' lives to which we can add the greatest value. There is something special about interacting with kids who have developed the habit of saying "please" and "thank you," who work hard and never think of quitting, who treat one another with uncommon respect, and who generally conduct themselves in ways that should make themselves and their families extremely proud.

**Figure 2.4**    Habits of Character

| | |
|---|---|
| Cooperation | Positive Attitude |
| Courage | Pride |
| Fairness | Respect |
| Honesty | Responsibility |
| Kindness | Self-Discipline |
| Patience | Service |
| Perseverance | |

Figure 2.5 extends the diagram shown earlier and offers a framework within which we can place our four student goals. Locating the academic focus areas at the bottom of the diagram visually reinforces the point that the standards must be viewed in their proper context. They do not represent the educational "holy grail," and they cannot be the sole focus

**Figure 2.5**    A Framework That Unites All Four Year-End Student Goals

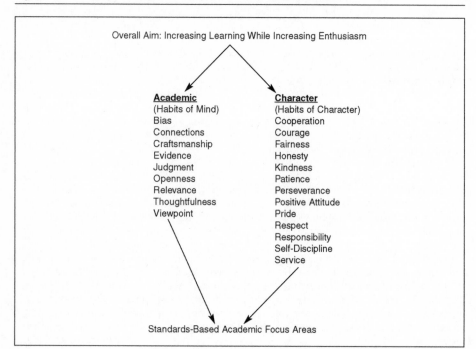

Overall Aim: Increasing Learning While Increasing Enthusiasm

**Academic**
(Habits of Mind)
Bias
Connections
Craftsmanship
Evidence
Judgment
Openness
Relevance
Thoughtfulness
Viewpoint

**Character**
(Habits of Character)
Cooperation
Courage
Fairness
Honesty
Kindness
Patience
Perseverance
Positive Attitude
Pride
Respect
Responsibility
Self-Discipline
Service

Standards-Based Academic Focus Areas

of our work. Even in this age of high-stakes testing, our content standards are not the be-all-end-all with respect to our mission as teachers. Rather, the standards represent the foundation of our work, on top of which we must add other important goals that will help our students develop as thinkers and as people. Furthermore, the diagram underscores the point that in our quest to help our students develop enduring habits of mind and habits of character, we cannot view these two entities as add-ons developed in isolation, but as vital components that must be woven into the fabric of the curriculum on a consistent basis. It diminishes our work as professionals if we believe that the primary purpose of our job is so narrow that it only involves teaching the standards that enable our students to pass standardized tests.

The diagram, then, illustrates a broader, more balanced view of learning and supports the notion that a quality classroom focuses on the whole child. Taken together, the goals address critical issues that go far beyond standards: how students feel about the subjects they are studying, how they relate to one another, how they operate as thinkers, and how they manage themselves throughout the learning process. Returning to Crosby's definition of quality as conformance to requirements, we can say that a quality education is one that empowers students to reach all four of these goals. Specifically, quality has been achieved when students

- are enthusiastic about the work they do and are eager to put their learning to use in new ways
- demonstrate proficiency with the various skills and standards set forth by our state, district, or school

- display habits of mind that predispose them to think and act in certain ways consistently
- exhibit habits of character that encompass strong work habits, attitudes, and social skills

Conducting our classrooms in ways that facilitate these outcomes is certainly not an easy task, but when we do our jobs with these important priorities in mind, the brass ring to which Sizer refers as the ultimate standard will be within the reach of every student. Now that the *what* of quality classrooms has been introduced, we turn our attention to *how* we begin making these outcomes a reality.

## KEY POINTS FROM ESSENTIAL 2

- Four types of worthwhile goals, stated in terms of year-end student outcomes, guide curricular and instructional planning for the school year and comprise a user-friendly framework that acts as yet another critical reference point for decision making.
- Quality, the ultimate classroom goal, must be defined as conformance to requirements. Defining quality in this manner facilitates classroom communication and increases the likelihood of academic progress.
- The first goal, increasing student enthusiasm for learning, connects directly to the second part of the aim introduced in the previous chapter.
- The second goal calls for students to learn the content standards for the subjects and grade levels we teach. The standards offer a foundation, not a ceiling.
- The third and fourth goals involve developing enduring habits of mind and habits of character. These two entities enrich the foundation provided by the content standards and help students become better thinkers and better people.
- Taken together, these four goals focus on the whole child and address the broadest possible range of academic skills and knowledge, work habits, attitudes, social skills, and dispositions.

## REFLECTION QUESTIONS

- As you begin to define quality as "conformance to requirements," what examples from everyday life could you use that would resonate with your current or most recent group of students?
- With which habits of mind and habits of character will you start your next school year?
- Which ones might you add later in the year as your kids gain experience with these ideas?
- Will you simply present the habits of character to your students, or will you brainstorm and refine your list as a class?
- Will you measure student proficiency with the habits of mind formally or informally?

# Essential 3 | BUILDING QUALITY INTO THE PROCESS

s Dr. Deming worked to help companies improve the quality of their manufactured goods, he initially faced opposition from business leaders who believed that improving quality would cost, rather than save, money. Leaders held this notion due to the prevailing belief that the only way to improve quality was to improve inspection, the process of systematically checking products as they come off the assembly line with the goal of removing the defective ones from the lot. How could inspection be improved? By hiring more inspectors. That way, fewer defective products found their way into the hands of customers. Hence, the added cost.

Deming demonstrated, however, that the road to better quality need not involve better inspection. He sought to sever the tight association between inspection and quality by arguing that inspection focused attention on the wrong end of the assembly line. His main point: quality cannot be inspected into a project after it has already been made. At that point, it's too late to do anything about it. Rather, Deming asserted that quality must be built into the process from the beginning, and he taught that it is more important to focus on what happens step-by-step from the beginning of the process to the end than it is to evaluate quality once a process has concluded. Furthermore, according to Deming, relying on inspectors to be the sole arbiters of quality absolves other workers of *their* obligation to focus on quality. In successful organizations quality is everyone's responsibility.

In the classroom, building quality into the process means that we focus significant time and attention on how things get done so that we get the biggest bang for our buck. Specifically, this endeavor demands that we take the best available information about how children learn and incorporate it into our daily practice to make our limited time together as efficient and effective as possible. We build this knowledge into the learning process from the outset so that by the end of the process we have done everything possible to set our students up to be successful, step-by-step. This chapter explores the concept of building quality into the process and offers several examples that illustrate the variety of ways in which we can bring this idea to life for the betterment of children.

## THE INSPECTION ROLE PLAY

Before proceeding with these examples, I would like to describe a role-play activity you can do with your students to raise their awareness of the importance of process. This exercise helps students understand that quality is everyone's responsibility and that they must pay careful attention to how they do their work before they can ever expect themselves to produce quality on a consistent basis.

Create a short stick of unifix cubes using five different colors. Present the stick to your class and announce that this "toy" is the hottest product on the market. Because consumers are buying them at record rates, stores can't keep these sticks on their shelves. Never has a fad drawn this much interest—not beanie babies, not slinkies, not pet rocks, not pogs, and not whatever else might be in vogue as you read this. Unable to keep up with demand, factories have asked for your help manufacturing these sticks. So, you decided to help out the cause and make some in class.

Begin by recruiting five volunteer assembly line workers and have them face the rest of the class. Assume each stick of five cubes contains a blue, red, orange, yellow, and green cube. You will need approximately 10 cubes of each color. Worker #1 will connect a red cube to a blue and pass the combination down the assembly line. Worker #2 adds an orange cube before continuing the stick down the line. Worker #3 adds a yellow cube, and Worker #4 finishes off the assembly with a green cube. You will also need a special volunteer to act as inspector. You, as the foreperson, are entrusting the inspector with the job of analyzing each stick as it comes off the assembly line to ensure that it looks exactly like the one shown at the beginning—same colors, same order. The inspector places the products that conform to requirements in one pile and the defectives in another. (Secretly tell one of the workers to make a couple of mistakes, but be subtle about it. Without these defects, the exercise will fail. I try to meet with the chosen student privately well in advance of the activity so that I don't have to whisper instructions while the exercise is in progress.) The Inspection Role Play continues until all the cubes have been consumed by the production process. Most important, no talking is allowed during this activity.

When all the sticks have been manufactured, ask your students, both the workers and the audience members, for their comments. Challenge them to ascertain whether any lessons can be taken from this activity and applied to classroom life. Your kids will likely point out that the process would have been more effective and more enjoyable if the volunteers were allowed to work together, communicate orally, and help one another. Some students will offer specific suggestions for improving the process so that no defects would have existed at the end of the line. A few children may even observe that the inspector is like a teacher in that both are "in charge" and both traditionally determine whether work is quality. Their comments will show that they understand the relationship between the quality of the final product and the quality of the processes that are needed to produce it. This activity shows students that if the group is interested in quality, everyone has to do his or her part, not just the inspector. Emphasize that everyone's opinions and everyone's suggestions for improvement matter. Everyone has a part to play in the process, and when processes are improved, the final products become better.

## THE WRITING PROCESS EXAMPLE

Let's use the area of writing as our first classroom example of building quality into the process. The task calls for students to write interesting stories. Our initial question becomes, "How do we design a process that empowers students to write the highest quality stories possible?" Since standards-based instruction provides the foundation for our work, we must first identify the language arts standards we wish to address with this project and then proceed from there. As a third-grade teacher in California, I identify the following state standards as appropriate:

- **Writing Applications (Genres and Their Characteristics)**

  Write narratives: (a) provide a context within which an action takes place, and (b) include well-chosen details to develop the plot.

- **Writing Strategies**
  ○ *Evaluation and Revision*

  Revise drafts to improve the coherence of ideas by using an established rubric.

- **Written and Oral Language Conventions**
  ○ *Sentence Structure*

  Understand and be able to use complete and correct declarative, interrogative, imperative, and exclamatory sentences in writing.

  ○ *Punctuation*

  Punctuate correctly dates, city and state, and titles of books.

  Use commas in dates, locations, and addresses, and for items in a series.

  ○ *Capitalization*

  Capitalize correctly geographic names, holidays, historical periods, and special events.

  ○ *Spelling*

  Spell correctly one-syllable words that have blends, contractions, compounds, orthographic patterns (e.g., *-y to -ies*), and common homophones.

## GUIDING APPROACHES

Once I have selected the applicable standards, I then turn my attention to the issue of how to bring these objectives to life for students in the most effective way possible. It is crucial to understand that though the standards serve as our starting point, they don't teach themselves. As professionals, *we* decide how we will deliver our instruction, *we* decide how to provide a meaningful, engaging context within which we can place these standards, and *we* decide how to create the conditions that will give students the greatest possible chance of becoming proficient writers.

To help us bring the standards to life, we can employ a number of what I call *guiding approaches*. Dozens of guiding approaches currently exist; I describe only a handful. My descriptions are brief because my purpose is not to provide a comprehensive treatment of each approach.[1] Instead, I seek to show how much more thorough and effective our standards-based instruction will be when we capitalize on the value these approaches add.

## DISCIPLINARY UNDERSTANDING

Disciplinary understanding is the first approach I usually seek to employ when planning a unit or designing a process for a four- to six-week project. Although we commonly think about our work with kids as involving different subjects, it is more accurate to say that we are introducing students to various academic disciplines, such as science, history, mathematics, and art. These disciplines can be seen as lenses, as different ways of approaching and making sense of the world. Each discipline contains its own methods, its own questions, its own moves. Scientists, for example, approach phenomena far differently than do artists. Howard Gardner, author of *The Disciplined Mind,* argues that the purpose of education is for children to study and master these fundamental ways of knowing.[2]

Authenticity is the key to disciplinary understanding. For students to learn about a given discipline, they must be able to experience it directly and face the issues and grapple with the challenges that their adult counterparts working in the discipline encounter. The seven life roles, because of the limitless possibilities they afford in this regard, fit naturally with disciplinary understanding. So, under this learning-by-doing approach, students would learn about art by being artists, learn about history by being historians, and learn about science by being scientists. Returning to our story-writing example, the disciplinary understanding approach helps us begin our planning with authenticity as one of our highest priorities so that students can learn about writing by being writers.

As writers, then, our students should be given opportunities to do the things that adult writers do—make meaningful choices about the topic and substance of their writing, share their work with peers, give and receive feedback throughout the process, even keep a notebook or tape recorder at bedside to capture valuable ideas. If the standards were our only concern, then we could have our students complete an avalanche of workbook pages that address each one. The kids may learn the standards eventually, but their experience would not at all be authentic, meaningful, or engaging. Disciplinary understanding, then, enriches our standards-based work by helping us approach our planning with a certain mindset, one that embraces valued priorities.

A further advantage of disciplinary understanding lies in the fact that learning-by-doing provides a natural context for developing several of the habits of mind and character discussed earlier. Writing is difficult. (As evidence to this point, consider the fact that I began this chapter in 1996.) To do it well requires patience and perseverance. Rather than shield kids from moments of frustration and rush to their sides the instant they become stuck, we embrace these occasions and view them as learning opportunities. Similarly, good writing requires thoughtfulness, judgment, and craftsmanship. Discussions of these and other habits are built into the fabric of our writing instruction. Consequently, by the end of the process, the students have gained important writing skills, but they have also learned something far more valuable. They have learned what it's like to be a real writer.

## THE FUNDS OF KNOWLEDGE APPROACH

The Funds of Knowledge Approach, articulated by Luis Moll of the University of Arizona, focuses primarily on how educators can empower low-achieving students. Traditionally, deficit-model theories have frequently been used to explain why low-achieving students are not meeting academic expectations. These theories account for such performance by identifying and emphasizing characteristics that students and their families are believed to be lacking or missing (Gonzales et al, 2005).

In contrast to the deficit-model theories, Moll emphasizes what all households *do* possess, not what they don't. Specifically, he argues that all families engage in productive activities, all families accumulate knowledge and strategies for survival, and all families have ways of obtaining and distributing their material and intellectual resources. Moll refers to these collectively as a household's "funds of knowledge."

It is necessary, according to Moll, for educators to develop strong relationships with families to learn more about the unique funds of knowledge that they possess. Moll claims that the knowledge gained from these relationships will help teachers work with students in ways that build on and "tap" these funds. Thus, teachers would be able to capitalize on the knowledge, strengths, and experiences that students bring with them to school. As a result, academic success becomes more likely, and the home-school relationship becomes stronger.

With story writing, teachers would actively encourage all students to write about what they know best. If students want to write about some aspect of their home life or culture, we value those ideas. If low-achieving students claim that they can't think of anything or don't have anything interesting to write about, we strongly disagree and use what we know about the children's home lives and interests to offer suggestions. Though the choice of story topics and ideas always remains with the students themselves, we are always there to make suggestions, validate student ideas, and serve as cheerleader for any home or culture or family-related topic the kids brainstorm.

## DIFFERENTIATED INSTRUCTION

Every summer I attend an elementary physical education workshop at Cal Poly San Luis Obispo. One year, well before the term *differentiated instruction* became well-known, Coach John Thomson began his presentation by holding up a jump rope parallel to the ground, waist high. He said that if we asked students to jump over the rope at that height, the task would be too difficult for many students, too easy for some, and just right for others. Then, he turned the rope diagonally. Now, he claimed, if we asked children to jump over the rope, everyone could be successful because there were more options, more entry points, more spots where students would be optimally challenged. Thomson's "slanty rope principle" remains the best introduction to differentiated instruction I have ever heard.

In the classroom, with standards-based instruction, I often view each standard as the jump rope at Thomson's waist. For some children a given standard offers an appropriate challenge. For some it doesn't pose enough of a challenge, and for others it poses too much of a challenge. The purpose of differentiated instruction is to ensure that we are meeting the needs of children in all three situations. In other words, we are attempting to empower everyone to meet the standard and encouraging those capable of exceeding it to do so. With story writing, our next issue becomes, "How do we ensure that our writing process meets the needs of every student?"

According to Carol Ann Tomlinson, author of *The Differentiated Classroom*, teachers have the ability to differentiate three primary variables: resources, process, and product.[3] Resources are usually differentiated when a project involves substantial reading or research and where the reading level of these resources may not match that of all the students. At these times, it is advisable to provide a variety of resources so that all children are reading from texts that offer an appropriate level of challenge. With story writing, however, dictionaries and thesauri serve as the main resources students might be expected to use, and when they do, it is only in the later stages of the process. I have never differentiated these resources, but one easily could. Simpler or more complex dictionaries could be provided, as could glossaries from other texts or computerized versions of these resources, should the need arise.[4] In addition, we could help struggling students to access dictionaries and thesauri more effectively by providing additional instruction with alphabetizing or reducing the number of words they are asked to locate.

Most of the differentiation that occurs with story writing will pertain to process. In recent years, use of the writing process, and formats such as Writer's Workshop that embrace the writing process, have become common. Although countless variations of the writing process exist, most include stages that allow kids to do the following:

- Brainstorm topics and ideas
- Express their thoughts in draft form freely, without focusing unnecessarily on issues such as spelling
- Discuss the draft with peers at various points in the process to share strengths as well as suggestions for improvement
- Revise ideas
- Edit for punctuation, grammar, and spelling
- Publish a final draft

Each of us will determine the multistep approach that we believe works best. Within that structure, however, lies great flexibility and great potential for differentiation. Many children will be able to proceed through the stages independently with little assistance. Katie, for example, might hole up in a corner, and I may not see her again until her draft is complete and ready for the shelves at Barnes & Noble. Others will struggle at various points along the way and need substantial assistance. I may need to have a conference with Shaun for a few minutes each day as he works on his draft to give him whatever support he may need. Even better, I can ask Katie to meet with Shaun, giving him the help he needs, providing her with the extra challenge she may need, and building the skills of cooperation in both. With regard to process, we can differentiate the amount and type of support children receive, strategically determine which students work with which, and, if necessary, adjust the amount of time certain kids have to complete various stages of the process. One process does not fit all.

Finally, the type of product students submit at the end of the process can be differentiated. Figure 3.1 conveys the expectations that one third grade class was asked to meet with its published Writer's Workshop stories. As a class, we discussed and clarified these expectations before the kids began writing. You will notice two sets of expectations on this sheet. The first relates to five elements that comprise a story (character, setting, plot, problem, resolution). The second refers to a series of traits that exemplify quality writing. (These characteristics are taken from the well-known Six Traits writing program, itself a guiding approach. This list, though, varies slightly from the actual Six Traits list.) Looked at another way, these expectations are the requirements to which I expected all my students' stories to conform. Each third grade California standard identified earlier in this chapter is represented somewhere on this sheet. Thus, students whose stories conform to these requirements are also demonstrating proficiency with the identified standards.

Should there be times when a struggling student, for a compelling reason, simply is not yet ready to meet all these expectations, we can modify what the final product will look like. Perhaps, for the first story, we omit "Setting" or one of the other story elements so the child is expected to include four out of five. Or, with the traits, maybe we focus on one or two, instead of five, so the child can focus greater attention on fewer areas. Modifying the requirements doesn't mean we provide a free pass or forget about the other requirements; it means we select

**Figure 3.1** Expectations for Round 3 of Writer's Workshop

---

Name _____ Date _____

### Expectations for Round 3 of Writer's Workshop

*Character*—Have no more than three *major* characters. Describe each major character completely so your readers will care about what happens to them. Include information from all three parts of the 3D Bone Structure (physiological, psychological, and sociological).

*Setting*—Paint a picture in your readers' minds so they feel like they are actually there. Have at least 10 sentences that describe what the setting looks, sounds, tastes, smells, and feels like. About half the sentences should appeal to the sense of *sight*. You may either do one whole paragraph about the setting or mix in your description throughout your other paragraphs.

*Plot*—Establish what your characters are trying to accomplish in the story. In other words, establish what's at stake in your story so your reader can get excited about it.

*Problem*—Your problem is only a problem when it's a problem. For each of your problems, you must make it clear that something is really wrong.

*Resolution*—Stretch out the resolution to each problem so there's drama, suspense, uncertainty, new problems, and/or false resolutions. Your resolution shouldn't be quick, easy, or predictable. Keep people guessing.

---

*Organization*—Your story should be logically organized into paragraphs. Every time you change speakers, places, events, or topics, be sure to start a new paragraph and indent.

*Word Choice*—Pick the best, most active, most descriptive words possible. Don't use the same words over and over and over and over and over.

*Sentence Fluency*—Use a variety of sentence types. Don't use all statements. Include questions, commands, and exclamations. Start your sentences in different ways and vary your sentence length.

*Voice*—Your story should sound like you. It should be honest and sincere.

*Conventions*—Have capitals, commas, periods, apostrophes, question marks, exclamation points, and quotation marks in the right places.

---

a different entry point, another spot on the slanty rope, if you will, where the child can attain success through effort. Once success has been achieved, we can always add requirements the next time around.

How students publish their work is another way products can be differentiated. Depending on the availability of technology at your school, students can print their stories, type them on a word processing program, or go all out and create an impressive presentation using HyperStudio, PowerPoint, or other software. Furthermore, this choice can belong either to you or the students. When I have students for whom printing neatly is consistently an issue, I ask them to publish by hand. Otherwise, whenever multiple options exist, I usually allow them to choose for themselves. Once again, my point is not to provide an exhaustive list of possibilities. Rather, it is to show that the list of possibilities is often longer than we think it is.

## MULTIPLE INTELLIGENCES

Although I mentioned Howard Gardner earlier when describing the disciplinary understanding approach, he is best known for his work with the multiple intelligences, a theory stating that all humans are born with eight broad types of ability: bodily-kinesthetic, intrapersonal, interpersonal, linguistic, logical-mathematical, musical, naturalist, and spatial.[5] Because each of us differs in our combinations of strengths and weaknesses in these areas, we all learn somewhat differently. Therefore, according to Gardner, we, as educators, must incorporate into our teaching a variety of activities that address these different intelligences to increase the likelihood that learning will occur.[6]

Returning to our story-writing example, one of our goals throughout the writing process is for the kids to master a series of language arts standards. To illustrate how the multiple intelligences approach applies to this situation, I focus on one standard in particular: students will capitalize geographic names, holidays, historical periods, and special events correctly. Assume we are using a Writer's Workshop format. Under this format, the period begins with a 10-minute minilesson before the kids spend the bulk of the time working on their stories and the final few minutes sharing their work with the class. If I wanted the kids to master this capitalization standard, I could have them complete worksheets for several days in a row, but those exercises would address only the linguistic intelligence. Plus, it would be boring.

Instead, I choose to structure my week's worth of minilessons so they'll be more consistent with Gardner's theory. Here's what the first three days might look like.

- *Monday:* I introduce the standard to the kids, and we practice with some examples on the board *(linguistic).* Then, we play the Slouch Game *(bodily-kinesthetic).* In the Slouch Game the students sit in chairs. Every time I say a common noun, the kids slouch in their chairs. When I say a geographic name, holiday, historical period, or special event that requires capitalization, they sit up super tall in their chairs. Sitting tall brings their heads to the approximate height of a capital letter; slouching moves their heads down to the approximate height of a lower case letter. The heights, of course, aren't perfect, but the kids enjoy it and quickly grasp the lesson I'm trying to impart. This will probably be the only time in a youngster's school experience where expert slouching will be valued.
- *Tuesday:* We review the standard from yesterday and go over some more examples *(linguistic).* We then participate in a card sorting activity *(logical-mathematical* and *bodily-kinesthetic).* In card sorting I set up a series of shoeboxes on desks around the room,

labeled with the following titles: "geographic names," "holidays," "historical periods," "special events," and "words that are not capitalized." I then pour a few dozen index cards (laminated if I want to use them in future years) onto the floor. The kids then work with partners *(interpersonal)* to place each index card into the appropriate shoebox. Once all the cards have been placed, we check each box for accuracy and make any necessary changes.

- *Wednesday:* After a couple days of non-pencil-and-paper activities, I have the kids complete a workbook page or two. They choose whether to work alone or with a partner *(intrapersonal* and *interpersonal).*

In only three days, we are able to address five of Gardner's intelligences. When we use a variety of activities, the children who struggle linguistically have other ways to make sense of and acquire information. Especially important in this regard is the bodily-kinesthetic intelligence. The current wave of brain research (another guiding approach) indicates that a large majority of students are highly receptive to active learning strategies and suggests that teachers incorporate movement into the curriculum as much as possible. With greater variety comes greater enjoyment and a greater likelihood of learning.

## WRAPPING UP THE STORY WRITING EXAMPLE

Some sheets that my students have used as they progressed through the various stages of our writing process, from prewriting to publishing, are shown in Figures 3.2 to 3.6. Over time, working through these stages helps students develop not only valuable writing skills, but also the habits of patience, cooperation, perseverance, responsibility, self-discipline, judgment, thoughtfulness, and craftsmanship in a genuine manner. On two occasions, I have also had my students dictate their stories into a tape recorder, thus creating a set of books on tape, which we then donated to the Foundation for the Junior Blind in Los Angeles. This activity brings in the habit of service, as well as a series of oral language standards.

To promote student ownership of the revision stage, I frequently ask my kids to create their own revision plans. Using the sheet provided in Figure 3.2, students check the items that they believe will help them improve their stories the most. Once completed, these plans guide the kids as they meet with their revision partners. If Julio, for example, decides he wants to focus on paragraph structure, voice, and word choice, then his partner Megan knows what to look out for when the two read Julio's story together. After Megan and Julio read each other's work, offer suggestions for improvement, and then make these improvements, they sign each other's revision plans at the bottom. If time permits, they will then meet with a different partner.

Signing the bottom of these sheets offers a measure of accountability. Should I notice a glaring weakness as I read Megan's story, I will definitely speak with her about it; however, if this issue pertains to something that Julio had already signed off on, I will speak with him as well. I want students to understand that serving as someone's revising partner is an important responsibility and that they should care as much about improving their partner's work as they do their own.

Students self-edit their work using the checklist shown in Figure 3.3. Employing the four-color pen at this stage simplifies the complex task of editing by associating each part of this endeavor with a specific color. Before adopting the four-color system, I noticed that many students tended to rush through or neglect certain aspects of editing. When this system was first introduced, the kids appreciated the novelty of using these pens at this stage, and editing suddenly became cool. In fact, children who showed little interest in editing their work or who struggled to edit proficiently suddenly looked forward to it and displayed greater dedication to this detail work.

The evaluation sheets shown in Figure 3.4 contain writing rubrics for all six traits, with the score of 3 being the standard. Both the students and I use these rubrics to evaluate their writing. The kids get the first turn. After underlining the specific descriptors that they believe apply to their own work, students indicate on the bottom of each rubric the scores they would give themselves and then include any comments they want me to read. Next, I follow these same steps. Using the same evaluation sheet facilitates fruitful conversations because together we can compare scores, analyze the descriptors we underlined for each trait, and discuss any areas of disagreement. Finally, students respond to the reflection questions listed in Figure 3.5. Reflecting on the process of writing their stories promotes metacognition, raises student awareness of their strengths and weaknesses, and plants the seeds for future improvement.

Now that I have described in detail how I attempt to build quality into the process with regard to story writing, compare this way of working with its polar opposite: simply distributing the expectations sheet shown in Figure 3.1 and providing students with time to work on their own to create stories however they wish. The contrast between these two options is sharp. With the latter, we create a situation where the kids do their work, and we serve as inspector. With the former, where the students are working within the structure of a thoughtful, well-designed process, the results will be far better, the experience more authentic, and the teacher's role as end-of-the-line inspector de-emphasized. Time that we invest on the front end to help set our students up for success will pay off big time on the back end.

Planning a process in this manner (beginning with the applicable standards and choosing the most appropriate guiding approaches to enrich and add value to the standards) may seem time consuming and overwhelming, but with experience it becomes second nature. As we plan future processes and units, we will find that some guiding approaches, such as differentiated instruction, and tools, such as checklists, serve us well yet again. In addition, we may discover that other approaches, such as constructivism, are more suitable to the task at hand and that others that we've used successfully in the past are less well suited. That's fine. The guiding approaches, though influential, are merely options for us to use at our discretion. Also, during the course of our future planning, the habits of mind and character that may not have been emphasized in the writing process will eventually fit well somewhere. Thus, by the end of the year, you will have found several opportunities to build quality habits into the process successfully.

In Figure 3.6 is an updated version of the framework introduced in the last chapter. This new format adds a few of my favorite guiding approaches to the bottom left-hand corner where their enriching effect on the content standards can be best demonstrated. Also, the seven life roles have been added to the bottom right-hand corner. They serve as a constant reminder of the importance of establishing purpose and providing context with all our academic work with children. As a whole, this entire diagram acts as a critical reference point, reminding us (a) of the goals we hold for our students and (b) that the best way to empower our students to reach these goals lies not with greater evaluation and inspection, but with building quality into the process from the beginning.

## BUILDING QUALITY INTO THE PROCESS: OTHER EXAMPLES

Thus far, the main example of this chapter has involved using guiding approaches to enrich standards-based instruction in the design of a writing process lasting for a period of weeks.

*(Text continued on page 48)*

**Figure 3.2** Creating My Revision Plan

Name _____ Date _____

### Creating My Revision Plan

Directions: Think about what you hope to accomplish during revision. Remember, revision is the stage of the process where we improve the quality of our ideas. We work to ensure that our writing makes sense, that we organize our ideas well, and that we use the best words possible. In revision we can add, subtract, or change words and ideas. Which of the following goals will you focus on during revision? (Check as many as you want.)

_____ I want to make sure that everything makes sense.

_____ I want to make sure that each paragraph has a clear focus.

_____ I want to make sure that all my paragraphs follow appropriate paragraph structure (topic sentence, supporting details, concluding sentence).

_____ I want to lift a line every time I see a sentence that I think I can improve.

_____ I want to make sure that my writing sounds honest and personal (VOICE).

_____ I want to make sure that I maintain a consistent viewpoint (VOICE).

_____ I want to take out parts that just don't fit.

_____ I want to improve my WORD CHOICE.

_____ I want to improve my SENTENCE FLUENCY so that my sentences vary in terms of their length, structure, type, and beginnings.

_____ Other: _____

_____

Revising Partner #1 _____ Initial when done _____

Revising Partner #2 _____ Initial when done _____

Revising Partner #3 _____ Initial when done _____

**Figure 3.3** Four-Color Editing

Name _____ Date _____

### Four-Color Editing

Directions: Use this paper as an Editing Checklist. As you complete each step, be sure to check the appropriate blanks. Edit your work carefully using each color of your four-color pen.

Black is the color for **indented paragraphs** and **dialogue**.

**What to do:** Check to see if all your paragraphs are indented. Also, check to see if your dialogue has quotation marks, commas, and periods in the right places.

_____ I checked to see that all my paragraphs are indented.

_____ I checked the punctuation of my dialogue.

Red is the color for run-on sentences and other punctuation.

**What to do:** Read your work aloud to yourself. Correct any run-on sentences you find. Also, check that you have commas, question marks, and exclamation points in the right places.

_____ I corrected all the run-on sentences I saw.

_____ I have commas (1) between cities and states, (2) for all lists of three or more items, (3) whenever I connected two short sentences, (4) for all direct addresses, (5) before all transition and introductory words.

Blue is the color for **capitals**.

**What to do:** Read your work aloud to yourself a second time. Check to see that you have capitals

_____ at the beginning of every sentence.

_____ for days of the week and months of the year.

_____ for holidays and special events.

_____ for all titles.

_____ every time you use "I."

_____ for names of people, places, and things.

Green is the color for **spelling**.

**What to do:** Read your work aloud for a third time. Point to each word carefully. Circle any word you are not 100 percent sure about. Then, check these words in the dictionary.

_____ I pointed to each word and circled the ones I wasn't 100 percent sure about.

_____ I looked up the circled words in the dictionary.

**Figure 3.4**     Evaluation Sheets

Name: _____     Date: _____

## Evaluation Sheet

Ideas Rubric

Conventions Rubric

4 = Exceeds Expectations

- It all makes sense.
- The writing has a clear focus or main idea.
- Details give the reader important, interesting information that goes well beyond the obvious or predictable.

4 = Exceeds Expectations

- There are few, if any, errors with spelling, capitals, punctuation, grammar, and indenting.
- Conventions may be used creatively to enhance the writing.
- Difficult spelling words and other above-grade-level conventions are well done.

3 = Meets Expectations

- It all makes sense.
- The writing has a clear focus or main idea.
- The writing contains important, interesting details that support and adequately develop the main idea.

3 = Meets Expectations

- The writing is clean and polished. It looks proofread.
- There may be some mistakes with spelling, capitals, punctuation, grammar, and indenting, but the mistakes do not interfere with the reader's ability to understand the writing.
- Errors may occur with difficult spelling words or other conventions that are beyond the grade level.

2 = Below Expectations

- It may or may not make complete sense.
- The writing may or may not have a clear focus or main idea.
- The writing may or may not contain important, interesting details that support and adequately develop the main idea.

2 = Below Expectations

- Conventions errors are frequent and may interfere with the reader's ability to understand the writing.
- Errors may occur with basic spelling words, beginning-of-sentence capitalization, and end punctuation.
- Errors may occur inconsistently. Writing may not look well proofread.

1 = Significantly Below Expectations

- It may or may not make sense.
- The writing may lack any sense of focus.
- Details may be completely lacking, irrelevant, or unimportant.

1 = Significantly Below Expectations

- Errors are so numerous that it is very difficult to read and understand the text.
- Extensive editing (virtually every line) would be required to polish the text for publication.

Student Score: _____ (pencil)

Teacher Score: _____ (pen)

Comments:

Student Score: _____ (pencil)

Teacher Score: _____ (pen)

Comments:

Name: _____     Date: _____

## Evaluation Sheet

<u>Organization Rubric</u>

### 4 = Exceeds Expectations

- The order of ideas is logical, perhaps unusually clever or original.
- The writing follows appropriate paragraph structure when necessary.
- Transitions from one idea to the next are clear.
- Introduction and conclusion are effective, perhaps unusually clever or original.

### 3 = Meets Expectations

- The order of ideas is logical and easy to follow.
- The writing follows appropriate paragraph structure when necessary (topic sentence, supporting details, concluding sentence).
- Transitions from one idea to the next are clear.
- Introduction draws in readers; conclusion provides effective closure.

### 2 = Below Expectations

- The order of ideas may or may not be logical or easy to follow.
- Writing may or may not follow appropriate paragraph structure when necessary.
- Transitions from one idea to the next may or may not be clear.
- Introduction and conclusion may be ineffective or lacking.

### 1 = Significantly Below Expectations

- The order of ideas may or may be illogical or very difficult to follow.
- Writing may or may not follow appropriate paragraph structure when necessary.
- Transitions from one idea to the next may be unclear or not present.
- Introduction and conclusion may be ineffective, lacking, or confusing.

Student Score: _____ (pencil)

Teacher Score: _____ (pen)

Comments:

<u>Voice Rubric</u>

### 4 = Exceeds Expectations

- The writer speaks to the reader in an unusually engaging or original manner.
- The reader feels an unusually strong connection with the writer.
- The writer maintains a consistent viewpoint.

### 3 = Meets Expectations

- Non-narrative writing reflects a strong commitment to the topic.
- The writing sounds like the person who wrote it.
- The writer maintains a consistent viewpoint.

### 2 = Below Expectations

- Non-narrative writing may or may not have a consistent commitment to the topic.
- The writing may or may not consistently sound like the person who wrote it.
- The writer may or may not maintain a consistent viewpoint.

### 1 = Significantly Below Expectations

- Non-narrative writing may or may not have a consistent commitment to the topic.
- The writing may or may not sound like a person who wrote it. It may sound mechanical, dry, or lifeless.
- The writer may or may not maintain a consistent viewpoint.

Student Score: _____ (pencil)

Teacher Score: _____ (pen)

Comments:

*(Continued)*

**Figure 3.4** (Continued)

Name: _____     Date: _____

### Evaluation Sheet

Word Choice Rubric

**4 = Exceeds Expectations**

- Use of advanced vocabulary is evident and purposeful.
- Words and phrases are powerful and engaging; they catch the reader's eye.
- The words and pictures paint a strong picture and linger in the reader's mind.

**3 = Meets Expectations**

- Words are specific and accurate; it's easy to know what the writer means.
- Words appear to be purposefully chosen by the writer.
- The author chooses words that are rich, colorful, interesting, and natural.

**2 = Below Expectations**

- Many words may be vague. It may be difficult to know what the writer means.
- Attempts at rich, colorful language may be lacking or may go too far.
- Some words appear to be purposefully chosen; many appear to be the first thing that popped into the author's mind.

**1 = Significantly Below Expectations**

- Many words may be vague. It may be difficult to know what the writer means.
- Few, if any, words are rich, colorful, interesting, or natural.
- Few, if any, words appear to be purposefully chosen; most, if not all, appear to be the first thing that popped into the author's mind.

Sentence Fluency Rubric

**4 = Exceeds Expectations**

- Sentences feature advanced or creative sentence structure.
- Sentences begin in several different ways and are of varying length.
- There is an unusually strong rhythm to how the sentences sound. The writing is easy to read aloud.

**3 = Meets Expectations**

- Sentences begin in several different ways.
- Sentences are of varying length.
- There is a rhythm to how the sentences sound. The writing is easy to read aloud.

**2 = Below Expectations**

- Sentences may begin in mostly the same way.
- Most sentences may be of similar length.
- Some sentences may be choppy, incomplete, awkward, or difficult to read aloud.

**1 = Significantly Below Expectations**

- Sentence beginnings may be all alike.
- All or almost all sentences may be of similar length.
- All or almost all sentences may be choppy, incomplete, awkward, or difficult to read aloud.

Student Score: _____ (pencil)

Teacher Score: _____ (pen)

Comments:

Student Score: _____ (pencil)

Teacher Score: _____ (pen)

Comments:

SOURCE: Based upon Culham, R. (2003). *Six + One Traits of writing: The complete guide grades 3 and up: Everything you need to teach and assess student writing with this powerful model.* New York: Scholastic Professional Books.

**Figure 3.5**     Writer's Workshop Reflections Sheet

---

Name _____     Date _____

### Writer's Workshop Reflections Sheet

1.  What did you enjoy the most about working on your story?

    _____

    _____

    _____

2.  Which part of your story or the writing process makes you the proudest? Explain why.

    _____

    _____

    _____

3.  What was the biggest challenge you faced as you worked on your story?

    _____

    _____

    _____

4.  What did you learn about yourself as a writer as you worked on this story?

    _____

    _____

    _____

5.  What are your next steps as a writer? In other words, what part of your writing are you the most determined to improve in the future? Explain why.

    _____

    _____

    _____

---

**Figure 3.6**    Expanded Version of Framework Introduced in Last Chapter

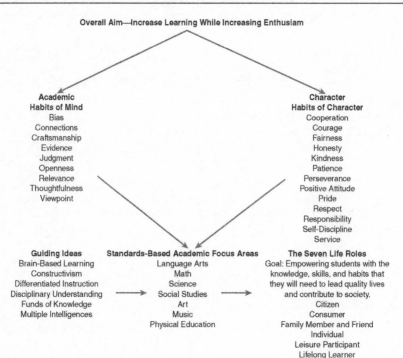

The remainder of this chapter includes other examples that illustrate the flexibility with which the concept of building quality into the process can be applied. After all, this third Essential, along with the others, is primarily a mindset, a way of thinking about the work we do and how we do it. Having begun by focusing on processes requiring multiple weeks to complete, we can now adjust our time frame however we wish. We can expand our view and take a look at the school year as a whole, or we can narrow our focus and consider a single week, a single school day, or even a single lesson.

## THE YEARLONG PERSPECTIVE

Figure 3.7 shows one example of a planning calendar I've used to organize our major units, assessments, and projects throughout the year. All dates, of course, are tentative. By positioning our major priorities on the calendar in advance, we are being proactive. In education we learn quickly that if we don't control our schedule, our schedule will control us. In addition, laying out the year ahead ensures that there's adequate time for each priority—that weeks won't go by without anything important happening or that three important

## An Idea From a Teacher:
## Putting Essential 3 Into Practice

Darlene Fish

*Corinne A. Seeds University Elementary School*

*Los Angeles, CA*

*Primary Demonstration Teacher (7–9-year-olds)*

I try to build quality into the process by having circle time with my students both in the mornings and at the end of each school day. At the start of the day, students can do a brief check-in, and later at the closing circle they can offer highlights of the day, something they learned, or something they want to share. These circle times help me build stronger relationships with the students and help the students bond with one another. I strongly believe that affording my students these opportunities to express themselves gives them purpose, power, and choice in the classroom.

SOURCE: Darlene Fish, Corinne A. Seeds University Elementary School.

**Figure 3.7**   Calendar of Assessments

|    | A | B | C | D | E |
|----|---|---|---|---|---|
| 1 |  | Week 1 | Week 2 | Week 3 | Week 4 |
| 2 | September | Reading Assessment #1 |  |  |  |
| 3 | October |  |  | Math Problem Solving | Social Studies Project #1 Due |
| 4 | November | Reading Assessment #2 | Story #1 Due | Math Problem Solving | Parent Conferences |
| 5 | December |  | Science Project #1 Due | Math Problem Solving |  |
| 6 | January |  |  | Math Problem Solving |  |
| 7 | February | Reading Assessment #3 | Story #2 Due | Math Problem Solving | Student-Led Conference #1 |
| 8 | March |  | Social Studies Project #2 Due | Math Problem Solving |  |
| 9 | April |  |  | Math Problem Solving |  |
| 10 | May |  | Final Math Problem Solving | Reading Assessment #4 | Story #3 Due |
| 11 | June | Science Project #2 Due | Student-Led Conference #2 |  |  |

events don't sneak up on us all at once. Furthermore, the calendar helps us see the progression of our units of study.

I recommend dividing the calendar into three smaller time periods. Organizing the calendar into more manageable blocks of time sharpens my focus and prevents me from being overwhelmed by a whole year's worth of work all at once. As you can see from Figure 3.7, the first period ends in November with parent conferences, the second in February with the first round of student-led conferences, and the last in June with the second round of student-led conferences. I constructed this calendar around both our school's parent conference schedule and its official reporting periods. Our school district was somewhat unique in that it scheduled only one set of parent conferences during the year. These meetings were planned for late November. By ending the first assessment period right before parent conferences, I ensured that I would have information about each child's progress toward many of the academic standards to share with parents.

After the February and June assessment periods, parents have two other opportunities to review their children's progress toward the standards. Because our school has no parent conferences scheduled during these times, I like to conduct the meetings in the form of Student-Led Conferences, a variation of the traditional parent conference that has become quite popular in recent years. Student-Led Conferences give kids a genuine opportunity to take charge of their own learning. The teacher plays no active role in these meetings. Students are entrusted with the responsibility of choosing all or part of the work that will be discussed, planning the agenda, and leading their parents through a tour of their work. The next chapter explores this preparation process in greater depth.

The calendar of assessments, then, is a tool designed to make life easier for you once the school year begins. It may take time to construct initially, but this investment of energy will pay off. Your planning time, for instance, will be greatly reduced throughout the year because the calendar provides so much structure for your instructional program. You will know what goals you are working toward, how you will measure progress toward them, and when and how often you will assess progress. Focusing your curricular, instructional, and assessment efforts in this manner to give your students their best chance of reaching our four year-end goals is the hallmark of building quality into the process.

## A SINGLE SCHOOL DAY

Shortening our time frame to that of a single day, we begin with a simple question: "How can we help our students become as focused and productive as possible for the time they are at school?" Under the inspection model, we would begin each morning with the expectation that the kids would behave appropriately and then at the end of the day evaluate that behavior—either by recognizing positive conduct or by calling attention to inappropriate conduct. An approach more consistent with the lessons of this chapter, though, would cause us to shift emphasis away from the end of the day and have us look for proactive steps we could take at the beginning of the day and throughout the day to help students become and remain focused and productive.

One such step that yields marvelous results involves the use of Paul Dennison's Brain Gym program, specifically its PACE (Positive, Active, Clear, and Energetic) component, part of which I use to begin each day.[7] Brain Gym (another example of the brain-based learning guiding approach) consists of a series of movements designed to help individuals to relax, concentrate, and channel their energies in a positive direction. Here is a brief description of three PACE components.

- *Cross crawls:* Standing in place, touch the left elbow to the right knee and then the right elbow to the left knee. Continue alternating in this pattern. Cross crawls should always be done slowly, emphasizing excellent posture and clean contact between the elbow and knee. This movement activates both hemispheres of the brain and builds nerve networks between the two hemispheres. Moving slowly, students move in an alternating pattern, connecting their elbow to their knee.
- *Hook-ups:* Place both arms straight out, thumbs facing down. Cross one arm over the other and interlock your fingers. Then, roll the locked hands straight down and in toward the body so they rest on the chest with elbows down. Cross one leg over the other and rest your tongue on the roof of your mouth behind the teeth. While the kids are standing in hook-ups, I have them think about the upcoming day and what they hope to accomplish while at school.
- *Drink water:* If you allow students to keep water bottles by their desks, they can take a minute to get a drink.

Since incorporating the PACE series into our morning routine, I have noticed a significant effect on the children's ability to work in a calm, productive manner. We also use PACE and the other Brain Gym movements throughout the day, either at predetermined times, such as before assessments, or as the need arises. In addition, the Brain Gym movements are wonderful problem-solving tools. Instead of getting frustrated with students who have the tendency to lose their concentration and distract their classmates, I now give them the option to stand outside the room for a few moments and do one or more of the movements until they have regained their focus.

Another important factor that impacts how productive students will be relates to how we schedule our daily activities. All time periods are not created equal. In my experience, children tend to be the mentally freshest and most alert first thing in the morning. From there, the ability to concentrate slowly but steadily diminishes as the day progresses. Rather than fight this phenomenon, I try to use it to my advantage and craft each day's schedule so that the most cognitively demanding activities occur early, and the remaining activities are sequenced from most to least demanding as the day progresses. On a typical day our math activities usually require the most rigorous thinking and the greatest attention to detail. I, therefore, schedule math first. I then do an informal ranking of the "demandingness" of the remaining activities I have planned for the day and slot them into our schedule accordingly. This type of "demandingness prioritizing" builds quality into the process by putting students in situations where they are most likely to be successful.

## INDIVIDUAL LESSONS

Volumes have been written about lesson design and lesson planning, and my intention is not to add to this knowledge base. Rather, it is to point out the number of variables over which we have control when we are deciding how to structure our daily lessons. Decisions relating to these variables exert an enormous influence on the ultimate success of our teaching and, as such, provide us with valuable opportunities to build quality into the process.

Think about a math lesson in which students attempt to solve a complex problem that you have posed. As you read the following list of questions, consider the instructional decisions you would make for this lesson:

- Which teaching strategy will I employ for this lesson (e.g., direct instruction, guided discovery, cooperative learning, reciprocal teaching, divergent discovery)?
- How will the students complete their work (e.g., alone, in pairs, or small groups? If partners or groups, who chooses these partners?)?
- What will I be doing while students are working (e.g., circulating to provide assistance and encouragement, working with a small group, offering one-on-one assistance)?
- Will all students complete the same work or will differentiation options be provided to simplify, enrich, or extend the core activity?
- Where will the children sit (e.g., at their desks, on the rug, some at desks and some on the rug)?
- Will any manipulatives or learning tools be used (e.g., counters, rulers, number lines, calculators)?
- Will there be a period of whole class sharing or debriefing at the end of the activity?
- How will successful student strategies be shared with the class a whole (e.g., volunteers present their work, group members nominate members of their group, we conduct a gallery walk, teacher-selected volunteers present work, we pair-share)?

As you think about these variables, remember that there's never only one right combination, one right answer. The items in parentheses are merely options. From these options and others, we use the knowledge we possess about pedagogy and the knowledge we possess about our students to make the best decisions we can. Over time we learn from experience. We will repeat what proves to be effective and tweak what doesn't. The most important fact is that we are doing everything we can to build quality into every lesson we teach.

The examples provided in this chapter only scratch the surface of what is possible once we adopt the mindset of consistently analyzing the work we do and searching for ways to use our knowledge to set our students up for success every step of the way. Over time we will come to see familiar educational practices in new ways. Consider the high stakes tests our states administer every spring to determine whether students are meeting academic expectations. These tests are textbook examples of inspection. They occur at the end of the school year, and regardless of what the results show, we usually receive our scores well after the school year has ended, when it is too late to put them to meaningful use for that group of students, too late to address any identified deficiencies. Politicians and the public focus exclusively on scores; they pay little to no attention to the learning processes or classroom practices that preceded the assessment period. Imagine what could happen if our states took the millions allocated for end-of-the-line testing and instead shifted emphases and spent part of that money on teachers, helping us improve the way we plan and deliver instruction throughout the year. In this collaborative effort, think of the genuine quality that could be added to the learning process.

## KEY POINTS FROM ESSENTIAL 3

- Building quality into the process means that we focus significant time and attention on how things get done in the classroom so that we operate as efficiently and effectively as possible.
- The Inspection Role Play helps students understand that quality is everyone's responsibility and that the better our classroom processes are, the better the learning will be.

- In terms of academic planning, teachers can build quality into the process by using a variety of effective guiding approaches to enrich standards-based instruction.
- The concept of building quality into the process can be flexibly applied to different time frames, from a yearlong perspective, to a four-week unit, to a single school day, to even a single lesson.
- The concept can also be flexibly applied to different aspects of managing a classroom, such as unit planning, scheduling, lesson planning, and even incorporating movement into the school day.
- Whichever time frame and whichever aspect of managing a classroom we consider, the goal of building quality into the process remains the same: to take the best information available about how children learn and how groups of people work together most effectively and use it to get the biggest educational bang for our buck.
- The end of the line is the wrong time to focus on quality. Quality must be built into the process from the beginning.

## REFLECTION QUESTIONS

- As you work to enhance and enrich your standards-based instruction, which guiding approaches appeal to you the most?
- What are some ways you might be able to incorporate checklists or other tools and strategies into your teaching to foster student independence and build quality into the process?
- What are the major units, assessments, and projects that will comprise the foundation of your yearlong planning calendar?
- Are there any practices currently in your teaching repertoire that resemble end-of-the-line inspection? If so, how could you end this reliance on inspection and instead focus greater time and attention on the steps of the process itself?
- In addition to the ideas and strategies described in this chapter, how else might you be able to take the best information available about how children learn and how groups of people work together most effectively and use it to get the biggest educational bang for our buck?

# Essential 4     INVOLVING PARENTS

Growing up on the beaches of Santa Monica, California, as a competitive paddle tennis player, I learned some valuable lessons that would later influence my teaching philosophy. Paddle tennis is a game very similar to tennis; in fact, the scoring system and basic rules are virtually identical. Paddle tennis, however, features a smaller court, lower net, and different type of racquet. Despite its court size, paddle tennis is primarily a game of doubles. Every major tournament, as well as most recreational play, pits teams of two against each other. For a doubles team to succeed, both players must possess strong skills. But a pair of powerful backhands and effective serves, by themselves, will not be enough to guarantee victory. The players must also work well together, functioning as a cohesive unit.

The ability and willingness to play as a team is so important because doubles partners sink or swim together. For example, with my partner Richard, it was impossible for one of us to achieve victory without the other; our fates were inextricably linked. Of all the people gathered at any given tournament, Richard was the only one who cared as much about our team's winning as I did. We had equal stakes in the outcome. It made sense, therefore, that we valued each other as the most important assets we had in our quest to succeed. When he missed shots, it did me no good to blame, criticize, or alienate him. Doing so would have served only to damage our relationship. No matter how intense the action became, we had to make an unconditional effort to offer encouragement and support. We needed to bring out the best in each other.

When my days as a competitive paddle tennis player ended and my days as a teacher began, I carried these notions of partnership and teamwork with me to the classroom. My mission, which had involved winning paddle tennis tournaments, was now to increase the learning and enthusiasm of my students. As a new teacher, it was easy for me to think that I was alone in this mission, but I wasn't. There were others who had just as much of a stake in my ultimate success as I did: the parents of my students. They were my new partners. After all, we were both striving for the same outcome—for our kids to have the best school year possible. I couldn't do my part without help from the parents, and they couldn't do theirs without me. We needed one another. Like two members of a doubles team, our fates were inextricably linked.

Consistent parent involvement dramatically increases the likelihood that quality learning will occur. Parents play such a crucial role in their children's academic, physical, social, and moral development that we, as teachers, make a huge mistake if we view them as anything other than indispensable collaborators. It's not enough to keep parents pleased, appeased, or out of our hair. If we're committed to bringing the best out of our students, we need to build and maintain long-term relationships of loyalty, trust, and respect with their parents. Investing the time and effort to work closely with parents throughout the year maximizes our chances of fulfilling our aim and mission and achieving our goals. In addition, Alan Blankstein, author of *Failure is Not an Option*, asserts, "Educational research clearly shows that the support and involvement of students' families . . . is fundamental to achievement." (p. 167)

## NINE REASONS TO MAKE THE EFFORT

The following points provide a strong rationale as to why teachers should make parent involvement a top priority:

1. Parents are their children's first and most important teachers. Although not all teachers are parents, all parents are teachers. As such, they have the greatest impact on a student's motivation to learn. Parents are usually eager to play a significant role in their children's education, but they often don't know how. By establishing caring relationships with parents, we can help them help their children.

2. Consistent communication between the home and school enables parents to reinforce the skills, knowledge, and habits that we emphasize in class.

3. It's important that teachers are aware of students' strengths and weaknesses, likes and dislikes, areas of special sensitivity, and any factors at home that are affecting school performance. Parents are in the best position to provide this information.

4. Students act, behave, and perform differently when they know that their parents and teachers communicate frequently.

5. Frequent communication earns parents' confidence, trust, and respect. With open lines of communication, it's unlikely that feelings of uncertainty, mistrust, and alienation will ever arise. The favorable impression that we create makes problems easier to solve when they occur.

6. When teachers and parents communicate in a respectful manner, we model positive adult interactions for the kids. These occasions serve a prosocial function because many children, unfortunately, don't often have the opportunity to observe this type of relationship.

7. Parents can become our biggest supporters and most loyal allies. Should a colleague or supervisor ever doubt our methods or question our approach to teaching, these allies will be there to come to our defense.

8. Parents are often valuable classroom resources. The better we know parents, the more we'll be aware of the various ways in which they can assist the class.

9. Forming trusting relationships with parents can reduce the feelings of isolation that so many teachers, especially newer ones, often experience.

## GUIDING PRINCIPLES FOR HOME-SCHOOL COMMUNICATION

The principles that follow set the tone for all communications with parents. Together, they constitute a comprehensive framework designed to make our interactions as positive and productive as possible.

*Thinking Long Term*—Forming trusting relationships occurs over time; it is not a one-shot deal. Don't be discouraged if your early efforts to contact parents don't bring an immediate response. During my first year of teaching, I didn't meet a certain parent until February. After months of one-sided communication, I could easily have given up on him, but I didn't. Finally, he found me one afternoon on the playground and introduced himself. Because of his busy work schedule, he was unable to stop by sooner. He informed me that he had read everything I had been sending home and promised to become more involved. Leaving the door open allows parents to come in when they are ready.

*Communicating Frequently*—The more frequently we communicate with parents, the better. Parent communications come in two forms, standardized and individualized. "Standardized" means that every parent receives the same message. At a minimum, I send home one standardized communication, such as a newsletter, per week. Doing so establishes consistency and keeps parents informed about important class business. Individualized communications, on the other hand, are unique to each student and usually relate to issues of academic progress and behavior. Phone calls are one example of this form. While I hold myself to a set routine with standardized communications, I allow myself greater flexibility with individualized ones. I generally strive for one or two per month, depending on the time available and the needs of each child. You must decide how much time you are willing and able to devote to this aspect of your teaching. As a rule of thumb, start small and build from there. It's much better to begin the year sending newsletters home every month and then increasing the frequency later in the year than it is to begin with weekly bulletins and then lose steam.

*Creating a Sense of Inclusion*—In my communications with parents, both written and oral, I try to create the feeling that we're all in this together. I welcome each family's participation by encouraging every parent to take an active role in class. I extend this invitation, though, fully understanding that many parents will be unable to devote time because of heavy work or family commitments. It's important, therefore, not to alienate parents by putting too much pressure on them to get involved.

*Listening With Understanding and Empathy*—Listening is one of the most important life skills a person can develop. Because of its significance, teachers spend a tremendous amount of time trying to help students improve in this area. With listening, we need to practice with parents what we preach to the kids. Listening, though, isn't easy. It takes patience, caring, and a genuine desire to understand what the other person says and means. When we are talking one-on-one with parents, listening is all the more difficult because the conversations generally take place right before school, when we have a great deal on our minds, or right after school, when we've often just about lost our minds. When parents take time out of their day to speak with us, however, it's usually for an important reason. We must do our best to listen intently and understand matters from their perspective so that we can effectively address their concerns.

*Encouraging Cooperative Problem Solving*—When a problem arises, I work with parents to solve it. Working together as a team allows us to create solutions that benefit all parties involved. Covey calls this approach "win-win thinking."[1] The emphasis is on producing mutually beneficial results, not on winning an argument or finding fault with one another. Placing blame serves no useful purpose. Fix the problem, not the blame.

*Showing Appreciation*—Parents work hard to raise their children. The sacrifices they make to feed, clothe, assist, and support their kids remain largely hidden from the view of teachers, but they are very real. Many parents spend so much time satisfying their children's needs that they rarely take time for themselves. Because of all the time and energy parents spend on behalf of their kids, make a concerted effort to thank them for any service they provide to the class. Express appreciation for contributions large and small.

*Conveying a Sense of Optimism*—Because each school year is full of possibility, use your communications to convey a sense of excitement and optimism. Tell parents, for example, how happy you are to have their child in your class and how much you are looking forward to a wonderful year together. Making this effort is especially valuable for students who have never before had successful school experiences. When their teachers communicate in an enthusiastic, upbeat tone, these kids will sense that this year may be different. They will know that they are in a new place with a new attitude, and they will feed off this optimism.

*Being Proactive*—Being proactive has two major benefits. First, it gives you the opportunity to package your ideas and articulate them in the best possible light. Acting first, you shape the conversation, saying your ideas in the way you want to say them, not in the way someone else has already characterized them before ever having the chance to hear from you. Proactivity increases your credibility, strengthens your voice, and reaffirms your position of leadership.

Second, proactivity is the best approach to problem prevention. Consider the following example: Imagine that a brand new shipment of expensive, state-of-the-art math manipulatives has just arrived at school. Because the school could only afford one set, the staff decided that each class would get the manipulatives for three weeks. When our turn comes, I lengthen the daily math period from 45 minutes to 2 hours so we can try all the hands-on activities shown in the accompanying teacher guidebook. To compensate for the extra time that we spend on math, I don't give any math homework for the next three weeks.

Immediately, parents become concerned. "Where's my child's math homework?" they ask. "Why did you stop assigning math homework?" they wonder. "Don't you know that my child will fall behind without math practice every night?" they insist.

Now, I have to react. The parents have already made up their minds. Based on the information they have received from their kids, they have concluded that I have stopped assigning math homework, and they don't understand why. I have dug myself a hole, out of which I must climb.

All this trouble could have been avoided had I been proactive. Before the first day of our three-week manipulative exploration, I should have sent home a newsletter explaining the situation. Then, the parents would have known in advance of the unique, short-term opportunity that we had to use these manipulatives and understood the value of these types of experiences. I could have told them that to take full advantage of this opportunity, I would be lengthening our daily math period, and that because of the extra time the kids spent on math in class, I would be decreasing the time they spend on math at home. I could have emphasized that this hiatus from math homework would only last three weeks and that the kids would not be at all disadvantaged because they were gaining valuable practice in class. Informing parents beforehand would have enabled me to accentuate the positive.

Experience has taught me that teachers' greatest difficulties with parents often arise from a lack of proactivity. When parents are not informed in advance about rules, units, grading policies, and the like, they have every reason to come back after the fact and say, "I didn't know." Once that happens, teachers are forced into a reactive, often defensive, position. The trouble is, no matter how effectively we later explain ourselves, the damage has already been done. Furthermore, by the time we have responded to one problem situation, the next crisis has occurred and needs to be addressed. A pattern soon begins. We find ourselves spending a tremendous amount of time putting out fires instead of using it to communicate proactively.

*Building Goodwill*—In his *The Seven Habits of Highly Effective People*, Stephen Covey introduces the concept of an Emotional Bank Account, a metaphor that can help teachers build and maintain strong relationships with parents.[2] Unlike a traditional bank account where people keep money, an Emotional Bank Account is where we store feelings of trust and goodwill. Covey makes the point that each individual has an Emotional Bank Account with every other person with whom we come into contact. With these friends and acquaintances, there are times when we add positive feelings to our accounts (deposits) and times when we take away some of these feelings (withdrawals).

There are several ways to make deposits in another person's Emotional Bank Account. These include the following: giving compliments, sharing, doing favors, taking the time to talk, and being polite. Similarly, there are numerous ways of making withdrawals: arguing, blaming, lying, and showing disrespect. When a relationship between two people is strong and their Emotional Bank Accounts contain a large reservoir of goodwill, then an occasional withdrawal won't cause a great deal of harm. When a relationship is weak, however, a single withdrawal may have a severe negative effect. Therefore, when dealing with parents, commit yourself to making frequent deposits so that your relationships are strong and the trust level is high.

## WAYS TO BUILD AND MAINTAIN RELATIONSHIPS WITH PARENTS

In this section, I present a number of specific, proven ways to put the guiding principles into action. These options help you keep parents informed and involved throughout the year.

### Begin With a Bang

Prior to my second year, I came across an idea I just had to try. First, I obtained a class list of my first graders' names and phone numbers. I went home and called every family, introducing myself to the parents and telling them that I was tentatively scheduled to be their child's teacher this year. I used the word "tentatively" to cover myself and the school in case any last minute enrollment changes were made. Since I knew I'd be setting up the classroom during the week before school started, I invited each family to stop by to meet me in person. About 10 of my 32 students accepted this offer. With these 10, I was able to learn their names, talk with them briefly, and get a sense of who they were. I greatly enjoyed and appreciated this one-on-one time.

I then found the previous year's kindergarten class pictures in the yearbook. By matching the names on my list to the faces in the yearbook, I learned the names of the rest of my returning students. In addition, I was only expecting two new students, one boy and one girl. So, I quickly learned their names. On the night before school started, I made a simple name tag for each student and arranged the tags on a table by the front door of the classroom.

That next morning I was ready. I stood at the door eager to welcome my new students. While I was praying that none of them had gotten haircuts over the summer, they began to arrive. I greeted each one by name, handed them a name tag, and invited them to sit down on the rug. Standing outside on the yard, a number of parents watched the whole thing, wondering how I could possibly know the names of people I had never met. I felt fantastic. Before the school year was barely three minutes old, I had created a very favorable first impression and made a major deposit in the Emotional Bank Accounts of my students and parents. This proactive gesture had set the tone I wanted.

Begin the year with some sort of powerful, dramatic initiative. If you are unable to obtain a class list before the start of the year, do something the first day. Write a short, personalized note to each student, call each parent after school expressing how much you are looking forward to the year ahead, or send a postcard through the mail. Just do something. The more novel, the better. A thoughtful gesture on your part will be remembered.

### The First Day Letter

Making a proactive gesture to introduce yourself and build goodwill will capture parents' attention. Capitalize on this momentum before it disappears. Send home a detailed letter discussing the upcoming year. Although I refer to it as the First Day Letter, it's a good idea to wait a few days before sending it home. On the first day of school, parents are so inundated with paperwork from the school office that a letter from you may get lost in the shuffle. What I do is send a very brief note home the first day of school, maybe one paragraph long, introducing myself once again and alerting parents to watch out for a more detailed letter that I will be sending home in a few days.

The First Day Letter is the educational equivalent of a movie trailer. It offers a sneak preview of the year ahead, whetting parents' appetite for what's to come. The First Day Letter is a sincere articulation of who you are, what you value, and what you hope to accomplish. Your words paint a picture for parents of what the upcoming months will look like and create a sense of possibility, optimism, and excitement by charting the direction in which you want to take the class. Writing a First Day Letter provides you with your first and best opportunity to establish your leadership of the class, saying what you want to say in the way you want to say it.

The following list contains ingredients you may want to include in your First Day Letter:

- Biographical information about yourself
- Your educational philosophy
- Your personal goals for the year
- Introduction to class aim, goals, and other quality-related concepts with which parents may not be familiar
- Major curricular emphases
- Your classroom management system
- Highlights of the year
- How you will communicate with parents and how they can reach you
- A blank page at the end of the letter for parents to use to inform you about any special concerns, abilities, or interests that either they or their children have. Asking parents about *their* interests and abilities is a great initial step when employing the funds of knowledge approach mentioned in the previous chapter.

The First Day Letter that I send home is shown in Figure 4.1. I used the concept of "quality education" to structure my thoughts. By organizing the letter around this central theme, I was able to present my beliefs, ideas, and expectations in a coherent, integrated fashion. With quality education as my umbrella topic, I was able to connect essential ideas such as character, teamwork, and communication. Without a broad theme, First Day Letters can too easily become long laundry lists of topics, unconnected to one another or to any larger idea.

### The Weekly Newsletter

Once you have sent home the First Day Letter, don't stop there. Continue to inform parents on a regular basis about important classroom matters. The best vehicle for

**Figure 4.1**     First Day Letter

September 12, 2005

Dear Families,

This is the letter I promised you last Wednesday. As I mentioned in my earlier note, my name is Steve Reifman, and I am delighted to welcome you to what I know will be an outstanding year. I consider myself very fortunate to be at such a special place as Roosevelt School. The quality of its staff, the dedication of its volunteers, and the supportiveness of its families and neighboring community are truly precious assets. In this letter I would like to share with you a little bit about who I am and what I hope to accomplish this year.

I am strongly committed to providing your child with the highest quality of education possible. To me, quality education means several things. First, quality education begins with the recognition and appreciation of the fact that each child is unique and special. I believe that all children should be valued for who they are and encouraged to discover their full potential. Each child has something to offer, and each child is a potentially valuable resource to his or her community. I strive to bring out the best in every child. I want all children to take pride in who they are, have a healthy self-esteem, and become independent, self-directed learners.

I place particular emphasis on the importance of character. My top priority is that my students become good people. We will talk about principles such as honesty, kindness, self-discipline, and perseverance. I want to develop students who try their best, never give up, and conduct themselves in a courteous manner. I will try my very best to lead by example.

Second, quality education involves taking each individual student and bringing everyone together to form a cohesive, supportive team. Just as I try to develop a sense of identity and self-esteem in each child, I also try to develop a sense of group identity and group esteem. I want students to be proud of being members of our classroom. As a community of learners, we will spend a great deal of time discussing ideas such as respect, cooperation, responsibility, service, and fairness. We will work together, help one another, and make meaningful decisions together. I will do whatever I can to create an emotionally safe, nurturing environment where students feel comfortable taking risks, sharing information, and being themselves. The whole can be greater than the sum of the parts.

Third, quality education focuses directly on the habits of mind and habits of character that students will need in order to make a contribution to society and lead quality lives. I will attempt to connect classroom learning to these higher purposes. Specifically, I hope to show the kids how what they learn in school will help them become lifelong learners, productive workers, active citizens, intelligent consumers, and caring individuals. I seek to empower my students so that they will be able to perform these roles successfully now and in the future. When students understand the purposes of their learning and when they are encouraged to find meaning in it, motivation increases and greater learning gains result.

Fourth, quality education demands high expectations for everyone. All students are capable of achieving excellence. My job involves getting the students to expect great things from themselves. Once students believe in themselves and are motivated to put forth consistent effort, wonderful things start happening. It is my goal to build the students' confidence and nourish the intrinsic motivation that lies inside of them so that they experience the joys of learning. I will demand a great deal of responsibility from everyone, but I will be there to support them every step of the way. I will set them up for success any way I can.

Fifth, quality education requires the active involvement and support of parents. It is crucial for us to remain in close contact throughout the year. Every Monday you will receive a weekly newsletter containing important information about our class. It is absolutely essential that you read this newsletter every week and discuss it with your child. I will also contact you by phone or with a note whenever the need arises. Please feel free to do the same. I am always happy to discuss school matters with you.

Parental involvement and support also mean that you closely monitor your child's performance at home and at school. Every time you ask your child about a homework activity, every time you take an interest in one of his or her projects, and every time you make sure your child has a designated time and place for homework, you are showing that you value education and that you think schoolwork is worthy of the time and effort your child puts forth. This is a message your child needs to hear constantly.

I actively encourage parents to volunteer in the classroom. I hope to have parent volunteers in the classroom on a daily basis. The assistance that parents provide is invaluable. For those of you who are interested, I will be distributing a volunteer sheet in the near future. If you are unable to volunteer in the classroom but would like to help out in other ways, such as with xeroxing or by providing supplies, that would be fantastic as well. Any help that you could give us this year would be much appreciated.

There are many more things I would like to share with you about the upcoming year, but I feel it is best if I stop here. In this letter I hope I have made it clear how important it is for all of us to work together this year. When parents, students, and teachers form trusting relationships and work together, then we give the kids their greatest chance for success in the classroom. I hope this letter finds you in good spirits, and I look forward to speaking with you soon.

Sincerely,

Steve Reifman

Please use the following sheet to provide any information about your child that you believe would help me perform my duties more effectively. You may choose to describe strengths, weaknesses, hopes, fears, previous school experiences, personality characteristics, hobbies, or anything else that you think I would find helpful. Even if you write nothing at all, please print your name and child's name and fill in the date below so that I know you have read this letter. Thanks.

Child's Name _____

Your Name _____     Date _____

maintaining this type of communication is the Weekly Newsletter. Use the Weekly Newsletter to do the following:

- Summarize the previous week
- Offer a sneak preview of the week ahead
- Describe various features of the classroom
- Highlight pieces of student work
- Promote upcoming events
- Ask for special favors
- Introduce units and policies
- Give "State of the Class" updates
- Suggest tips that parents can use to help their children at home more effectively
- Remind parents of important dates (assessments, due dates, field trips)
- Continue discussing ideas and themes you introduced in the First Day Letter
- Recognize class improvements and successes
- Thank those who have helped the class in important ways

Sample newsletters are shown in Figure 4.2. Begin creating your own by choosing a title and making a template so your newsletter has a distinctive look that parents will recognize immediately. Reproducing these bulletins on a different color paper will further distinguish them from other school correspondence. I write my newsletter every Thursday and send it home the following Monday, attaching it to our weekly homework packet. When you have a consistent routine, parents know to watch out for the newsletter on the same day every week.

Initially, writing weekly newsletters requires a substantial amount of time. During my first year of teaching, I usually spent 30 to 45 minutes per week writing them. But the good news is that the time commitment decreases each year because you will be able to reuse many of the newsletters, sometimes in their entirety, and because you will become more proficient with this style of writing. Remember, start small and build from there. If you're comfortable with monthly newsletters, then try sending them home every two weeks.

Invite students to contribute articles or entries to the newsletter. This will also decrease your workload, but that's not why you do it. Including their submissions represents another way of sharing ownership and building teamwork with the kids. You may also want to consider creating your newsletters together, as a shared writing activity. This collaborative venture enables you to produce meaningful correspondence and practice important writing skills simultaneously. Your willingness to incorporate student writing into the newsletter shows that you value the contributions of everyone and that you are committed to making this truly a *class* newsletter.

## Home-School Journals

A Home-School Journal is a single-subject spiral notebook that students transport back and forth to class. These notebooks are readily available at office supply stores, and an entire class set can usually be purchased for a few dollars. Home-School Journals are wonderful complements to the Weekly Newsletters. Parents very much appreciate the important information that you present in the newsletters, but they will also want specific information about how their child is doing in class. Home-School Journals enable you to provide this type of individualized communication in an informal way.

Use these journals to communicate about a wide variety of issues. Of course, there will be times when you need to notify parents about their child's misbehavior, but make sure that

**Figure 4.2**    Sample Class Newsletters

---

Volume 1, September 11, 2006

# What's Going On in Room 27?

## A Weekly Newsletter

### Homework Packets

Welcome to the first edition of *What's Going On in Room 27?* a newsletter that you will receive every week along with your child's weekly homework packet. The homework packets and newsletters will be sent home every Monday. Please tear off the newsletter and keep it at home. Underneath, you will always find the cover sheet to the homework packet that lists and explains the activities that the kids will work on during the week. The completed packets are due each Friday. Please sign on the bottom of the cover sheet to show that you monitored your child's work throughout the week.

According to guidelines, third graders should generally spend between 30 and 40 minutes per night on homework. The first 20 of these minutes will always consist of WEB Reading, which is what we call silent reading in our class. The remaining activities will connect directly to the standards and academic focus areas of our curriculum. If you notice that your child seems to be spending significantly more than an average of 30-40 minutes per night on homework, please let me know so we can discuss the situation.

The kids should arrive home with a full understanding of how to do their homework because we will have gone over the directions to each activity thoroughly in class. If they need to stay after school for a minute to clarify some of the directions, I am always happy to do that. Students who do not turn in a completed, neat packet will work on their homework in class on Friday during a special Choice Time, in which the kids will pursue topics and projects of interest.

Finally, it is very important that homework be done carefully and that the packet be turned in on Friday free of wrinkles, folds, and tears. Homework should always be kept in a folder or notebook during the week. Feel free to use the PTA folders we give out as homework folders.

*(Continued)*

**Figure 4.2** (Continued)

Volume 6, October 16, 2006

# What's Going On in THQ?

### Getting Deeper Into Reading

During our daily Reading Workshop, the kids and I participate in a variety of activities designed to help us "get deeper" into the books we read. Throughout the year we will spend a significant amount of time reading, talking about what we read, and writing about what we read. In this week's newsletter I'm providing some suggestions that you can use to help your child get deeper into books at home.

- Read aloud to your child frequently. Even if your child can read at a high level independently, there are still many benefits that come from reading aloud to children as they get older.

- Pay close attention to the strategies I include on the homework packet cover sheet. As you read with your child, see which ones your child already uses and offer guidance as to how others can be implemented.

- Find ways for you and your child to weave reading into your interests, hobbies, and home lives.

- Strike up a book conversation with your child and discuss the books you are currently reading.

- Encourage your child to interview an enthusiastic adult reader to try to find approaches, strategies, or ideas that your child can emulate.

- In order to find more reading time throughout the day, take books with you on trips or errands. You never know when you'll find a few minutes here or there that can be spent reading.

- Spend some time looking through the sections of your new Parent Guidebook that pertain to helping your child with his or her reading.

## An Idea From a Teacher:
## Putting Essential 4 Into Practice

Amy Argento

*Seaside Elementary School*

*Torrance, CA*

*4th Grade Teacher*

To improve parent involvement and correspondence, I have started a weekly newsletter that outlines homework for the week on one side and a newsletter on the other. The newsletter, titled "Week at a Glance," is attached to the front of the student's homework packets each week and is copied on yellow paper to make it prominent. The front page incorporates spelling words, parent reminders, and homework outlined for the week including due dates. Most of the weekly homework only changes slightly, other than special projects. The newsletter sections on the back include an author of the week, how parents can help, announcements, looking ahead, and a note from the teacher. I utilize the first newsletter to talk to the parents about quality, habits of character and mind, classroom procedures, and to encourage practices at home that will help their child succeed. At first, the use of a newsletter seemed overwhelming and time-consuming, but over time, it became much easier and actually saved me time.

SOURCE: Amy Argento, Seaside Elementary School.

your entries are not limited to the issue of behavior. You don't want children to develop a negative association with the journals, viewing them as "those things that are only going to get me in trouble at home." Instead, the journals should contain such items as recognitions of student progress, requests for favors, questions, suggestions to help parents help their children at home, and amusing anecdotes.

Using Home-School Journals has a number of advantages over communicating by phone. First, to speak with parents on the phone, we generally have to call during the evening hours. I have never liked calling at this time because I worry about interrupting family dinners and because I make a concerted effort not to take work home with me at night. Instead, I prefer to write my journal entries while I'm still at school. Second, when I send the journals home with students, I know that their parents will almost always receive my notes that day; thus, it only takes me one attempt to deliver the information. With phone calls, however, there is no such certainty. Busy signals, answering machines, and pagers mean that I will frequently have to contact parents again at least once to share my original message. Writing notes offers a more efficient use of time.

Finally, writing notes allows parents to preserve important milestones. For example, when I was a student-teacher in a fifth grade classroom, I noticed a boy who seemed to be having a hard time in class. His spirits were low, and I could tell that he didn't feel connected to what was going on in the room because he didn't talk much and he chose to sit away from the other kids. After my supervising teacher asked me to choose new monitors to perform various class jobs, I decided to make the boy one of the line leaders. He took to his new position right away. I wanted to make a big deal out of the good job he was doing, hoping that it would change his outlook and improve his morale. I wrote a brief note to his mom, telling her how well he was performing his new responsibility. The next day, she wrote me a short note back, explaining how happy he was to be recognized for a job well done and how appreciative she was to hear from me. Gradually, he began to open up; he appeared happier. His mom told me that they kept the note and that he looked at it often. They were able to revisit this correspondence because it was tangible. There was a sense of permanence with the note, one that doesn't exist with phone calls.

Using Home-School Journals to communicate with parents also has a number of advantages over the more traditional practice of writing notes on individual pieces of paper. First, single sheets are more often lost or wrinkled than single-subject notebooks. Second, individual notes are generally thrown away after they are read. The pages of the journal, on the other hand, remain in the notebook where they serve as a record of all your communications and allow you to observe each child's progress over time.

There are a number of ways to use the Home-School Journals. The easiest is to keep them stored in a box somewhere in the room. Whenever you need to write to a parent, simply find that student's journal, make an entry, and send it home. Once the parent reads and responds to your note, the student brings the journal back to you. You then read the reply and place the journal back in the box. This use-as-needed approach offers you tremendous flexibility in terms of when and how often you write in the journals.

A more structured approach involves writing in a certain number of journals per day so that each child receives one entry per week. For example, if you have 20 kids, you would write in four journals per day so that by Friday every student has an entry to take home. This approach ensures that nobody falls through the cracks. With the use-as-needed approach, there is the tendency to write in some journals more than others while neglecting some students entirely. If you choose this more structured approach, don't feel obligated to maintain this pace every week. You may want to write in the journals every other week or once a month. Again, remember to start slow and increase the frequency when you are ready. Don't commit yourself to doing this every week and then find that you're unable to continue the pace.

A third alternative, one better suited to the upper grades, transfers the primary responsibility of writing in the journals to the students. With this Parent-Teacher-Student Journal approach, set aside time once a week for the kids to write notes to their families. In these entries they can discuss their day, explain what they're learning, or introduce their parents to some unique aspect of the class. A mini-brainstorming session held at the beginning of the period will help every student find a topic that will make for interesting conversation later that evening.

While the students are taking about 20 minutes to make their entries, use this time to write to parents. I place an empty chair next to me and invite one child at a time to sit with me. This is fantastic quality time between teacher and student. It's one of the few opportunities I have during the school day to focus attention on only one child. While we talk, I write a short note to the parents. Sometimes, I address the note to the child and ask him or her to take it home, thus facilitating smooth three-way communication between parents, teachers, and students. Typically, I will write four journal entries during this time. Keep a checklist handy so that you are aware of how many times you have called up each student. Along with the quality time you spend with the kids, the other advantage of this approach is that you do all of your writing during class time; it requires no afterschool commitment. If your day is an extremely busy one, and you just don't think there's any way you can write in the journals, this is the approach for you.

Whichever approach you choose, keep in mind a few pointers:

- Always date the entry.
- Be complete, yet brief (3–4 sentences).

**Figure 4.3**     Sample Home-School Journal Entry

February 21, 2005

Dear Mr. and Mrs. Harper,

I was very surprised this morning to hear Michael using inappropriate language in class. Considering how well he usually conducts himself, I'm hoping this was a one-time occurrence.

Still, I would appreciate it if you could talk with him tonight so he knows that you are aware of the incident. Please respond to this note as soon as possible.

Thanks,

Steve

- Be specific so parents know exactly what you mean.
- Ask for a response.
- Phrase your thoughts in the most positive way possible.

A sample journal entry is shown in Figure 4.3.

## OTHER WAYS TO PROMOTE WORKING TOGETHER

In addition to the ideas mentioned in the previous section, there are a number of other ways to involve, assist, and strengthen relationships with parents. When we make the most of these options, our students reap the benefits:

- Assemble a list of community organizations whose addresses and phone numbers parents may need.
- Invite parents to participate in special class events such as holiday parties and cooking activities.
- Organize workshops and arrange for guest speakers on matters of interest to parents.
- Have a potluck meal in your classroom. You may want to schedule it to coincide with one of the workshops mentioned earlier.
- Incorporate the expertise that parents possess into your curriculum (e.g., Funds of Knowledge Approach). Whenever you begin a new unit of study, ask parents if they have any knowledge or experience in that area that they would like to share. Your

effort to include parents in this manner shows that you are truly committed to building a classroom community where every team member is valued as an important resource.

- Consider making a home visit. Parents are often more comfortable relating to teachers at home where the setting is more familiar and the atmosphere more informal.

- Survey students and parents periodically about various aspects of your classroom. This is another way to demonstrate that you value their input.

- Actively solicit parents to volunteer in your classroom. Their labor helps out tremendously while their mere presence shows students that they care about the education of young people.

- Distribute a homework sheet for parents to sign in order to show that they have monitored their child's efforts. Many teachers attach a sheet of this kind to a homework packet that contains all the activities for a given week.

- Have your students write invitations to their families for major class events. Invitations written by students are more personal and more meaningful to parents than those done by the teacher.

- Maintain a reasonable open-door policy in your classroom. Parents should feel comfortable approaching you, but they need to know that it must be done during nonschool time.

- Try to become involved in neighborhood and community events. Participating in community clean-ups, canned food drives, and recycling rallies sends the message that you view the school as not just the place where you work, but as part of a larger community about which you care deeply.

- Encourage parents to observe in your class. They are more likely to want to volunteer and more likely to understand your point of view once they have seen part of an actual school day.

- Distribute a calendar of major school and class events. Doing so gives parents the advance notice they need to organize their schedules around these occasions.

- Establish a phone tree. A phone tree serves as an effective way to communicate important messages to all parents quickly.

## HELPING PARENTS HELP THEIR CHILDREN

A significant aspect of the home-school relationship involves helping parents help their children at home. Parents are usually eager to play a major role in the education of their children, but they are rarely shown how to do so. Unfortunately, teachers often interpret this parental uncertainty as unwillingness or apathy. Share the following suggestions with parents to assist them in this endeavor:

- Commit yourselves to playing an active role in your child's education. Many parents leave the responsibility for their child's education with the teacher. No matter how dedicated your child's teacher may be, this practice is unwise. Parents must remain involved on a consistent basis.

- Repeatedly express to your child that doing well in school and getting an excellent education are essential prerequisites for living a happy, productive life. You can never repeat this message too many times. (The seven life roles include dozens of examples that illustrate this point, and you may want to provide your parents with a list of some of these options or with a copy of the Tower of Opportunity foldout.)

- Develop a homework policy with your child: No television until all homework is complete? No play time? Discuss questions such as these with your child so that both of you are clear about your expectations for home study.
- Provide your child with a quiet study area. If possible, supply a desk and a spot to keep all necessary books and materials organized. With or without a desk, however, it's critical that children have a consistent place to study where nobody will disturb them. Providing such an atmosphere will not only enable your child to have an easier time studying but also let him or her know that you think doing homework is an important priority.
- Encourage your child to complete homework activities as independently as possible; offer help only when necessary. Giving too much assistance can cause your child to become too dependent on you while not giving enough can cause frustration. Strive to achieve the right balance so that your child exercises responsibility and you still remain actively involved in overseeing his or her efforts, both on daily homework activities and during long-term projects and test preparation.
- Respond promptly to all paperwork and notices that your child's teacher and the school office send home.
- Discuss school events and happenings with your child as often as possible.
- Don't hesitate to express to the teacher any concerns you have about your child's progress
- Make sure that your child takes all needed supplies to school every day.

I conclude this section by describing the Parent Guidebook, an important resource with which we can provide families in our efforts to help them help their children at home. My friend Lorie and I created our school's first Parent Guidebook during the summer of 2001, and now third grade parents receive a copy every year at our annual Back to School Night. The guidebook contains five sections: (1) a list of the third grade California Language Arts and Math standards, along with user-friendly explanations and examples; (2) homework suggestions, reading strategies, decoding tips, and other information designed to help parents work with their children at home; (3) a section on Howard Gardner's multiple intelligences, including indicators of all eight, along with activities and strategies consistent with each that students can use to help them study; (4) instructional suggestions to which parents can refer throughout the year; and (5) reference papers.

Our grade level has received wonderful feedback as a result of this outreach effort, and we are always looking for ways to improve the guidebooks. Whether you are able to provide a similar resource for parents at your school or one that includes only some of the contents, please know that any effort you make in this regard will go a long way toward helping parents build quality into the process for their children all year long.

## BACK TO SCHOOL NIGHT, CONFERENCES, AND OPEN HOUSE

Back to School Night, Conferences, and Open House are well-known, annual events. Each one provides you with a golden opportunity to communicate with families in a meaningful way. Use these occasions to strengthen your Emotional Bank Accounts with parents and to inform them about what you're trying to accomplish in the classroom.

## Back to School Night

A Back to School Night presentation is like the State of the Union address the President delivers to the nation at the beginning of each year. It is a chance to speak with a sense of optimism and articulate a compelling vision of the upcoming year. Because your presentation provides such a strong introduction to the school year, it is important to have as many parents there as possible to hear it. Do whatever you can to maximize turnout. Consider the following ideas:

- Have students create personalized invitations to the parents.
- Highlight the event in your Weekly Newsletter.
- Write a Home-School Journal entry, inviting parents to come.
- Create a Countdown Sheet like the one shown in Figure 4.4 to provide a series of reminders for the event.

Use the evening to emphasize the major ideas you introduced in your First Day Letter. Explain what your aim is and how it drives what you do in the classroom. Share your class mission statement and discuss the results of your first Enthusiasm Survey. Present your year-end student goals so that parents understand what you expect of their children and how you will assess them. Also, discuss the major emphases of the curriculum, the classroom management system, your home-school communication system, homework policy, and any other issues of special interest or importance to you. Be sure to leave time for questions because many of these ideas will be new to parents and may require further clarification. By focusing on high priority issues, you will make a strong impression on those parents whom you are meeting for the first time.

Here are some other tips for getting the most out of this evening:

- Prepare for the parents a folder of handouts that includes copies of all the information you share that evening (e.g., class mission statement, student goals, Enthusiasm Survey results). These handouts will make it easier for everyone to follow along with your presentation. Also, by putting the students' names on the folders, you can take attendance for the evening by seeing which folders remain at the end. (You will want to have a sign-in sheet as well.)
- Post a parent volunteer sign-up sheet on the wall so you can recruit willing workers.
- Be careful about offering specific information about individual students to any parents. With so many people around, this isn't the time for in-depth, one-on-one conversations, and you don't want to say something you might later regret. If parents ask you about their child, offer to schedule a private meeting so you can have an opportunity to talk in a less congested atmosphere.
- Have student-created name tags waiting for the parents as they enter the room. Placing the name tags on the students' desks enables parents to see where their children sit each day.
- Simulate an actual school day as much as possible so that parents can appreciate what it feels like to be a student in your class. For example, if music is playing each morning as the students arrive in class, play music as the parents arrive. Perhaps even have the parents go through the Brain Gym movements described in the previous chapter. Little touches matter.
- Start off the evening with some ice-breaking activities to build camaraderie among the parents.
- Distribute and discuss any form of Parent Guidebook you are able to provide.
- Attach a sentence to the bottom of your next newsletter thanking the parents for attending.

**Figure 4.4**   Countdown Sheet

Starting a week before the event, give out one strip per day in order to promote the event and maximize attendance.

---

# Only 7 Days Until Back to School Night!

**Wednesday, September 18th at 7:00 P.M. in Room 27.**

---

# Only 6 Days Until Back to School Night!

**Wednesday, September 18th at 7:00 P.M. in Room 27.**

---

# Only 5 Days Until Back to School Night!

**Wednesday, September 18th at 7:00 P.M. in Room 27.**

---

# Only 2 Days Until Back to School Night!

**Wednesday, September 18th at 7:00 P.M. in Room 27.**

---

# Only 1 Day Until Back to School Night!

**Wednesday, September 18th at 7:00 P.M. in Room 27.
See you tomorrow.**

---

## Parent Conferences

The most productive Parent Conferences include teachers, parents, *and* students. For a number of reasons, the students' presence at these meetings is highly desirable. First, involving the kids provides another of those rare opportunities when I can focus my attention on only one child. One-on-one time with each student allows me to strengthen relationships and discuss sensitive issues away from the other kids. Second, I learn a great deal by observing how the children interact with their parents. Specifically, I discover more about the inner workings of each family and develop a greater understanding of each child's home life. Possessing this knowledge helps me do my job better.

Third, because the students are the subjects of these meetings, they need to hear what their parents and I are saying about them, and they have a right to express their thoughts and feelings about their own learning. Fourth, with all of us there together, I know that parents and students are hearing the same message from me. When the students aren't there, they hear second hand what I said about them. As a result, the message they receive from their parents may not be the one I intended to send. Fifth, I occasionally like to assess students at these conferences. These assessments couldn't occur without the child present. Finally, when students attend the conference with their parents, they get a feel for what these meetings are like. Consequently, when Student-Led Conferences roll around a few months later, the kids will be more prepared and less anxious about leading them. Above all, however, inviting the students to attend Parent Conferences is a matter of respect. Because I truly value my students, I believe they deserve to be present when I discuss their progress with their parents. In the event that I need to discuss a piece of sensitive information with only a parent, I simply ask the child to wait outside the room for a moment.

As you plan for the conferences, create an agenda containing all the topics you intend to discuss. Following this agenda during the meetings keeps everyone's attention focused on the business at hand. See Figure 4.5 for a sample agenda. Give parents a copy of these sheets so they can take notes throughout the meeting. Each item on your agenda should connect directly to one of the year-end student goals. With assessment data by your side, explain to parents how their child is progressing toward each goal. Be careful not to focus exclusively on the academic goals, though; be sure to discuss the enthusiasm survey and the habits of mind and character as well. As you move through your agenda, invite the students to offer their own opinions and self-assessments as often as you can. Asking the kids to discuss their strengths and weaknesses encourages them to take ownership of their learning. Leave time at the end of the conferences for parents to ask questions and share concerns, and remind them that you are always available should they ever want to meet with you again in the future.

As you share assessment data with parents, pay special attention to ensuring that they understand your rubrics, scoring methods, and terminology. Nontraditional scoring systems can cause quite a bit of confusion. For example, one year many parents viewed the 6-point writing rubric we used at the time as identical to the traditional A–F letter grades they encountered in school. As a result, they interpreted a 6 to be an A, a 5 a B, a 4 a C, and so on. This correlation, however, was inaccurate. No connection whatsoever existed between any number and any letter grade; the two systems were completely unrelated. Number 4 was the standard. Our goal was for all students to earn at least that score. Two parents whose children earned a 2 were shocked at what they perceived to be failing scores. Once they realized, however, that the goal was 4, not 6, and understood the requirements and criteria on which the rubric was based, they had a better grasp of how our assessments worked. Taking the time to discuss this matter with parents prevents them from misinterpreting the data and from viewing either their child's abilities or mine more unfavorably. Make the effort to educate and clarify during these meetings.

**Figure 4.5**    Parent Conference Agenda

1. Habits of Character Self-Evaluation Sheet

2. Reading
   • WEB/Accelerated Reader Report
   • Reading Workshop
   • Read Aloud

3. Writing Workshop
   • Writing Notebook
   • Small Moment Stories

4. Math
   • Place Value Audit
   • Multiplication Assessment
   • Weekly Facts Quizzes

5. Spelling
   • High Frequency Word Bank
   • Practicing/Reinforcing at Home

6. Santa Monica Historical Society Museum Project

7. Personal Learning Plan
   • Summary Sheet

8. Home-School Communication
   • Weekly Newsletters
   • Parent Guidebook
   • Homework

9. Other Issues
   • Fall Enthusiasm Survey Results

10. Questions

Here are some other suggestions to improve your Parent Conferences:

- Provide a private, comfortable setting. Place some chairs outside the room in case the next parents arrive early.
- Welcome each parent. Smile and make eye contact.
- Express appreciation for their presence and establish a rapport by talking informally for a few moments at the outset.
- Have data and work samples to support your opinions.
- Discuss ways for parents to help their children at home.
- Ask parents for their questions, comments, and suggestions.
- Remind parents of the procedure for reaching you at school.
- End on a positive note and thank the parents again for coming.
- In the following week's newsletter thank the parents once more for coming and explain how beneficial you believe the conferences were and how important it is for all of you to continue communicating on a regular basis.
- Follow through with your meetings by informing parents the first time their child shows improvement in one of the areas you discussed.

## Student-Led Conferences

Student-Led Conferences offer kids meaningful opportunities to take ownership of their own learning. These meetings work like traditional Parent Conferences except that the student assumes the role of teacher. Because the kids have taken our place, we have no active involvement in these conferences. We are not even there at the table watching; family members only are present. Our job is to stay out of the way. Don't even walk around to take a peak. Your presence may interrupt the flow of the meeting and take the spotlight off the student. This is their moment. Our role involves greeting families as they enter the room, thanking them for coming, and talking with them briefly when the conference concludes.

Because we're not involved in these meetings, many can occur simultaneously. In fact, an entire set of conferences can be completed in a relatively short time. Pick one afternoon, and block off two hours, say from 3:30 to 5:30 p.m. Send home a sign-up sheet asking parents to choose a half-hour time slot within this window. At any given time, as long as there are enough tables in the room to accommodate each family, space will not be an issue. Of course, some parents may need to reschedule for a different day due to work or other commitments.

Families first learn about Student-Led Conferences early in the school year. Inform parents by sending home a newsletter, like the one shown in Figure 4.6, sometime in October or November. Also at this time, introduce your kids to the concept of a Student-Led Conference by explaining what they are, how they will work, and how they connect to the class mission. Informing the students about these conferences well in advance is another form of building quality into the process. Armed with this knowledge, they will take greater pride in their work because they know that *they* will ultimately be the ones sharing it with their families. In addition, the first round of Parent Conferences becomes more meaningful to the kids because it serves as a form of dress rehearsal for the Student-Led Conferences.

Actual preparation for Student-Led Conferences begins approximately one to three weeks before the event. First, the kids create and send home invitations to their families.

**Figure 4.6**    Student-Led Conferences Newsletter

---

Volume 11, November 20, 2006

# What's Going On in THQ?

## Student-Led Conferences

This week we conclude our first round of parent conferences. These meetings provide us with a chance to discuss in depth your child's progress in the various subject areas as well as in our habits of character. Though the November conferences are the only official ones that Roosevelt schedules for the year, I am planning a second set a few months from now. I have not set an exact date yet, but the conferences will probably occur in late February or early March.

This time around, however, the meetings will take the form of a Student-Led Conference. In a Student-Led Conference each child is entrusted with the responsibility of conducting the meeting. I will be present in the room during these conferences, but I will not have an active role in them. The conferences will be private meetings between you, your child, and any other family members you would like to invite.

During the conference your child will share with you the contents of his or her portfolio. The portfolio will include work samples from the various subject areas along with a few other special items. Some of the items in the portfolio will be chosen by the kids, others by me.

I believe that allowing students to have the opportunity to lead their own conferences is an important step in helping them build responsibility and take charge of their own learning. The students will decide how they will organize their conferences and how they will explain their portfolio contents to you.

We are very excited to begin the process of planning these conferences. In the future I will send home a sign-up sheet for time slots that are convenient for you. Please remember that I am always happy to meet with you to discuss your child's progress. Student-Led Conferences are designed to supplement my ongoing efforts to keep you informed and involved, not replace them.

Have a Wonderful Thanksgiving!

Then, they begin assembling portfolios of their work. These portfolios may include any combination of the following:

- Work samples from the different disciplines
- Academic assessments showing progress toward the content standards
- Habits of Character Self-Evaluations (the next chapter provides more information about these self-evaluations)
- Personal mission statements
- Photographs or videotapes of performances or presentations
- Reflections, journals, and learning logs
- Special papers or projects
- Enthusiasm Survey results

You must decide which portfolio items you will select and which you will ask the students to select. One way to achieve a balance is for you to determine broad categories of work and then let students pick specific examples of work within these categories to put in their portfolios. For instance, within the category of Writer's Workshop projects, have the kids choose their favorite one to share with their families. Once you and your students have decided which items the portfolios will include, create a form like the one shown in Figure 4.7 to help organize the assembly process.

After the students assemble their portfolios, the next step involves deciding what they are going to say about these items during the meetings. Using a form similar to the Student-Led Conference Outline sheet shown in Figure 4.8, have the students put the portfolio contents in the order in which they would like to share them. Then, ask the kids to write down at least two specific points or comments that they would like to make about each item. There is also space on the outline sheet for brief introductory and concluding remarks. This sheet serves as each student's personal conference agenda.

A few days before the conferences, have the kids practice giving their presentations to a partner. By first rehearsing with peers, your students can work out the kinks and gain confidence. Some students will choose to follow their outlines as they share their work; others will not. Either way is fine. I have even had students go a step further and prepare their entire presentations on index cards for a more professional look. Brainstorm other such possibilities with your kids so that they can benefit from one another's clever ideas.

On the day of the conference, lay out all the portfolios on a large table. Greet the families as they arrive, and once they locate their child's portfolio, show them to an empty table. Most families will stay for 20 to 30 minutes while others will stay for well over an hour. It is wonderful to watch the kids share their work with pride. Being a fly on the wall enables you to hear a number of interesting comments from parents and students alike.

Make a special effort to speak with all the families before they leave. Thank them for coming and ask for their feedback. In addition, remind them that you are always available should they ever want to schedule a meeting with you. I learned this lesson the hard way. The only negative reaction I've ever heard about Student-Led Conferences came from a parent who felt that I was abdicating my responsibility as a teacher by having her daughter lead the conference. The mother felt that I should have led it. Her comment caught me completely off guard. I had always viewed Student-Led Conferences as a supplement to my communications with parents, not a replacement.

Follow up on these meetings by asking your students to reflect on their presentations, either in class or for homework. Have them write down what they liked, what they might

**Figure 4.7**    Portfolio Organization Form

Name _____    Date _____

## What Should Be In My Portfolio?

Directions: Put a check on the appropriate line for each item.

| Subject Areas | Complete | Not Yet | Missing |
|---|---|---|---|
| 1. Division Audit | _____ | _____ | _____ |
| 2. Fraction Creatures | _____ | _____ | _____ |
| 3. Math Facts Graph | _____ | _____ | _____ |
| 4. Math Problem Solving Menu | _____ | _____ | _____ |
| 5. Accelerated Reader Report | _____ | _____ | _____ |
| 6. Writer's Workshop Story | _____ | _____ | _____ |
| 7. *The Talking Cloth* Project (Computer) | _____ | _____ | _____ |
| 8. Social Studies Maps | _____ | _____ | _____ |
| 9. Kwakiutl Timelines | _____ | _____ | _____ |
| **Habits of Character** | | | |
| 10. Habits of Character Update | _____ | _____ | _____ |
| 11. Personal Mission Statements and Boxes | _____ | _____ | _____ |

**Figure 4.8**    Student-Led Conference Outline

Name _____    Date _____

### Student-Led Conference Outline

I. Introduction
   A. Greet families and thank them for coming.
   B. _____

II. First Item _____
   A. _____
   B. _____

III. Second Item _____
   A. _____
   B. _____

IV. Third Item _____
   A. _____
   B. _____

V. Fourth Item _____
   A. _____
   B. _____

VI. Fifth Item _____
   A. _____
   B. _____

VII. Sixth Item _____
   A. _____
   B. _____

VIII. Seventh Item _____
   A. _____
   B. _____

IX. Eighth Item _____
   A. _____
   B. _____

X. Ninth Item _____
   A. _____
   B. _____

XI. Tenth Item _____
   A. _____
   B. _____

XII. Eleventh Item _____
   A. _____
   B. _____

XIII. Conclusion
   A. Thank families for coming and ask if there any questions.
   B. _____

not have liked, and how they would improve these conferences in the future. In addition, invite the parents to write their child a letter expressing what they enjoyed about the meeting, what they learned, and how much they appreciated being able to spend that time together. I have seen many heartwarming letters that significantly strengthened the parent-child bond.

A more advanced form of Student-Led Conferencing shines a spotlight directly on the habits of mind and habits of character and offers a wonderful opportunity to reinforce these valuable ideas. Start by selecting 8 to 10 habits that will serve as the foundation of the portfolio. Figure 4.9 shows the 9 habits I chose for our March 2007 conferences. Students build their portfolios by choosing one piece of work that best represents each habit. To help guide the students in their selections, I distribute a sheet listing the major projects and activities that occurred during the preceding few months (see Figure 4.10). To make their selections, students write down the number of the habit from Figure 4.9 on the blank line to the left of each desired item on Figure 4.10. Once these decisions are made, we then proceed through the same steps I described earlier: (1) placing the work inside the portfolios and (2) completing the Student-Led Conference Outline sheet. As a final preparation step, I ask the kids to reflect on and describe the rationale for each of their choices. Specifically, using the strips shown in Figure 4.11, students explain how a given piece of work exemplifies the habit to which they matched it. We clip these strips to the work samples so parents can see them during the conferences. Reflecting on their choices in this manner promotes thoughtfulness and judgment and also reinforces the meaning of each habit.

## Open House

I have mixed feelings about Open House. On one hand, I believe it can be a valuable opportunity for teachers and students to display with pride the work they've done during the preceding months. On the other hand, Open House often becomes a big show, a form of end-of-the-line inspection where visitors walk through your room to evaluate you and your students. At its best, Open House shows the school community what you are all about. Visitors learn about your aim, mission, goals, and what you did to bring these ideas to life. There is a sense of celebration and accomplishment in the air as you and your students highlight the quality work you did together. At its worst, Open House resembles a fashion show. An emphasis on making things look good overrides any attempt to inform observers about the important work that occurred in the classroom. Too often, an informal competition develops as to who has the most attractive bulletin boards or the most attention-getting art projects.

One way of maintaining the focus on student work and moving away from the idea of Open House as end-of-the-line inspection is to host a series of mini–Open Houses throughout the school year. A mini–Open House is an exhibition of student work that occurs at the completion of a specific unit of study. It is an exciting, enjoyable way to culminate any unit. Mini–Open Houses can be held for any subject area or for any type of long-term project. They focus directly on the quality of student work and offer parents a clear view of the kinds of learning activities you believe to be most beneficial. In addition, they require very little time to plan and stage. If you hold enough of them regularly, by the time Open House rolls around, visitors will already have a strong understanding of your approach and philosophy.

When my third and fourth graders finished a math unit on patterns and functions a few years ago, we held a mini–Open House to show parents what the kids had learned. We also invited administrators and other classes to attend the event. Each student described a real-life situation where one would find a numerical pattern and made a table representing this pattern mathematically. We divided the event into two parts. During the first part, half the students stayed at their desks presenting their work and answering questions while the

**Figure 4.9**    Student-Led Conferences: Habits of Mind and Habits of Character

Name _____    Date _____

### Student-Led Conferences: Habits of Mind and Habits of Character

During your conference you will share nine categories of important work. Each category will either be a habit of mind or habit of character. You will choose one piece of work for each category. After you make your nine choices, you may also decide to share other work as well. Here are the nine categories.

**Habits of Character**

1. Courage — Choose the piece of work where you took the biggest risk, tried something new, or stepped out of your comfort zone the most.

2. Perseverance — Choose the piece of work that is your best example of perseverance. When things became difficult, you kept going, didn't give up, and did what you needed to do in order to succeed.

3. Pride — Choose the piece of work that you were the most intrinsically motivated to complete, cared the most about, or felt the most proud of.

4. Positive Attitude — Choose the piece of work that you enjoyed working on the most or that brought the biggest smile to your face.

5. Responsibility — Choose a piece of work where you took charge and managed yourself in an independent way from beginning to end.

6. Self-Discipline — Choose a piece of work where you showed tremendous focus and did a great job, without starting and stopping.

**Habits of Mind**

7. Craftsmanship — Choose the piece of work where you paid the greatest attention to detail and did your neatest and most careful work.

8. Judgment — Choose a piece of work where you were a great decision-maker and were very happy with the choices you made.

9. Thoughtfulness — Choose a piece of work where you took your time, thought things through, and put a great deal of thought into your work.

**Figure 4.10**   Student-Led Conferences: Portfolio Options

---

Name: _____   Date: _____

### Student-Led Conferences: Portfolio Options

<u>Directions</u>: Put the habit of mind or character number from the other sheet on the line next to your choice for that habit. Be sure to choose work from many different sections of this paper.

<u>Writing</u>

_____   "All About" Book

_____   Letter

<u>Social Studies</u>

_____   Economics UVF³

_____   The Symbol and Landmark Project
(includes both your actual symbol and your written explanation)

<u>Division</u>

_____   The Doorbell Rang Retelling

_____   The Doorbell Rings Again

_____   Division Audit

<u>Fractions</u>

_____   Fraction Creature

_____   Fractions Audit

<u>Other Math</u>

_____   Math Facts Graph

_____   Problem Solving Menu (either a whole menu or part of a menu)

<u>Reading Workshop</u>

_____   Reading Notebook

<u>Nonfiction Unit</u>

_____   Web of Big Ideas and Details

_____   Venn Diagram Comparing Two Topics

<u>Five Story Elements Unit</u>

_____   Literary Essay 2
(Which of the five story elements adds the most to your book?)

_____   Five Story Elements Chart

<u>Astronomy</u>

_____   The Telescope Project

_____   Constellations Painting

_____   Planets Painting

_____   Moon Phases Illustration

<u>Other</u>

_____   Personal Mission Statement and Box

_____   Purple Practice Book page

_____   Math Workbook page

_____   Work from any folder

---

**Figure 4.11** Student-Led Conferences: Reflections Sheets

Name _____    Date _____

### Student-Led Conferences: Reflections Sheets

I chose this piece of work to represent the habit of:

_____

because _____

_____

_____

_____


I chose this piece of work to represent the habit of:

_____

because _____

_____

_____

_____

_____

_____


I chose this piece of work to represent the habit of:

_____

because _____

_____

_____

_____

other half walked around visiting each project. The two groups switched roles halfway through. By the end, every child had an opportunity to demonstrate his or her learning to a genuine audience in an authentic manner.

Whichever specific communication tools you choose to incorporate into your repertoire, make a consistent effort to keep parents informed and involved throughout the year. It does take time, and there are roadblocks that make building and maintaining relationships difficult. You may, for example, encounter parents who speak a different language, who lack the time to get involved, or who are hard to reach. There's too much at stake, though, for us not to act. By persevering, trying a variety of communication approaches, and providing parents with genuine opportunities to become involved, we give ourselves and our students the very best chance to have a successful school year.

## KEY POINTS FROM ESSENTIAL 4

- Consistent parent involvement dramatically increases the likelihood that quality learning will occur.
- Because parents are their children's first and most important teachers, we must make a consistent effort to inform and involve them throughout the year.
- Nine important reasons remind us why taking the time to build and maintain trusting relationships with parents is worth the effort.
- Interactions with parents should be frequent, positive, proactive, and characterized by both a problem-solving orientation and a sense of inclusion and optimism.
- Beginning the year with a significant outreach effort to welcome students and their families makes a powerful first impression.
- The First Day Letter, Weekly Newsletter, and Home-School Journal are three of the many tools we can use to build and maintain a close working relationship with parents.
- A significant aspect of the home-school relationship involves finding ways to help parents help their children at home.
- Back to School Night, Parent Conferences, Student-Led Conferences, and Open House provide us with invaluable opportunities to strengthen the home-school connection.
- Although roadblocks exist that can make building and maintaining relationships with parents difficult, there is too much at stake for us not to act. By persevering, trying a variety of communication approaches, and providing parents with genuine opportunities to become involved, we give ourselves and our students the very best chance to have a successful school year.

## REFLECTION QUESTIONS

- What communication tool or strategy will you use to begin the next school year with a bang and grab the attention of your students and their parents?
- What are the main priorities that you will emphasize in your First Day Letter?
- Which of the strategies described in this chapter will you use consistently to keep parents informed and involved throughout the year?
- Given the grade level you teach, which type of Student-Led Conference do you think you will try with your current or next group of students?
- What priorities will you emphasize to get the greatest possible benefits from your next Back to School Night and Open House?

Essential 5

American swimmer Mark Spitz captured a record seven gold medals in the 1972 Summer Olympics. His time of 51.22 seconds in the 100 Meter Freestyle established a new world record, one of four individual marks he set during the games. Just eight years later, Spitz's time would have placed him fourth in the U.S. Olympic Trials. With only the top three finishers qualifying for the games, he wouldn't even have earned a spot on the team.

Two or three generations ago, the American economy was at a point in its history when a strong work ethic enabled millions to earn middle-class wages despite low levels of educational attainment. Technological advances and the increasing globalization of the economy, however, have rendered most of these jobs obsolete. Today, the world economy demands considerably more from its workers than determination and desire. Employers expect workers to possess a broad range of knowledge, skills, and personal characteristics. Specifically, recent reports tell us that to compete, individuals need to work well with others; be active learners; read, write, and speak effectively; know how to solve problems; and understand technology.[1]

Gaining admission to our nation's top colleges becomes more difficult every year. In 1991, for example, 21,650 students applied to become part of UCLA's freshman class. By 1999 that number had increased to 35,621. As the number of students seeking admission continues to grow, so too do the academic credentials of each group of incoming freshman. In just two years, from 1997 to 1999, the average, fully weighted grade point average of the admitted freshman class had climbed from 4.13 to 4.25. During this same period the average Scholastic Aptitude Test  score jumped from 1298 to 1330, and the average number of high school honors courses taken had risen from 15.6 to 17.4.

The three previous examples illustrate that what was once good enough to survive and succeed in our society no longer suffices. Competition has intensified, technology has exploded, and the limits of human performance have expanded. As standards, conditions, and circumstances change, we must adapt to keep pace. More than ever before, our success as individuals and as a society depends on our ability to learn and improve.

Continuous improvement is one of the central tenets of Quality Theory. Although progress in any given area is generally measured in numerical terms, the idea of improvement involves much more than simply comparing swimming times or grade point averages. Above anything else, continuous improvement is a way of thinking. It's an attitude, a mindset. The Japanese have a word for it, *kaizen*, meaning the spirit of continuous improvement.[2] I do everything possible to build this spirit of improvement into my classroom culture, encouraging students to find a way to get a little bit better at what they do every day. There is value in improvement, a certain satisfaction that kids experience when they realize that as readers, for example, they are better today than they were just a short time ago.

It's important to encourage and recognize incremental improvement throughout the school year. Let's return to the story-writing example described in Chapter 3. The goal for this task is for every student to earn at least a 3 on the 4-point trait rubrics shared in Figure 3.4. You will remember that a score of 3 indicates proficiency with these traits. For many students such a large gap will exist between the level of proficiency needed to score a 3 and the level of proficiency with which they enter the school year that just thinking of earning a 3 on these rubrics would be overwhelming. For these children a more reasonable short-term goal would be to score a 2. While a 2 is not a 3, it represents progress, a step in the right direction. Every step forward shrinks the original gap. After earning a 2, then they try for a 3, and then perhaps a 4.

As students achieve short-term successes, they develop a hunger for more success. They feel better about themselves and take more pride in their work. Their confidence increases. They begin to believe that they can achieve demanding goals. By recognizing the value of improvement and emphasizing it constantly, we break the long journey toward accomplishment of these goals into more manageable trips, empowering our students to work hard, persevere, and perform to their potential. The spirit of continuous improvement takes students from where they start to where they want to get.

This chapter highlights the importance of continuous improvement in building a classroom culture of quality. It features examples that illustrate how the idea of improvement can pervade every aspect of class functioning. In these examples I examine the concept of improvement on the individual and class level, focusing on both product and process. These examples are not limited to academic improvement; they pertain to character and enthusiasm improvement as well.

## IMPROVING OUR HABITS OF CHARACTER

In this section I describe an approach designed to help students continuously improve their performance with the habits of character throughout the year. This approach emphasizes reflective thinking, self-evaluation, and goal setting. The first step involves defining each habit clearly so that everybody in the class is speaking the same language. As Crosby emphasizes, children need to know the requirements of each habit to conform to those requirements.

Figure 5.1 lists the habits of character mentioned in Chapter 2 along with the definitions my students and I currently use. As you can see, these definitions attempt to break down complex character traits into a reasonable number of concrete, measurable behaviors that are essential to productive classroom functioning.

With these definitions in place, we now proceed to the next aspect of this approach, self-evaluation. It is a fundamental truth that people, whether they are children who experience difficulty treating others with respect or adults looking to lose a few pounds, will only affect genuine behavioral change when they make a personal commitment to do so. If, for example, I want my kids to become more honest, talking at them all day long about the importance of honesty is not the answer. Furthermore, no amount of scolding, imploring, or chastising is likely to bring about lasting results. If I am constantly telling my students how to act and how not to act, they will eventually tune me out. Instead, I have to understand that the most effective step I can take to promote these ideals is to create the conditions where students can assume ownership of their behavior so they can attempt to improve it themselves.

**Figure 5.1**   Habits of Character Definitions

---

### Habits of Character Definitions

1. Cooperation
   - working well with others

2. Courage
   - asking for help when I need it
   - willing to take risks

3. Fairness
   - sharing equally
   - taking turns
   - raising hand before speaking (not calling out)

4. Honesty
   - telling the whole truth

5. Kindness
   - thinking about the needs of others
   - being polite

6. Patience
   - staying calm and relaxed when I have to wait in line or in class

7. Perseverance
   - trying my best and never giving up

8. Positive Attitude
   - pleasant to be around
   - looking at the bright side of things
   - trying to enjoy the work I do

9. Pride
   - driven by intrinsic motivation
   - caring deeply about my work
   - keep trying to improve

10. Respect
   - treating others how I want to be treated
   - listening attentively (sit flat, eye contact, not interrupting, listen carefully)

11. Responsibility
   - owning my actions
   - turning in homework completely and on time
   - bringing WEB book and library book
   - using restroom, water bottles, and drinking fountain at proper times
   - keeping the room clean and keeping my papers and supplies neat and organized

12. Self-Discipline
   - working quietly at seat
   - lining up on time
   - entering room quietly
   - following signal and directions the first time
   - quick and quiet transitions

13. Service
   - trying to be helpful to other kids and adults
   - giving support without giving answers

---

In this endeavor the greatest service we can do for our students is provide daily opportunities to reflect on their performance in the various habits. My students use the Weekly Evaluation Sheet shown in Figure 5.2.

Using the 4-point rubric mentioned earlier (4 = Exceeds Expectations, 3 = Meets Expectations, 2 = Slightly Below Expectations, 1 = Well Below Expectations), the kids give themselves scores in five of the habits every week. In the past I have asked kids to self-evaluate in all 13 of the categories but found it to be too much. With our current five-category-per-week format, the children and I each make two choices. For Boxes 2 and 3, I always choose the habits of respect and self-discipline because I believe the components of these categories make them the two most difficult ones to develop. The students, individually, are free to choose any of the other habits for Boxes 4 and 5. Box 1 is our "Spotlight Category," where each week we simply rotate alphabetically through all 13 habits. Doing so ensures that every habit will be represented at least once every 13 weeks and also enables us to give special attention to our Spotlight Category, such as tell stories, share quotes or newspaper articles, or participate in role-play scenarios involving that habit.

The kids sit quietly at their desks during the last few minutes of the day to perform their self-evaluations. For each category the kids first refer to the definition of that habit and then think about how they have performed in that area. For example, if I am evaluating myself in the habit of fairness, I first read that fairness involves sharing equally, taking turns, and not calling out. If I did all those things (in other words, if I conformed to requirements), I would write down a 3. If I did most of those things but had a little trouble taking turns earlier that morning, I would write down a 2. If I somehow went above and beyond the call of duty (I leave that judgment about whether they have exceeded expectations to the kids), I'd give myself a 4. Of course, there will always be some kids who are too easy or too hard on themselves, but over time, with practice and adult guidance, the children become more accurate in their self-assessments. On those days when time for written reflection simply isn't available, a quick flashing of one to four fingers in the air for each habit (with eyes closed to preserve everyone's privacy) or some type of voluntary oral sharing will do the job.

Goal setting is the final piece to this puzzle. Every week the kids set a goal in one of the habits of character. The goal can pertain to any of the five boxes on their Weekly Evaluation Sheet. When setting a goal, the kids first decide which category and which number they are targeting and then state that goal in a complete sentence. For example, they may say, "I want to be a 3 in Fairness." They then refer back to the definitions sheet and write down one or two specific actions related to that category that they will do during the week to help themselves reach that goal. Once the kids have become a 3 in every habit of character, I allow them either to set goals where they try to become a 4 or to move on and set goals involving the habits of mind. They keep track of their progress on the Habits of Character Progress Sheet shown in Figure 5.3, which I describe shortly.

There's a special Friday routine we use to keep this process on track. The kids first give themselves scores for the day in that week's five categories, the way they do Monday through Thursday. They then move to the bottom of the sheet and fill out the "Friday Comments" section. There, they write whether they have reached their goal. To reach a goal, the kids need to have that score for every day of that week. So, if I wanted to be a 3 in honesty, I'd need to have a 3 for all five days. After signing their names at the bottom, the kids prepare their sheets for the following week. (I make double-sided copies of these sheets so that I only need to provide a new paper every other week.) The kids write down the Spotlight Category in Box 1 and then decide what to write in Boxes 4 and 5. They then write down their new goal and what they will do to reach it. If a child does successfully reach a goal that week, he or she records it on the sheet shown in Figure 5.3. Recording successes builds confidence and increases self-esteem, but it also has another practical effect: it ensures that

**Figure 5.2**    Weekly Evaluation Sheet

Name _____    Date _____

## Weekly Evaluation Sheet

| Category | Monday | Tuesday | Wednesday | Thursday | Friday |
|---|---|---|---|---|---|
| 1) | | | | | |
| 2) Respect | | | | | |
| 3) Self-Discipline | | | | | |
| 4) | | | | | |
| 5) | | | | | |

Goal For the Week: (ex. "I want to be a <u>3</u> in <u>Respect</u>.")

---------------------------------------------------------------------------------

---------------------------------------------------------------------------------

What I Will Do to Reach My Goal (ex. "I will <u>make eye contact</u>.")

---------------------------------------------------------------------------------

---------------------------------------------------------------------------------

---------------------------------------------------------------------------------

Friday Comments: (ex. "I did/did not reach my goal because . . .")

---------------------------------------------------------------------------------

---------------------------------------------------------------------------------

---------------------------------------------------------------------------------

Signature _____          Teacher Signature _____

**Figure 5.3** Habits of Character Progress Sheet

Name _____

### Habits of Character Progress Sheet

| | A | B | C | D | E |
|---|---|---|---|---|---|
| 1 | List of Habits | I Became a 3 on: | Teacher Initial | I Became a 4 on: | Teacher Initial |
| 2 | Cooperation | | | | |
| 3 | Courage | | | | |
| 4 | Fairness | | | | |
| 5 | Honesty | | | | |
| 6 | Kindness | | | | |
| 7 | Patience | | | | |
| 8 | Perseverance | | | | |
| 9 | Positive Attitude | | | | |
| 10 | Pride | | | | |
| 11 | Respect | | | | |
| 12 | Responsibility | | | | |
| 13 | Self-Discipline | | | | |
| 14 | Service | | | | |

students eventually address all the different habits of character. Before implementing this progress sheet, I found that some students would play it safe and set goals in the same categories for weeks at a time. For improvement to occur, however, it's crucial for kids to understand that we must acknowledge and address our weaker areas, not avoid them.

Once all the students have finished their sheets and moved on to the next activity, it only takes me a few minutes to walk around the room and check what they have done. At that point, I am able to praise students for reaching a difficult goal, offer encouragement to those who didn't reach their goals, provide feedback, make suggestions, and hold students accountable for assessing themselves honestly and accurately. More important, however, than whether students reach a goal for a given week, is the fact that we, as teachers, are empowering children by helping them develop their judgment, better their reflective thinking skills, and improve their ability to chart their own path.

## ACADEMIC IMPROVEMENT AT THE INDIVIDUAL LEVEL

When I was in fourth grade, I gave an oral report on the life of baseball great Willie Mays. I worked hard on the project, spending the night before my presentation preparing a speech on index cards and making a big poster showing Mays as a child, a teenager, and a professional. I remember feeling confident the next morning as I walked to the front of the room to share my work. With my poster on the chalk tray behind me, I delivered what I thought was an interesting, comprehensive account of the slugger's life. My teacher disagreed. Although she did offer some positive comments about my work, she told me that the report was missing a few necessary components and that I would have to address these areas and give my entire report again the next day.

That afternoon I went home and cried. Without a doubt, some of my sadness stemmed from the fact that my teacher shared the weaknesses of my report publicly. Nobody likes hearing criticism in front of classmates, and I am no exception. But there was more to it. I was upset that I had to give my presentation again. I had taken my turn in front of the class, and I was done. Having to do it again was a real imposition. I wanted my project behind me, and I was ready to move forward, not backward.

Looking back on that moment now, I realize that all my teacher wanted me to do was improve my report. Granted, for self-esteem reasons, I would have preferred her request to be made privately, but, nonetheless, her goal was quality. She had defined the requirements for that project, and I had yet to meet them. She was giving me another opportunity to get the job done.

Now that I'm a teacher myself, I notice that most of today's students think the same way I thought back then. There seems to be something magical about being "finished." There's a certain satisfaction that students take in knowing that they have completed a task. I wish I had a dime for every time I've heard a student announce, "Done!" after completing a classroom activity. Students don't scream the word. It just spontaneously comes out of them with a combination of pride and relief as if a great weight has been lifted from their shoulders.

An important part of building a classroom culture of improvement and quality involves taking the time to discuss the issue of "finishing." First of all, school is not a race, and there's no prize for finishing your work first. When students rush, quality suffers. They need to derive their satisfaction not from a job done, but from a job *well* done. Quality, not finishing, must be the primary objective. Second, in my view, a piece of work is never truly finished. If we are talking about ditto sheets, true-false exercises, or fill-in-the-blank worksheets, then those can be finished. But when referring to the more open-ended activities that require students to think deeply, such as a science project or a Writer's Workshop story, these types of activities are never really finished. They can always be improved somehow. We must encourage students to focus on quality and improvement, not completion and speed.

When my students turn in a paper and I evaluate it, I give them the same opportunity to improve their work that my fourth grade teacher gave me. As teachers, though, we must be very clear in telling our students that such an opportunity is neither a punishment nor a put down and that every student in the class will be asked to do the same thing at some point. It's not that their papers are "broken" and need to be "fixed."

Instead, I look at it this way. Our goal is quality work. As William Glasser explains in *The Quality School* (1990), any piece of work can be described as either as "Quality" or "Not Yet Quality." If the work conforms to our requirements for quality work, then that student may very well decide to stop at that point. But, if the work can't yet be considered quality, and quality is the expectation, then we need to ask that student, "Why would you want to stop now when this isn't your best work?" Posing this question to students reinforces the high expectations we hold for our class and sends the subtle yet powerful message that all our students are capable of producing quality if they are willing to put forth greater effort. In this situation, improving work until it can accurately be called quality work should become a natural part of the way your class conducts business.

In his book *The Quality School Teacher*, William Glasser (1993) encourages schools to adopt an evaluation system based on the notion of improvement. Using an approach he calls "Concurrent Evaluation," Glasser states that students should have frequent opportunities to meet with teachers to discuss their work. During these discussions students explain what they have done and how they believe they can improve their work. After continuing to improve the work, the students repeat the evaluation, explaining how the revised piece of work represents an improvement over the prior one. Students stop the process when they believe that further attempts to improve the work will no longer bring about significant change. Glasser asserts that under this system, "students would learn much more than now and begin to do quality work."[3] He goes on to say that "students would be better able to appreciate that education can increase the quality of their lives, and teachers would find their job much more enjoyable than they do now."[4]

Students working in this type of classroom culture will become far more likely to want to improve their own work, far less likely to settle for less than their best, and far more aware of the learning gains they are making. The habit of character "Pride" contributes greatly in the effort to build this mindset in students. Specifically, the parts of the definition relating to "caring deeply about my work" and "trying my best to improve" play a significant role in keeping this message alive and well throughout the school year.

## ACADEMIC IMPROVEMENT AT THE TEAM LEVEL

As part of the Writer's Workshop approach I frequently use, students take two stories in a row through the steps of the writing process. After students complete their first stories, it's critical that I gather data about the strengths and weaknesses of these papers so that I can improve instruction and boost performance the second time around. Without such an effort students will continue to make the same mistakes, and I will have missed valuable opportunities to add value to their work.

The primary improvement tool featured in this section is the Pareto Chart. Taking its name from an Italian sociologist and economist, a Pareto Chart represents data ranked by category.[5] I initially gather the data by keeping a tally of the significant weaknesses I notice as

## An Idea From a Teacher:
## Putting Essential 5 Into Practice

Jillian Esby

*St. Matthew's Parish School*

*Pacific Palisades, CA*

*K–5 Science*

When assessing my students' work, I look for completeness and quality. If I feel the work is not up to standard, I punch a hole through the top of the student's paper with an ordinary hole puncher to indicate that something is missing from making that assignment complete. The student can review the paper, ask his or her peers to take a look, or meet with me to find out what needs work before amending the assignment and turning it in again. If it still isn't up to par, it gets another hole punched in the top and the process repeats. Once the job is done well, I use a star-shaped punch (from a craft store) to indicate that all the criteria have been met for a quality assignment. The round punches and the star shaped punch really show all the work that goes into making an assignment complete. The kids are so proud when that star finally appears!

SOURCE: Jillian Esby, St. Matthew's Parish School.

I read each student's story. The tally shows which weaknesses were the most common. A Pareto Chart simply displays these areas of need in bar chart form. Proceeding from left to right in Figure 5.4, these need areas are listed from most to least common.[6] As the diagram shows, more students had difficulty satisfying the quality writing trait "Complete" than any other requirement. "Setting" was the second most common area of need with "Plot" and "Resolution" tying for third.[7]

The Pareto Chart provided valuable information that affected my writing instruction in the weeks ahead. Seeing which traits and story elements presented the kids with the greatest difficulty helped me determine how to spend my limited teaching time in the wisest possible ways (another form of building quality into the process). As authors Barbara Cleary and Sally Duncan point out, this visual approach focuses attention on the right things. So, when I gave writing activities for homework or when I taught minilessons at the beginning of our Writer's Workshop sessions, I knew that concentrating on the categories of "Complete," "Setting," "Plot," and "Resolution" would positively impact the greatest number of students. It would have been foolish to spend a week on descriptive language because the Pareto Chart had shown that to be an area of strength. Using a Pareto Chart adds discipline to an already disciplined instructional process.

Although the preceding example focuses on Writer's Workshop, the effectiveness of Pareto Charts extends far beyond story writing. This tool works equally well in any situation where a common assessment method will be used more than once and where valuable lessons can be learned from one assessment and used to improve instruction in the weeks that follow. Other excellent applications of the Pareto Chart include math problem-solving assessments, where the format remains consistent throughout the year, and standardized language arts tests, where the assessments are divided into discrete areas, such as vocabulary, decoding, reading comprehension, and grammar.

**Figure 5.4**    Writer's Workshop Pareto Chart

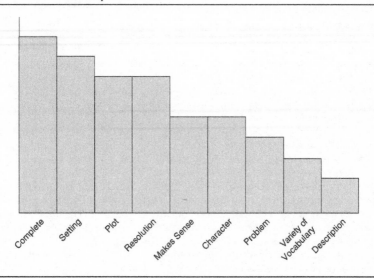

## INCREASING ENTHUSIASM THROUGHOUT THE YEAR

Like all teachers, my personal experiences as a student powerfully shaped my approach as a professional. It's amazing how many specific details we can remember about events that occurred so far in the past. I recall one morning in third grade when my teacher Mr. Lesner entered the room and, through a series of gestures, informed everyone that he had laryngitis. For that whole day, we were on our best behavior, trying to help him out however we could. (We were naive back then.) At the end of the day, as we gathered our backpacks and lunch boxes in preparation to go home, he held his hand up to wave goodbye and, in the healthiest voice I ever heard, said, "See you tomorrow everybody." We stood there in disbelief. The whole day had been a joke. He had successfully pulled the wool over our eyes.

Mr. Lesner's prank made a strong impression on me. I still remember the big smile that appeared on my face the moment he revealed his secret. He showed me how much fun school could be when teachers made an effort to inject humor and novelty into the day. To this day, I try to keep his legacy alive with little stunts of my own.

Unfortunately, not all school memories are pleasant ones. Most of us recall times when teachers yelled at us, embarrassed us in front of others, or punished us for something we didn't do. These types of experiences affect our teaching just as powerfully as positive ones. In fact, I believe that our negative experiences have an even stronger impact on how we approach our work with kids. It's as if negative episodes offend our sense of right and wrong so fiercely that they create within us a burning desire never to repeat these same mistakes. I have heard many teachers say things such as, "When I was in first grade, my teacher made me read a story out loud that I couldn't read, and I felt humiliated. I will never do that to one of my students."

My strongest negative memories came during my middle and high school years when I attended a highly regarded, college preparatory school in Los Angeles. My memories of the school itself are positive. I consider myself fortunate to have had dedicated teachers and coaches, good friends, and a supportive environment.

Academically, however, the program emphasized competition for grades, a staggering amount of rote learning, and a rigorous traditional curriculum. I studied extremely hard, but I didn't enjoy doing the work. I did whatever my teachers asked me to do, no more—unless I could get extra credit points. When I began my homework each night, my one goal was to finish it. If the assignment required me to read a 30-page history chapter, I read 30 pages, counting down after each one.

My love of learning decreased tremendously during my six years at the school. Learning was my job, and grades were my reward. In fact, I don't think I even became familiar with the idea of "love of learning" until I began my training as a teacher. Enjoyment occurred after school and on weekends.

Because of my largely joyless experiences, I made a commitment to create a different type of learning environment for my students. As I began to read the ideas of Deming and Jenkins and their call for an aim that gives equal attention to learning and enthusiasm, my resolve strengthened. Learning would not come at the expense of enthusiasm. My students would not have to pay the same high price I had. Kids would work hard in my class because they enjoyed learning and because they understood the purpose of it, not because they were after a grade or out of some sense of duty or obligation.

It is because of my prior experiences that I focus so much attention on the enthusiasm surveys that I administer four times per year. The data collected from these surveys let me know how I'm doing in my quest to increase the enthusiasm of my kids. Figure 5.5 shows how student enthusiasm changed during the 1997–1998 school year for each major subject area. Specifically, it shows how the number of happy faces changed. The ultimate goal, of course, is for every student to enjoy every subject. Since attainment of that goal may not be possible during the course of one school year, the more immediate goal is to have more happy faces at the end of the year for each subject than there were at the beginning. As Figure 5.5 shows, we successfully reached the latter goal. Although the increase in the number of happy faces was not always steady or consistent, enthusiasm was higher in June than it was in September.

Increasing the number of happy faces for a given subject doesn't happen naturally or automatically. A concerted, consistent effort is required throughout the year to bring about this type of change. After you administer the first survey in the Fall, talk honestly and openly with your students about the results. Ask them to identify the subjects that received the greatest and least amount of happy faces. Then, commit yourself to following a simple strategy that promises to yield better results the next time you give the survey. The strategy involves focusing on the one or two subjects that received the greatest number of happy faces and trying to determine why so many students found these subjects enjoyable. Once you and your kids have identified the most appealing features of these subjects, you can then look for ways to spread them throughout the curriculum. In other words, take the most enjoyable features of one subject and look for ways to apply them to other subjects.

My experience with these discussions has taught me that there are three primary ways to increase enthusiasm for any given subject.[8] First, make learning as hands-on as possible. According to my kids, the main reason why computers scored so high on our Fall survey (37 happy faces) was because they allow for hands-on learning. Everyone in the class readily agreed that activities are more enjoyable when you actually get to do something rather than just read about it or hear about it. Once we established that hands-on learning makes computers enjoyable, I encouraged my students to come up with ways to use this information to make other subjects more enjoyable. Soon, they began finding ways to

**Figure 5.5**   Team 1011 Enthusiasm Survey Results for the 1997–1998 School Year

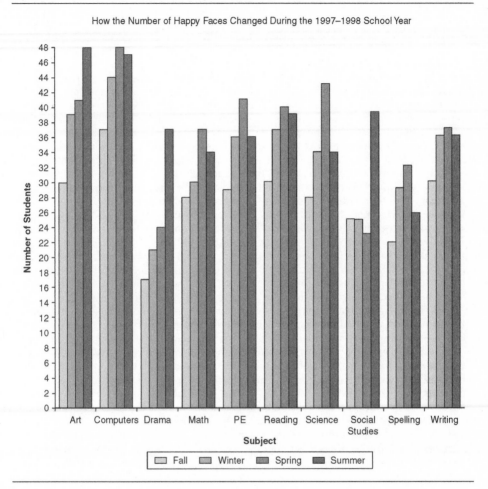

How the Number of Happy Faces Changed During the 1997–1998 School Year

incorporate hands-on learning into subjects such as spelling (by bouncing balls to practice their words), science (by participating in more frequent experiments and investigations), and art (by creating sculptures, prints, and architectural models). Every subject that we were able to make more hands-on experienced an immediate increase in enthusiasm.

Second, whenever possible, give your kids choices about what they will study. In art, for example, during the last few weeks of one school year, I wanted my students to have authentic experiences as artists. I didn't particularly care what they made; I simply wanted them to create works of art that they considered meaningful. When students choose for themselves, their motivation increases and greater learning gains result. In addition, when everyone in the room works on something different, the students learn a great deal from one another, and they gain exposure to a much wider variety of disciplines than if I, the teacher, would have had everyone do the same thing. For example, one boy decided to make a Japanese wood block print. When he announced his decision, the rest of us didn't even know what wood block prints were. But when we saw what he had created, the kids were impressed by his work, and I was glad that I had given him the opportunity to explore his own interests. During the mini–Open House that we held to display these projects, he even brought along his supplies and made a copy of his print for everyone who visited his table.

There are also multicultural benefits to this approach. Many teachers struggle with the issue of multiculturalism because it's so difficult to incorporate the contributions of so many cultures into the curriculum in meaningful ways. By transferring the responsibility for choosing project topics to the students, we allow the multiculturalism that already exists in our rooms to manifest itself. In fact, I strongly believe that a classroom where students are making choices about what they study will naturally become a multicultural classroom due to the fact that the kids will have regular opportunities to explore and share ideas that are important to them.

Third, students will enjoy a subject more when they can decide not only *what* to study but also *how* to study it. Here, we return to the issue of learning styles and multiple intelligences. Because, as Gardner points out, no two people learn the same way, teachers should encourage their students to discover how they learn best and then allow them to use those learning styles as often as possible. A dyslexic student I once taught used his drawing ability and creativity to help him learn his spelling words. Playing to his strengths enabled him to be successful at a task with which he had always struggled. Furthermore, making choices allowed him to use an area of strength to develop an area of weakness, thus boosting his confidence and preventing discouragement from overwhelming him. Such customization also fits neatly into our aim because it increases learning and enthusiasm.

Placing such strong emphasis on student enthusiasm doesn't mean that everything is fun and games. School isn't summer camp. It also doesn't mean that you lower academic expectations or sacrifice rigor or standards of conduct so that children will be happier. Focusing on student enthusiasm simply means that as our kids work to reach the year-end goals, we make every effort to ensure that the ride is an enjoyable one. Our role in this endeavor is to create the conditions where enthusiasm will flourish. We fulfill this responsibility by discussing each round of survey results with our students, analyzing the data thoroughly, valuing everyone's opinions and suggestions, and frequently encouraging everyone to find ways to make each subject more enjoyable. At the end of the year, take a minute to place your academic assessment results and your enthusiasm data side by side. For any subject, if you notice that your students' academic performance has improved *and* that they enjoy their work more than they did at the beginning of the year, then you have every reason to take pride in a job well done. School isn't summer camp, but we can make it more like summer camp.

## CONTINUOUS PROCESS IMPROVEMENT: THE PERSONAL SPELLING LIST EXAMPLE

All classroom processes can be improved. As I mentioned in Chapter 3, it's important to invest significant time initially to create the best processes possible; throughout the year we then work to improve these processes. Whether these processes pertain to academic matters, such as writing stories or conducting science investigations, or nonacademic matters, such as how to sharpen pencils or how to hang backpacks in the closet, we can always find ways to improve the way we do things. Continuously working to improve classroom processes results in better usage of time, fewer headaches, and, ultimately, higher quality learning.

**Figure 5.6**    PDSA Cycle

The most effective, user-friendly way to bring about this type of improvement is to follow the steps of one of the most well-known tools in the field of quality control, the Plan-Do-Study-Act (PDSA) Cycle (Figure 5.6). The PDSA Cycle enables teachers and students to solve problems and address concerns in a positive, team-oriented fashion.

Use the PDSA Cycle any time you want to call your students' attention to a problem or issue that you believe needs to be addressed. In the Spring of 1998, my class followed the steps of the PDSA Cycle in response to what I perceived to be a problem in the area of spelling. Our spelling goal called for our third graders to know the first 300 high frequency words and the fourth graders to know the first 400 by the end of the year. To support this goal and encourage the kids to go beyond it, I gave them the opportunity to create Personal Spelling Lists so they could choose words that suited their interests and offered an appropriate amount of challenge.[9] The kids could take as much time as they needed to learn their words, as the emphasis would be on mastery, not speed. In addition, they could choose as many as 20 words at once, but not fewer than 10, further allowing them to customize their lists. Finally, because I wanted the students to take the initiative to improve their spelling, I made use of the personal lists voluntary. (I was naive back then.)

I was initially attracted to the concept of a Personal Spelling List for many reasons. First, it transfers the responsibility of choosing the spelling words from me to the student. As a result, no longer could anyone complain about the words being too difficult or too easy. Every student could create a list that offered an optimal level of challenge. Second, the list provides a second chance for students to learn words that they missed on previous spelling assessments. Thus, these lists help me hold students accountable for their learning. A word remains on a student's list until that student spells it correctly during a personal spelling interview, which is conducted by either an adult or another student. When a student spells a word correctly, the interviewer erases it from the personal list and adds it to an ongoing list known as a Spelling Log. The Spelling Log contains every word a student has ever spelled correctly during an interview and documents progress over time.

I called my students' attention to this issue because I was disappointed that so few of them had been filling out personal lists and signing up for interviews. Considering that the lists were voluntary, was I foolish to expect otherwise? Probably, but in any event I was still frustrated. I really thought the kids would be scheduling interviews more frequently. To deal with this situation, I had two choices. First, I could get tough, blaming the kids for what I perceive to be laziness and then unilaterally making wholesale changes to this process. I could mandate weekly spelling interviews and threaten heavy punishment to those who didn't comply.

Getting tough, though, isn't the answer. Deeper, underlying reasons exist that explain why so few interviews had been conducted, and no matter how tough I get, these reasons will still be there. I may think I know why matters stand as they currently do, but without hearing from the kids, who know this process better than I do because they actually go through it, my perspective is limited. In a classroom built on trust, they are willing and able to suggest ways to improve the process. So, instead of getting tough, I chose a more thoughtful approach.

We held a series of class meetings to address this issue effectively. During the first one I posted the PDSA Cycle on the board and briefly explained each component. Then, we discussed what was happening with the personal lists. I shared my concerns and asked for everyone's help in creating a plan that would result in more interviews being conducted. Once we generated this plan, I told them, we would try it out and study its results. If the results were positive and the number of interviews increased, then we would make our plan standard operating procedure. If not, we would begin the process again to create a new plan. In this cycle there is literally no beginning and no end.

After discussing the PDSA Cycle as a whole, we focused on the first component of the "Plan" stage, "Define the System." In this component the group identifies the issue at hand and describes the process as it currently exists. We created the flowchart shown in Figure 5.7 to help everyone gain a better understanding of the steps of the personal spelling process.[10] Defining the system is an important first phase in problem-solving because, as Deming says, "if people do not see the process, they can not improve it."[11] Seeing the process broken down into its individual parts enables students to determine where exactly they run into trouble and where the greatest difficulties present themselves. It's also a great higher level thinking exercise.

Once you and your students have a clear understanding of the process under discussion, proceed to the next component of the Plan stage, "Assess Current Situation." In this stage, we collect data to show how matters currently stand. For example, it's not enough for me to say, "Kids, I feel that we're not doing a good job with the personal spelling interviews." They need more information than that; they need objective data to lend credence to my concerns. Having this data not only proves that a problem exists but also permits a comparison to be made between how matters currently stand and how they will stand in several weeks after our new plan has been in effect for a while. It is on the basis of this comparison that we will decide whether our new plan has been successful.

Different types of data can be used to assess the current situation. With regard to the personal spelling issue, the easiest data to collect was an actual count of how many interviews had been conducted since the beginning of the year. By looking in the book that the students used to sign up for their interviews, I determined that during the past three months only 15 had occurred. Information describing the students' attitudes about the personal lists also would have been helpful. Had I administered a brief survey asking the kids whether they found the lists to be useful, I would have known both how many interviews had occurred and how the students felt about the process as a whole. After we implemented our new plan, I would have been able to make two valuable comparisons, and thus, know whether the plan had been successful.

**Figure 5.7** Flowchart for Personal Spelling Interview Process

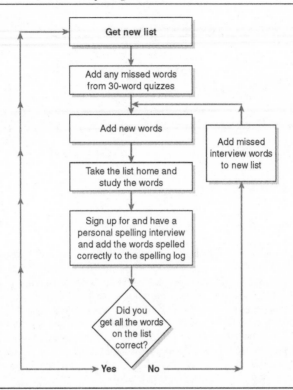

The third step of the planning stage, "Analyze Causes," involves determining why things are the way they are. To facilitate our search for explanations, my students and I employed what has undoubtedly become our favorite quality tool, the Fishbone Diagram (see Figure 5.8). Although it's also known as both an Ishigawa Diagram, after the Japanese mathematician who pioneered its use, and a Cause-and-Effect Diagram, due to the fact that it was designed to help individuals locate the causes of a phenomenon, students will forever remember this tool as a Fishbone Diagram because of its catchy name and distinct shape.

The Fishbone Diagram begins with a question, which is written in the box on the right. The question can be phrased in either a positive manner (e.g., What does it take for students to be successful early readers?) or a negative one (e.g., Why aren't we having that many spelling interviews?). How you phrase your question depends on the nature of the issue at hand. Here, it made sense to me to phrase the question negatively. The answers that students generate become the possible causes that may explain the current situation.

The diagram contains four distinct parts, or "bones," each representing one aspect of the total classroom system: people, equipment, methods, and environment. Arranging the diagram in this manner enables you and your students to observe how each part of the system

**Figure 5.8**    Fishbone Diagram for Personal Spelling Interviews

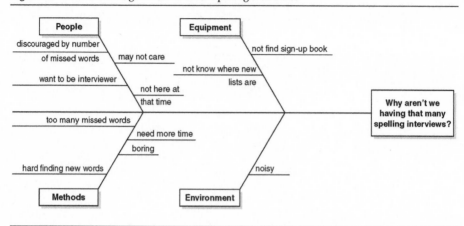

contributes to the bigger picture. Although there's always the tendency to blame or find fault with students when they don't perform to our expectations, Deming argues that individuals cause less than 10 percent of organizational problems. Most of the time, he points out, ineffective methods, inadequate supplies, faulty equipment, or a poor work environment trigger problems. Blame, then, serves no useful purpose in this activity. Rather, this is an exercise in group problem solving, a positive approach where everyone has an opportunity to contribute his or her best thinking and where everyone has a stake in creating the best outcome possible.

In Figure 5.8, I wrote down every possible cause that my students suggested. You will notice that they offered a wide variety of reasons to explain why we hadn't conducted that many spelling interviews. Of course, some reasons had more merit than others. For example, since the interviews occurred during silent reading time, I had trouble believing that the room was too noisy to take a spelling quiz. I had similar trouble believing that students needed more time to prepare and study their lists. They already had three months. How much more time did they need? Whether or not I agreed with every one of these reasons, however, I felt it was important to write them down so that the kids knew I valued their input and so they could see that rarely is there only one reason why a problem exists.

The fourth and final part of the planning stage requires you and your students to generate an Improvement Plan, which you will implement in the "Do" stage. Figure 5.9 shows the plan my class formulated to improve our spelling situation. Each point of our plan responds directly to one of the possible causes listed on the Fishbone Diagram. For example, Points 1 and 3, respectively, establish permanent homes for the sign-up book and the new personal lists so the kids will always be able to find them. Point 2 allows students who are unable to overcome the overpowering roar of silent reading time to conduct their interviews outside on the patio or off to the side of the room. In addition, Point 6 calls for the creation of a database to which students can turn if they are having difficulty finding words to put on their personal lists. This plan is much more comprehensive and thoughtfully done than any I could have crafted on my own.

Furthermore, it has more meaning to the kids because they created it themselves. Laying down the law would not have achieved nearly the same results.

After finalizing our plan, we proceeded to the "Do" stage where we made all the changes the students suggested. We implemented our new plan for about six weeks before attempting to evaluate its effectiveness. Data collection during this stage was very simple

Figure 5.9    Improvement Plan for Personalized Spelling List

---

**Improvement Plan for Personalized Spelling List**

1. Put interview book on the chalk tray in each room.

2. Conduct interviews on patio or off to the side of the room.

3. Keep new lists on kidney bean table.

4. People who aren't in the room during silent reading can have their interviews later in the day.

5. Use dictionary when possible.

6. Start database for spelling words.

7. Be sure to pick properly challenging words.

8. Lower the minimum to less than ten.

9. Have a sign up sheet to be an interviewer.

---

since all I had to do was check to see how many students signed up for spelling interviews. It turned out that after six weeks, there was indeed an increase in the number of interviews being conducted. Unfortunately, I was unable to determine whether the students felt any differently about these lists because I failed to collect that piece of data when assessing the current situation and had no basis for a comparison. Finally, in the "Act" stage, we decided to adopt our improvement plan for the remainder of the school year. During these remaining months, however, our eyes would always be open for ways to improve our personal spelling routine. The improvement process never stops.

Although I chose to make Personal Spelling Lists the subject of my PDSA example, there are two other occasions when you will find this tool especially valuable. First, whenever you administer an enthusiasm survey and notice that interest in a particular subject is alarmingly low, you will want to know why. For example, as Figure 5.5 indicates, only 17 out of my 50 students enjoyed drama in the Fall of 1997, a finding that took me completely by surprise. I employed the PDSA Cycle in an attempt to improve these results. When we reached the "Analyze Causes" phase, I asked my kids why they thought there were so few happy faces for drama. Their responses led to the generation of an improvement plan that more than doubled the number of happy faces by the end of the year.

Second, as you conduct academic assessments to determine how the students are faring in their quest to reach the standards, the PDSA Cycle can be an important part of your effort to build quality into the process. For each round of these assessments, if you are ever disappointed by the results, follow the steps of the cycle to generate an improvement plan to help students perform better next time. Specifically, you can use this tool to identify and address factors that may be interfering with your kids' performance. Should an issue ever arise, though, that you don't feel comfortable discussing with your class, invite your colleagues to share their input. Collaborating with fellow teachers to discuss common problems multiplies the power of this approach.

## INDIVIDUAL IMPROVEMENT PROJECTS

Alan Blankstein, author of *Failure is Not an Option*, writes "Ensuring achievement for *all* students means having an overarching strategy that encompasses the majority of learners— and then having specific strategies aimed at those who need extra support." (p. 110) This section includes some specific strategy ideas that can help students who may need additional assistance in their quest to meet classroom expectations.

Freddie (name changed to protect the guilty), an organizationally challenged student of mine, had a habit of leaving class each afternoon without some important items: his homework, his backpack, his jacket, and his books. He meant to take all these things home; they just rarely found their way into his hands. One morning I sat down with him and suggested that he create a flowchart to help himself remember what he needed to do before he left school each day.

Together, we constructed the step-by-step plan shown in Figure 5.10. Now, Freddie had a clear procedure to follow. The flowchart transformed what had been a confusing array of tasks into a visible sequence of simple steps. The flowchart empowered Freddie to take charge of his behavior. After reading this procedure day after day, he would eventually internalize it, and organization would soon become a habit. This approach builds his capacity while also sparing him quite a bit of nagging from his teacher.

The previous example illustrates how an individual component of the PDSA Cycle, the flowchart, can prove helpful even when it stands alone. Consider using one any time you and your students need to organize your thinking sequentially. For example, when you are absent, you can leave on the board for the substitute teacher your lesson plan in the form of a flowchart so that the kids know how to proceed from one activity to the next without adult guidance.

**Figure 5.10**    Freddie's End-of-Day Flowchart

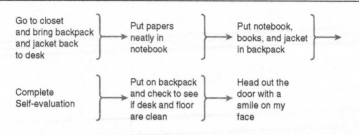

Fishbone Diagrams can also stand alone. Create one whenever you need help identifying possible causes of a phenomenon. I once heard a cute story from two teachers in North Carolina about a Kindergarten student who was growing frustrated by her classmate's annoying behavior. She took him over to the chalkboard and drew a Fishbone Diagram to find out why he was acting that way. In Chapter 7 I describe another terrific stand-alone improvement tool, the Plus/Delta Chart.

Serena was having trouble staying focused at her desk. During independent work time she would frequently look around the room and try to start conversations with other students. I suggested that she keep a checksheet by her side to record the number of times she found herself losing focus each day. I figured that if she became more aware of this tendency, her focus would improve. It didn't. After a week or so, the two of us sat down to talk. The checksheet hadn't been working. We realized that it wasn't serving a useful purpose because it required her to make a check whenever she did something that was viewed as negative. Not surprisingly, she wasn't too enthusiastic about commemorating her losses of focus with check marks.

We then tried a different approach. She would now keep by her side a checksheet similar to the one shown in Figure 5.11 to record happier occasions. Every time she lost her focus and then regained it without anyone having to remind her, she would put a check on her paper. Slowly, her focus began to get better. As she saw the number of check marks grow day by day, her attitude improved, and her confidence increased because she knew she was the one controlling her behavior. Serena's improvement also had a positive impact on those around her. Because she was no longer distracting them as much, they could focus better on their work. She made my job easier as well since I didn't have to keep as close of an eye on her.

Suddenly, other kids began asking me if they could create checksheets of their own. Some, like Serena, wanted to improve their focus while others wanted to improve a different aspect of their behavior, such as their attentive listening. Because this approach was flexible, the kids could apply it to any habit of character. Before long, half the class proudly displayed checksheets on their desks. I had a checksheet epidemic on my hands. The following week, many students carried this idea even further by incorporating checksheets into their goal-setting process. As these events unfolded, I took great pride in the fact that all of it was completely voluntary. The commitment was coming from the students themselves.

## OUR DEVELOPMENT AS PROFESSIONAL EDUCATORS

I conclude this chapter by focusing on how the spirit of continuous improvement applies to us as educators throughout the length of our careers. This section begins with a sports analogy. Many fans consider Michael Jordan to be the most outstanding basketball player

**Figure 5.11** Serena's Checksheet

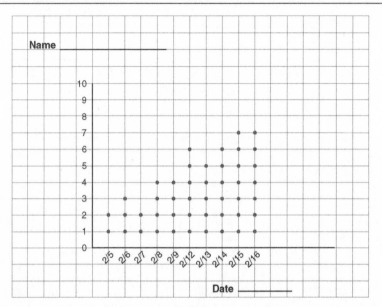

of all time. (Those people are right.) It's difficult to argue with his credentials. He earned two Olympic gold medals, led the league in scoring 10 times, won five Most Valuable Player awards, participated in 13 All-Star Games, and took the Chicago Bulls to six NBA championships.

Although he excelled as a player during each of his professional seasons, Jordan, at the age of 32, was far superior to Jordan at 22. In no way did he arrive in the NBA as a finished product. Of course, natural talent played a large role in his success, but hard work played an even larger one. Every summer, during the league's off-season, Jordan committed himself to improving specific aspects of his game. One summer, he would focus on his three-point shooting, another on his defense, still another on his free throws. By purposefully working to develop into a complete player, Jordan made the most of his vast potential.

Similarly, as teachers, we have the opportunity and, I believe, the responsibility to develop our skills over the course of our careers so that we may maximize our potential as educators. Of course, instead of basketball skills, our focus lies in developing our pedagogical skills (our ability to employ a variety of instructional approaches that give students their greatest possible chance of academic success) and our management skills. In some cases, our schools and districts take the lead in providing consistent, thorough training in these areas. For those of us who aren't as lucky, we take it on ourselves to build our repertoires—we read, reflect, plan, attend conferences, and participate in continuing education. Ultimately, responsibility for our own professional development lies with us as individuals.

Over time, our hard work pays off. All of our data collection, discussions with students, and efforts to build a culture of quality and improvement will yield substantial dividends. We will know more about how to do our jobs better. We will be more familiar with a wider variety of guiding approaches and have a better sense of how to use them for the greatest instructional benefit. We will know more about what works, what doesn't, and why. We will get a little bit better every day and significantly better every year. As a result, more students will demonstrate proficiency with the standards. More students will enjoy more subjects. More students will demonstrate the habits of mind and character that distinguish them as quality learners. The progress will not come right away, but it will be steady and consistent. In the end, we will all be able to take pride and satisfaction in a job well done.

## KEY POINTS FROM ESSENTIAL 5

- As with the other Essentials, continuous improvement is, above all, a mindset. It is important to build this spirit of improvement into our classroom culture so that students appreciate the satisfaction that comes from trying to get a little bit better every day.
- The spirit of continuous improvement can pervade every aspect of class functioning, influencing both the individual and the group, process and product, and the academic and the nonacademic.
- Genuine character development is best achieved through frequent reflection, self-evaluation, and goal setting.
- Quality learning occurs in an environment where high expectations are the norm and students are expected to improve their work until quality is achieved.
- Pareto Charts facilitate academic improvement at the group level by empowering teachers to focus instructional time and attention on the areas where they are needed the most.
- Enthusiasm for learning is likely to increase throughout the year when students are encouraged to make meaningful choices about their learning and when they are encouraged to share their ideas as to how classroom life can be improved.
- The PDSA Cycle is a user-friendly, problem-solving tool that enables teachers and students to bring their best thinking to bear on issues that matter.
- Individual students who experience behavioral difficulties can frequently benefit from customized strategies that involve data collection or that take advantage of the visual assistance provided by flowcharts and other quality tools.
- The idea of continuous improvement applies to teachers as much as it does to students. Over time, as we work to strengthen our practice and develop our skills, we will be able to do a better job of helping students reach their goals, we will experience greater joy, and we will be able to take a great deal of pride and satisfaction in a job well done.

## REFLECTION QUESTIONS

- What are some examples from your own life and from the lives of others that you can share with your students to help them develop the spirit of continuous improvement?
- In what ways do you, or could you, use data to improve your classroom instruction?
- For which academic projects might some form of Glasser's "Concurrent Evaluation" approach be suitable?
- Is there an issue with which you are currently grappling that would lend itself well to the PDSA Cycle?
- Are there areas with which individual students in your class may be struggling where a checksheet, flowchart, or other quality tool would be helpful?

# Essential 6 — INVESTING IN TRAINING

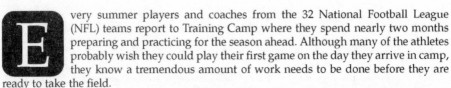very summer players and coaches from the 32 National Football League (NFL) teams report to Training Camp where they spend nearly two months preparing and practicing for the season ahead. Although many of the athletes probably wish they could play their first game on the day they arrive in camp, they know a tremendous amount of work needs to be done before they are ready to take the field.

Each team member has important responsibilities to fulfill during Training Camp. The head coach must take a group of diverse individuals, many of whom are strangers to one another, and assemble them into a cohesive, functioning unit. He must establish an environment of teamwork and discipline so that each athlete can perform to his potential. Players must learn how to play their positions well and understand that the team as a whole will only be successful when each individual does his part.

Together, players and coaches make many critical decisions. Perhaps each team's most crucial decisions involve determining its goals for the upcoming season. Struggling teams may decide that their seasons will be successful if they win half their games. Stronger teams set their sights higher; they will settle for no less than a trip to the playoffs. Elite teams will consider their seasons a failure unless they reach the Super Bowl. Clear, ambitious goals provide focus for everyone's efforts. They remind players and coaches what they are determined to accomplish.

During Training Camp players and coaches also establish routines, procedures, and guidelines that enable them to carry out their work in the most efficient and effective ways possible. For example, they determine where they will practice, what time practice will start, and how long practice will last. They reach agreement on where everyone stands in the huddle, what type of terminology they will use when calling the plays, and what kind of attire they will wear during practices, games, and road trips.

These expectations are set, reinforced, and rehearsed until they become second nature to the players. By the time training camp ends just prior to Opening Day, players will be prepared to succeed on the field because they will have accounted for nearly every situation that could arise during a game. Next time you watch the NFL on television, notice how well trained players are in their routines. They know where to go, what to do, when to do it, and how to do it. Professional football players may make these routines look easy to perform, but keep in mind, this ease comes as a direct result of weeks of diligent practice.

Setting aside time for focused training efforts is not a practice unique to professional sports. Training has long been an important part of both military and corporate life. In the military new recruits spend several months learning what it takes to be a soldier. Down to the last detail, they learn how to perform such functions as eating, dressing, grooming, marching, and communicating. They are thoroughly trained in the routines and procedures of their jobs. Expectations pertaining to their performance and conduct are set and clarified. Before they are ever asked to carry out the responsibilities of soldiers, recruits learn, practice, and internalize these responsibilities.

In the business world, quality-oriented companies pay careful attention to the issue of training. Specially designed programs help new workers learn the expectations of their jobs. According to Deming, the greatest strength of any organization lies in its people. Their skills, knowledge, and talents comprise a firm's most valuable assets. Before workers can contribute fully, however, they must be trained to do their jobs well. Trying one's best isn't enough. Recall author Mary Walton's quote from Chapter 2: "You have to know what to do, *then* do your best."[1] Writer Ted Cocheu adds, "Quality experts . . . all agree that a comprehensive training curricula is critical to providing everyone in the organization with the knowledge and skills to fulfill his or her quality-improvement responsibilities."[2]

Cocheu believes such a training program addresses the following issues:[3]

- Exploring the need for improvement as well as its individual and collective benefits
- Communicating the organization's quality goals
- Developing a common language to talk about quality-related issues
- Defining the structure and processes through which quality improvement will take place
- Clarifying everyone's responsibilities
- Providing people with the tools and techniques to manage the quality of their work

In this chapter I describe how to apply the aforementioned ideas about training to the classroom setting. Because we, as teachers, genuinely want our students to be successful, we must initially invest the time to train them in the various responsibilities we expect them to fulfill. In a quality classroom such a training program includes the following:

- Introducing and discussing the class aim
- Creating a class mission statement
- Clearly defining a set of habits of mind and habits of character
- Determining and clarifying goals
- Establishing requirements, rubrics, standards, and scoring systems so students understand how their work will be assessed
- Building an atmosphere of caring, trust, respect, and teamwork
- Establishing the routines, procedures, and expectations that will help you and your students complete tasks in the most effective and efficient ways possible

In general, four to six weeks of thorough training will be needed to address the priorities mentioned earlier. That time frame, of course, is simply a guideline. Yours may vary slightly due to such factors as the grade level you teach and the amount of prior experience your students have had working with one another, with you, or with teachers who share your basic teaching philosophy. Commonly, educators readily acknowledge the important benefits of training, yet neglect to follow through with sufficient attention to these matters due to the very real pressure to start teaching standards right away so the kids aren't disadvantaged come testing time. Such a decision is understandable, but it's also shortsighted. The long-term benefits of training far outweigh the short-term costs.

Investing time during the beginning of the year to set our students up for success will save considerable time down the road. As an example, let's take the issue of playground behavior. Specifically, let's focus on how we expect our students to solve problems and settle disputes on the yard. Inevitably, there will be times when a couple of kids return to your class from recess incredibly upset. At first glance, you can easily tell that they (a) argued with someone over a game or a piece of equipment, (b) had a fight, (c) got in trouble with the yard teacher, or (d) all of the above (usually progressing from a to b to c). Without any training as to how to solve playground disputes, your students won't be equipped to handle them. As a result, problems will occur repeatedly, and you will be forced to spend valuable instructional time dealing with the aftermath all year long.

On the other hand, if you spend the first few weeks of the year discussing this issue with your students and empowering them with strategies to solve their problems constructively, you greatly reduce the likelihood that intense, unpleasant episodes will occur. These efforts begin the first day of school. A short time before recess, I gather the kids together to talk about appropriate playground behavior. I tell them that we all know there will be times on the yard when people bother or try to start trouble with us. I pose the following question: "What should you do to handle this situation in a positive way?" Students usually suggest the following answers: ignore them, ask them to stop, walk away, or tell the yard teacher. I then call a student volunteer up to the front of the room to engage in a recess simulation. I pretend to bother that student in a variety of annoying ways. In response, he or she proceeds through our list of suggested remedies until I am ultimately hauled away by the yard teacher.

These simulation activities are incredibly effective for many reasons. First, they are enjoyable to do and entertaining to watch so the students pay close attention to the points I'm trying to make. Second, because the playground incident isn't actually happening as we speak, we can analyze and respond to it with some emotional detachment. The heat of the moment isn't clouding our judgment. Finally, our efforts to solve the problem are proactive. Because I timed the simulation to occur before the class ever went out to recess, kids don't feel like they're being put on the spot for something they just got caught doing. Everyone can participate in the simulation with a clean conscience.

As effective as they are, these simulations and discussions can't be one-shot deals. The power of a simulation is greatly diminished if it represents the only time students hear from you about important matters. Consistent follow-up efforts are needed if we expect our students to internalize these strategies and use them successfully. Returning to our recess example, I make sure to set aside a few minutes after the first recess ends to see how things went. We talk about how they spent their time, whether any problems arose, and, if so, how they were solved. I continue to set aside time both before and after recess to discuss playground matters for the first few weeks of the year. We spend this time practicing how to respond to a wide variety of recess situations either that have occurred or that we believe are likely to occur. After repeated discussions, simulations, and practice activities, the kids understand what their options are, when they should be used, and why they're important.

There's no getting around the fact that these training efforts require time. In fact, if you figure that I set aside 10 minutes a day for the first few weeks of school to focus on proper playground behavior, then we're talking an investment of a substantial amount of time, especially considering the amount of content the students are expected to learn. But there are worthy payoffs from this investment. As a result of these training efforts, the students will have safer, more enjoyable recesses. In addition, they become empowered with valuable communication and problem-solving skills that will help them handle a wide variety of situations in a constructive manner. Also, once I conclude that these efforts are no longer necessary, I know I won't have to devote significant time to this issue in the months ahead. So, while it may seem that training activities are taking a large chunk out of your day, keep in mind the time you're saving yourself later in the year and the quality you're adding to each day.

Of course, proper playground behavior is not the only area in which we will need to train our students. The kids also need to learn the routines, procedures, and policies that we expect them to follow in the classroom. Such matters include the following: how to sharpen a pencil, where to hang up backpacks, and how to sit in a chair. These aspects of classroom management aren't glamorous, but they are important. If they aren't done well, there's the potential for injury, confusion, distraction, disruption, and wasted time.

Before you can train your students in these matters, however, you must take the time to identify them. To generate this list, I close my eyes and pretend the bell has just rung to begin a typical school day. I visualize a complete day's worth of activities from start to finish. As I think about each one, I write down all the things students need to know to perform that activity effectively. For example, when the bell rings, the students line up in our designated spot. Immediately, I know that I have to teach my students where and how to stand in line. Next, I envision the kids walking peacefully inside the room and putting away their belongings. I note that I must show my kids how to walk in line, how to enter the room quietly, and how to put away their materials. Then, imagine that the first academic task I ask my kids to do is silent reading. As I picture the students reading silently, I add to my list that I need to teach them how to sit in a chair, how to hold a book, and how to keep track of their books and pages read in their reading notebooks.

When I finish my virtual tour of the school day, I wind up with a list similar to the one shown in Figure 6.1. It includes the routines, procedures, and policies that I use to organize my training efforts at the beginning of each year. Where appropriate, I have also included methods, strategies, and ideas that have proven to be effective.

No detail is too small. Although some items on the Training Routines list may appear trivial or unworthy of your time and some of the explanations may seem overly explicit, it's important for students to understand your expectations unambiguously. Often we assume that our students already know how to do many of the things on this list only to discover later that we had assumed incorrectly. When it comes to routines, don't assume that your kids have mastered *anything*. Save yourself the aggravation and start at square one.

Developing your list before the school year begins puts you in a terrific position to provide your kids with thorough training in these expectations. Once the year starts, I make sure that as I introduce each aspect of the curriculum to my students, I also teach them the routines, procedures, and policies that relate to it. Taking the kids step by step through each new feature of the classroom leads to greater success, and over time, completion of the routines becomes more and more automatic. For example, early in the school year, I ask my students to copy a paragraph from a health textbook so that I can have a baseline sample of their printing. Before the students begin their copying, however, I explain how they should head their paper and then model the procedure I expect them to follow. I show them where to write their names, the date, and the title of the activity. I indent the first sentence and write from margin to margin. Then, I answer all their questions so they are clear about my expectations. In addition, as the kids are working, I walk around the room to check everyone's paper. Finally, I follow-up on this initial effort for the next few weeks until the procedure becomes second nature to them.

The list of training routines itself can become an effective teaching tool. If you leave sufficient space between each item and provide all your students with a copy, the list serves as an advance organizer. During the first few weeks of the year, every time the students learn a new routine, procedure, or expectation, they can add it to the organizer. In addition, you can enlarge the list and create a poster-size advance organizer that you keep in front of the

**Figure 6.1** Training Routines

**Self-Management**

- How to sit in a chair
  *Bottoms on chairs, sitting tall with excellent posture*
- How to push in a chair
- How to sit on the rug
  *Cross sitting or hook sitting with eyes on speaker*
- How to raise your hand
  *Arms extended straight up (so I don't have to guess if students are raising their hands or just stretching)*
- How to follow the silent signal
  *Eyes on teacher, hands empty, hands touching forehead*
- How to follow the Acceptable Voice Indicator (AVI)
  *I describe the AVI more completely later in this chapter.*
- When to ask questions during an instructional lesson
  *I ask the kids to hold their questions until the end of the lesson so the flow of instruction isn't interrupted.*
- How to use hand signals
  *I frequently ask students to use hand signals during a lesson so that I can check their understanding. In response to my statements, kids show thumbs up if they agree with me, thumbs down if they disagree, or thumbs to the side if they're not sure. Their responses help me determine whether I should move on with the lesson or spend more time reviewing key points. In addition, their responses tell me which students may need individual follow-up with regard to the lesson's key points.*

**Getting Around**

- How to enter and leave class quietly
- How to line up and walk in line
- How to transition quickly and quietly from one activity to the next
- How to carry a chair
  *I ask my students to use two hands and to carry it in front of them for safety purposes.*
- When to use the bathroom
  *Preferably before and after school and during recess and lunch*
- When to use the drinking fountain
  *Before and after school and during recess and lunch*

**Materials**

- Where to put backpacks, jackets, and lunches
- Where all class materials are stored
- What to keep in your desk
  *Only books, folders, and pencil boxes that I provide all students on the first day of school. In the pencil boxes I provide two pencils, a large eraser, a glue stick, and a box of crayons. I give kids their own materials to teach responsibility and to avoid custody disputes.*
- How to hold and care for books
  *Books should never be left open facedown because it ruins the spines. Instead, students should use bookmarks. Each student has a bookmark that contains a list of reading strategies on it so the kids have easy access to these ideas while they are reading.*

- When and how to sharpen pencils

  *We don't use the electric sharpener during the school day because the noise is disruptive. Instead, the student leader sharpens a bunch of pencils after school or in the morning before class starts and puts them in a can labeled "Sharpened." Throughout the day, when a pencil no longer works, the kids trade it for a better one by putting it in the "Unsharpened" can and taking one from the "Sharpened" can. The two cans sit side by side on the counter in the back of the room.*

- Kleenex policy
- How to pass out and collect materials
- How to put papers into folders

  *Tuck papers all the way in so they don't become wrinkled or stick out of the top.*

- Where to turn in homework

**Class Work**

- How to head your paper

  *Name and date in the top right-hand corner of the paper and the title of the activity centered on the top line of the paper.*

- What to do when you finish work early
- How to use journals

  *I glue a page of writing prompts to the inside cover of student journals to give the kids ideas to write about during free choice journal writing. I also glue a list of writing guidelines to the inside cover of their take-home writing notebooks so they and their parents will both know how to complete homework activities correctly.*

- How to use the computer

**Policies**

- What students are allowed to bring to class (e.g., toys, gum, candy, water bottles, food)

  *I encourage students to keep water bottles at the foot of their desks to remain hydrated throughout the day. The bottles must be filled during their free time.*

**Dealing With Others**

- How to get the teacher's attention

  *Rather than approach me when they need help, the students raise their hands so I can come to them or call them up to me. This prevents a whole group of kids from coming up to me at once.*

- How to work in cooperative groups
- How to greet visitors
- How to act when delivering a message to another class or the office
- How to answer the phone or intercom

**Subject or Activity-Specific Expectations**

- How to record their reading in their reading logs
- How to progress through the stages of Writer's Workshop
- When it's necessary to skip lines while writing and when it isn't

  *As a general rule, I ask the kids to skip lines only when we're going to revise their written work. During these times the extra space will be helpful.*

*(Continued)*

**Figure 6.1** (Continued)

---

**General Class Business**

- How to take attendance
- How to do the lunch count
- How to perform the various monitor jobs
- How to perform the responsibilities of Student Leader
  *I describe these responsibilities in detail in Chapter 7.*

**Safety**

- How to use the first-aid kit
- How to handle problems on the yard
  *Many schools have adopted formal conflict resolution programs to address this need. If yours hasn't, your students will still be able to generate their own list of effective problem-solving strategies.*

---

room. With either of these options, you and your students can write detailed definitions of each new routine, jot down key words, or represent ideas with pictures or symbols. However you ask the students to fill out their organizers, the simple act of committing something to paper will help them (1) learn and remember what you expect of them and (2) understand that you take these expectations seriously. When complete, the organizers can function as a type of training manual to which your class can refer when necessary. Finally, should a new student arrive in your room later in the year, your organizer can help that child make a smoother transition to his or her new surroundings.

Holding students accountable for their performance with these expectations is an important aspect of our training efforts. For example, when the kids are working quietly at their seats, how quiet do they need to be? Does the room have to be completely silent? Can the kids talk softly? Can they talk loudly? To address this issue, I created a chart called the Acceptable Volume Indicator, AVI for short. The AVI includes three levels of noise: conversational tone, whisper, and complete silence. During the first week of school, I introduce the AVI to the kids, explain its purpose, model each level, and describe the types of activities for which each level will be used. Then, as the kids begin their work, we practice all three levels. Once we have practiced the levels sufficiently, the students need to know that I mean what I say. The first time students exceed the acceptable noise level I call their attention to it. If it continues to happen, we take a few moments to discuss the issue as a class. I continue to model what I expect, hold more simulation activities, give them more opportunities to practice, and explain why it's important to adjust to each level. When students understand the purpose of a procedure or routine and see the value in it, they will commit themselves to performing better.

Don't accept unacceptable performance. Once you do, you're sending a message, loudly and clearly, that such conduct will be tolerated. There's no room for indecisiveness or vacillating. Decide how good is good enough and stick with your decisions. As Crosby puts it, "The determined . . . [teacher] has no recourse except to make the same point over and over until everyone believes. The first time a deviation is agreed upon, everyone will know about it before the ink is dry. 'Oh,' people will say, 'there are some things that don't have to be right.'"[4] If, for example, a student hands you a paper without his or her name on it, hand it

## An Idea From a Teacher:
## Putting Essential 6 Into Practice

Jillian Esby

*St. Matthew's Parish School*
*Pacific Palisades, CA*
*K–5 Science*

In my elementary science classroom, I spend several days working with my students on practices to help keep them safe and working efficiently in the lab. We review several different types of checklists they will use frequently, from daily supply lists and to-do lists to weekly and monthly up-keep charts to ensure our materials are being cleaned and stored properly. We discuss how a science lab is different from other classrooms; it can be loud and chaotic at times, and needs to be still and silent at others. We discuss what it means to collaborate in group experiments to produce results.

SOURCE: Jillian Esby, St. Matthew's Parish School.

back. If your kids return to the room from lunch making too much noise, have them go back outside and line up again. Such actions are not punishments. They are effective responses to let your students know that you mean what you say. Over time the students will rise to your expectations. By holding them accountable early in the year, you will make the rest of the year much smoother.

An effective way to help students improve their ability to perform these routines is to use what educator Madeline Hunter calls "think-starters." Imagine Randy has just handed me a paper with no name on it. If I told him, "Put your name on it," that would be a "think-stopper" because I'm the one pointing out his mistake. On the other hand, if I asked, "What do you need to do before handing me this paper?" then I am helping Randy to discover his own mistake. That would be a think-starter.

Asking him instead of telling him shifts the responsibility to Randy. Think-starters give students ownership of their behavior. By encouraging kids to reflect on their actions, think-starters help them internalize these habits and build their capacity for the future. While Randy may have forgotten to put his name on the paper this time, think-starters increase the chances that he will remember to do it next time.

Figure 6.2 summarizes the steps I recommend taking every time you introduce a new routine or procedure to your students.

Four to six weeks into the year, you and your kids will be ready to conclude your training period. To culminate and reinforce these efforts, ask your students to prepare brief skits about the items on your Training Routines list. These presentations fit neatly with your class aim because they entertain the kids while also bringing their understanding to a new level. If you have the ability to do so, consider videotaping the skits. You can then use these performances, or at least some of them, as instructional videos for the following year's students.

The most common mistake teachers make with regard to Essential 6 is ending the training period prematurely. Sometimes we start a school year fully committed to training our students thoroughly, and the first two weeks go extremely smoothly. The kids

**Figure 6.2**    Summary of Training Steps

1. Introduce the new routine.

2. Discuss the importance of performing the routine correctly so students understand the purpose of it.

3. Explain how to perform the routine in a step-by-step manner.

4. Model the steps of the routine.

5. Hold simulation activities whenever possible.

6. Provide multiple opportunities for your students to practice the routine until it becomes second nature to them.

7. Hold students accountable for proper performance of the routine.

8. Use think-starters to help students internalize these habits.

respond well to our efforts, and they don't appear to need additional practice. After three weeks the routines become more automatic, and we are tempted to bring our training period to a halt. After all, there's a great deal of content for the kids to learn, and the thought of using the time we had earmarked for additional training to focus on that content is an attractive one. As attractive as this thought may be, however, resist this temptation. The extra time you take to build a foundation for quality learning will pay off. Effective training cannot be rushed.

Commit yourself to making the training of your students a high priority during the beginning of each school year. By February or March, you will be glad you did. An initial investment of time will not only save you considerable time down the road but also result in a more productive, more focused classroom environment. As any quality expert will tell you, individuals simply cannot perform their jobs well without proper training.

## KEY POINTS FROM ESSENTIAL 6

- Training students during the first four to six weeks of each new school year in the routines, procedures, and expectations we expect them to know and follow is an important priority.
- Training efforts do require a substantial investment of time and energy, but this investment will pay off. Our investment will result in better use of class time, smoother functioning, fewer problems, and higher quality learning throughout the year.
- Identifying and listing all classroom routines in a specific manner before the school year begins helps maximize the effectiveness of our training efforts.
- Each routine must be introduced and taught explicitly. Students must see each routine modeled in a step-by-step fashion and must understand the purpose of doing it correctly.
- Holding students accountable for their performance with these expectations is an important aspect of our training efforts. Students need to know that we mean what we say.

- The use of "think-starters" improves students' ability to remember and perform classroom routines consistently.
- A natural tendency exists to shorten our training period when students seem to grasp routines quickly. Resist this temptation. Students require multiple opportunities to practice routines before they become second nature.

## REFLECTION QUESTIONS

- What will be your highest training priorities the next time you begin a new school year?
- Which expectations will you include on your Training Routines list to set you and your students up for the greatest possible classroom success?
- What kind of simulation activities could you conduct to help students learn the routines, procedures, and policies you expect them to master?
- Of all the items on my Training Routines list, students usually have the greatest difficulty following the silent signal consistently. So, we spend extra time practicing this skill. Which of the expectations on your Training Routines list may require a little extra time and attention on your part?
- How will you hold students accountable for their performance with regard to the various items on your Training Routines list?

# Essential 7

## NURTURING INTRINSIC MOTIVATION

The eighth of Deming's 14 points counsels managers to drive out fear from the workplace. Although Deming established these points while working extensively with Japanese business leaders after World War II, he developed 8 after observing factory life in the United States. Managing by fear, according to Deming, was not an issue in Japan. It was chiefly an American way of supervising workers.

American managers used fear to control employees. They did this primarily through the application of the quota system, under which workers are responsible for producing a predetermined number or amount of output per day. The pressure placed on workers to meet their quotas made for a very stressful work environment. For example, assume I work in an auto parts factory, and my coworkers and I must produce 50 spark plugs each per day. Those who fail to meet the quota, or who otherwise displease the boss, are subject to intimidation, threats, pay deductions, and even termination. On the other hand, there's also strong pressure among employees not to exceed the quota. The thinking goes that if management sees some workers surpass the production target, they will then raise it for everyone.

According to Deming, whether workers are struggling to reach the quota or holding back not to surpass it, the fear associated with this approach presents serious problems to organizations concerned about quality. First, the constant stress prevents workers from feeling secure in their jobs. It also robs them of all pride in workmanship and destroys any joy they may experience from their efforts; workers can't enjoy their jobs when they are worried about losing their jobs. In addition, fear causes employees to focus on their own survival rather than on producing quality work. Quality must become and remain the emphasis if an organization and the individuals within it are going to live up to their full potential. Fear distracts workers from that emphasis.

As an outspoken critic of management by fear, Deming claims, "The economic loss from fear is appalling."[1] Fearful employees cannot produce quality work. As Mary Walton explains, "Many employees are afraid to ask questions or take a position, even when they do not understand what the job is or what is right or wrong."[2] Fearing that they will be blamed for the problem, fired, harassed, discriminated against, or given a less desirable job assignment, workers will continue to perform their duties wrongly or not at all. They will be afraid to report broken equipment, ask for additional instructions, or call attention to conditions that interfere with quality.

Why did companies choose to manage by fear? Were managers just cruel, uncaring people who enjoyed exerting their power? Was it because their desire to earn profits

**Figure 7.1**    Douglas McGregor's Theory X and Theory Y

---

**Theory X Assumptions of the Worker**

1. The average human being has an inherent dislike of work and will avoid it if he can.

2. Because of this human characteristic of dislike of work, most people must be coerced, directed, threatened with punishment to get them to put forth adequate effort toward the achievement of organizational objectives.

3. The average human being prefers to be directed, wishes to avoid responsibility, has relatively little ambition, wants security above all.

**Theory Y Assumptions of the Worker**

1. The expenditure of physical and mental effort in work is as natural as play or rest.

2. External control and the threat of punishment are not the only means for bringing about effort toward organizational objectives. Man will exercise self-direction and self-control in the service of objectives to which he is committed.

3. Commitment to objectives is a function of the rewards associated with their achievement.

4. The average human being learns, under proper conditions, not only to accept but to seek responsibility.

5. The capacity to exercise a relatively high degree of imagination, ingenuity, and creativity in the solution of organizational problems is widely, not narrowly, distributed in the population.

6. Under the conditions of modern industrial life, the intellectual potentialities of the average human being are only partially utilized.

---

SOURCE: Reprinted with permission from *The Human Side of Enterprise,* © 1960, McGraw-Hill.

overrode any concern for their employees' well-being? While these two possible answers will appeal to some, neither gets to the heart of the issue. Instead, the work of psychologist Douglas McGregor suggests another, more logical explanation why companies relied on fear to manage employees: they felt they *needed* to do so. McGregor developed two contrasting sets of worker assumptions, known as Theory X and Theory Y[3] (see Figure 7.1). Management, operating under Theory X assumptions, believed that without such a coercive approach, workers lacked the motivation of their own to put forth the effort required to get the job done. Because of this perceived lack of internal motivation, management felt the need to control their workers externally through the use of fear and punishment.

If managers truly embrace Theory X assumptions, then using fear in the workplace serves a constructive purpose. If I honestly believe that my employees dislike their work and will avoid it at all costs, then the survival of the firm depends on my finding a way to get them, and keep them, motivated. If that's my situation, then intimidating, punishing, and creating daily quotas for everyone to meet to receive a paycheck strike me as advisable courses of action to take. Sure, there are negative side effects to this approach, but our need to get work done around here justifies it.

## CLASSROOM PARALLELS

In American education, just as in business, an emphasis on control and punishment, rooted in Theory X assumptions, has dominated the way we manage our students. Punishment has traditionally come in a variety of forms. Without the ability to affect wages, as factory managers can, teachers have historically punished students by impacting two other commodities they hold dear: free time and grades. When kids misbehave, we take away their recess or send them to detention. Adding to the misery, we have them write standards during this time. We also punish by lowering their grades. Should the negative behavior become extreme, we suspend and expel. The fear created by such exercises of power is just as real and presents the same range of problems encountered by workers in the factory.

In recent years, however, the negative aspects of controlling students through the use of punishment have led educators to search for more positive ways to achieve the same effect. The result has been an increase in the use of rewards, both tangible and intangible. Throughout his well-known book *Punished by Rewards,* author Alfie Kohn (1993) defines a reward as any situation where the idea "if you do this, you will get that" is at work, such as telling students "if you spell all your words correctly, you will get a sticker." The idea of using rewards, rather than punishments, has obvious appeal. Because students are working to earn something positive rather than to avoid something negative, the classroom becomes a happier, more exciting place to be. Rewards appear to offer a win-win situation for everybody. Students win because they have opportunities to earn items that they value while teachers also win because our kids have to do exactly what we say to attain these rewards. They have to behave well and put forth effort.

Now, instead of taking away our students' recess time when they don't line up properly, we put five marbles in the jar when they do. When the students earn 50 marbles, they get a popcorn party. Now, when we discover that our class scores poorly on the weekly spelling quizzes, we offer a sticker to every student who gets all the words right. Now, to ensure that every table has a smooth transition from one activity to the next, we add another point to the board for each table that does a good job. Every time a table earns 10 points, we treat those kids to a pizza party.

## THE PROBLEMS WITH REWARDS

Although rewards may appear qualitatively different from punishments, both approaches suffer from the same underlying problems. Kohn, in his book *Punished by Rewards,* writes "that rewards and punishments are not opposites at all; they are two sides of the same coin. And it is a coin that does not buy very much."[4] He points out that while the negative effects of punishment may appear obvious, those of rewards are harder to detect. He has identified five specific problems associated with the use of rewards.

- **Rewards Punish**

  Rewards punish in two ways. First, they have the effect of controlling students' behavior. By offering a sticker to every child who shows me that he or she is ready to line up for recess, I can easily manipulate the class into action. Controlling students in this manner whenever we expect them to perform a task diminishes their autonomy. It denies them opportunities to act on their own, make decisions, and exercise responsibility. If our mission involves developing self-directed learners, rewards thwart that process by placing control squarely in the hands of teachers, not students. Our kids can't exercise self-control when their actions are being controlled.

Second, Kohn notes that rewards punish because "some people do not get the rewards they were hoping to get, and the effect of this is, in practice, indistinguishable from punishment."[5] For example, imagine I promise my class 20 extra minutes of Physical Education (PE) at the end of the day if everyone behaves well up to that point. After the morning goes very smoothly, the kids head to recess talking about how great our longer PE period is going to be. The group then returns from recess and continues its outstanding effort until lunchtime. As we walk to the lunch benches, I sense everyone's confidence growing. I hear one student tell another, "We've made it through the hard part. After lunch there's only one hour left until PE. We've got it in the bag." But, wouldn't you know it, just 15 minutes before PE, two students begin playing around during social studies. I ask them to stop, but they continue misbehaving. I have no choice but to tell the class that there'll be no extra PE today. Predictably, the kids are deflated. They feel as if they have just been punished even though I haven't, technically, taken anything away from them. They simply were unable to do what was necessary to obtain the reward.

- **Rewards Rupture Relationships**

Rewards rupture two sets of classroom relationships. First, rewards harm the relationships that students have with one another. This damage occurs commonly in situations of artificial scarcity where the teacher intentionally limits the number of rewards that will be given out. Imagine that I tell my kids that whoever constructs the best science project will receive a beautiful plaque. By turning this activity into a competition, I pit every child against his or her classmates. This type of system "sets people up as one another's rivals, [and] the predictable result is that each will view the others with suspicion and hostility and, depending on their relative status, perhaps with contempt or envy as well."[6]

Competition created by artificial scarcity also leads to other problems. According to Kohn, it produces "anxiety of a type and level that typically interferes with performance,"[7] discourages and demotivates those students who believe they have no chance of winning, and results in a diminished sense of empowerment and responsibility for future performance due to the fact that people tend to attribute the results of a contest to factors beyond their control, such as innate ability. Above all, competition destroys any sense of cooperation and community that teachers attempt to build in their classrooms. It replaces "the possibility that people will try to assist each other with the near certainty they will try to defeat each other."[8]

Rewards also rupture relationships among students when teachers offer collective incentives, as in the aforementioned example where I promised extra PE to the whole class if all the kids behaved well. Whenever the attainment of a reward depends on the efforts of everyone in the room, students quickly come to understand that any one individual holds the power to spoil it for the group. Kohn considers this approach "one of the most transparently manipulative strategies used by people in power. It calls forth a particularly noxious sort of peer pressure rather than encouraging genuine concern about the well-being of others."[9] Students watch over one another like hawks, snapping comments such as "Shh!" and "Do your work!" to ensure that nobody jeopardizes the promised reward. Should the class ultimately fail to earn the incentive, the kids will immediately turn on the individual causing, or suspected to have caused, the disappointment.

Second, rewards rupture the teacher-student relationship. As teachers, we try to create relationships with our kids characterized by trust, caring, and open communication. We want students to feel comfortable asking for help with something they don't understand, admitting mistakes, and coming to us with problems. This type of relationship, Kohn argues, "is precisely what rewards and punishments kill. If your . . . teacher . . . is sitting in judgment of you, and if that judgment will determine whether good things or bad things will happen to you, this cannot help but warp your relationship with that person. You will not be working collaboratively in order to learn or grow; you will be trying to get him or her to approve of what you are doing so you can get the goodies."[10] Rewards offer a strong incentive to hide problems, create an impression of total competence, and devote time and energy attempting to impress the person in power.[11]

- **Rewards Ignore Reasons**

For three straight days one of my most reliable students has failed to turn in her homework. Wishing to put a stop to this emerging trend, I offer her a reward if she brings it tomorrow. In doing so, I'm paying no attention to the possible causes of this sudden change in behavior. I'm only attending to the symptoms, wasting an opportunity to use this occasion as a teachable moment. By failing to focus on the reasons she hasn't been turning in her homework, I'm unable to help her in an effective way. Kohn points out that when acting in this manner, we really don't know what's going on beneath the surface because using rewards as a solution doesn't require us to know. "Rewards are not actually solutions at all; they are gimmicks, shortcuts, quick fixes that mask problems and ignore reasons. They never look below the surface."[12] There could be any number of reasons why she hasn't been turning in her homework, such as organizational difficulties or an illness. Until teachers stop using rewards to mask these deeper issues, we will never be able to address them in ways that lead to genuine solutions.

- **Rewards Discourage Risk Taking**

While rewards may increase the likelihood that individuals will engage in a certain behavior in the short run, they also change the way we engage in that behavior. Specifically, Kohn argues, when working for a reward, "we do exactly what is necessary to get it and no more."[13] Because the objective is simply to attain the reward, people are "less likely to take chances, think creatively, challenge themselves, play with possibilities, and follow hunches that might not pay off."[14] Psychologist John Condry has dubbed rewards "enemies of exploration."[15]

Rewards cause individuals to choose the easiest, fastest, most effortless route to completing a task. Because the task comes to be seen as something that stands between you and the reward, it's logical that people would attempt to get it over with as quickly as possible. The task loses any inherent meaning and becomes simply a stepping-stone to the reward. For example, when I was in first grade, my teacher gave a prize to every student who read 30 books. My friend Dean and I found the shortest book in our class library and read it 30 times. We then filled out the record sheet by writing the title of the book 30 times. Our goal was not to become better or more enthusiastic readers, but to read 30 books.

- **Rewards Decrease Interest**

Kohn's fifth reason explaining why rewards fail deals with the relationship between two types of motivation, extrinsic and intrinsic. Rewards and punishments are both examples of extrinsic motivation. I define extrinsic motivation to mean that *an individual desires to engage in a task not because of any connection to the task itself, but because of outside incentives.* (In fact, the Latin prefix "ex" means "out of.") For example, if

I begin listening to a certain radio station only because it's giving away $10,000 to caller 12, then I am extrinsically motivated. I'm not listening to the station because I enjoy the music it plays or the personality of the DJs. My desire to engage in the task of listening has nothing to do with the act of listening itself; I listen so that I can win money. I listen, not for its own sake, but because it is a stepping-stone to a greater good. Listening is simply a means to an end.

In contrast, intrinsic motivation focuses on what lies within the task, not on what successful completion of the task will earn. By intrinsically motivated, I mean that *an individual desires to engage in a task due to the nature of the task itself or because of something inherent in the task.* For example, I was initially attracted to paddle tennis because I enjoyed running around, hitting the ball, and planning strategy. I began playing the game for its own sake, not for extrinsic incentives such as prize money. For any task, whether it's playing a sport or solving a math problem, intrinsic motivation exists when one or more of the following conditions apply:

I find the task interesting.

I find meaning in it.

The task is important to me.

I feel a sense of mastery or accomplishment when I do it well.

I enjoy the challenge the task provides.

I take personal pride and satisfaction in doing the task well.

I value the learning opportunity the task offers.

The task offers opportunities for self-expression and creativity.

Extrinsic rewards reduce intrinsic motivation. Kohn shared this conclusion after reviewing scores of research studies examining the issue. The basic point is that "people's interest in what they are doing typically declines when they are rewarded for doing it."[16] The examples supporting Kohn's contention are numerous. One comes from my personal experiences as a paddle tennis player. These events taught me, first hand, how powerful the effects of rewards can be.

I first swung a paddle tennis racket at the age of five. My father had a regular Sunday morning doubles game down at the beach, and I would sit on a bench and watch for two hours, just hoping that he would have enough energy when they were done to hit the ball with me for five minutes. Once I began playing, I was hooked. Whenever my family spent the night at the beach, I would wear my shoes to sleep so that I could get right to the courts the next morning. There was no time to waste. I would play from early in the morning until dark. Lying in bed at night, I would visualize myself hitting shot after shot.

I started playing junior tournaments at the age of 7 and adult tournaments at the age of 13. I was pleased to find out that they give you trophies for finishing in the top three places. As I began to win these prizes, I wanted more of them. Soon, my desire to build up a trophy collection had eclipsed my intrinsic love of the game. My interest in accumulating trophies became a preoccupation, then an obsession. And it wasn't just trophies. Other extrinsics, such as my placement in the rankings, drove me to keep playing. My outlook on the game changed dramatically during my late teens and early 20s. Paddle tennis was becoming a job, not a hobby. Instead of lying in bed visualizing myself hitting great shots as I had done during my childhood, I stayed up calculating how many rankings points I needed to advance to a higher position. At the age of 23, the enjoyment was completely gone, and I retired from competitive play. From that point, it took me about two years of recreational play to rediscover the joy I knew so well as a child.

The motion picture *Searching for Bobby Fischer* provides another example that demonstrates how extrinsic rewards can decrease intrinsic interest. (I have shown the film to my students to illustrate this point.) As the movie begins, seven-year-old Josh Waitzkin walks home from school with his mother and baby sister. They pass through a park where a group of men are playing chess. He surprises his mom by asking if he could sit down to play with them. Although his mother has no idea that her son even knows how to play chess, she arranges a game for him. Josh's style of play attracts the attention of Vinny, Lawrence Fishburn's character, who compares the boy to a young Bobby Fischer. Having had his first taste of chess, Josh quickly develops a love for the game. He even tries to teach his sister how to play.

Sensing his son's potential, Josh's father hires a professional chess teacher, Bruce, played by Ben Kingsley. As part of his lessons, Bruce creates a variety of game situations and challenges Josh to choose the correct moves. Every time Josh makes the proper decision, Bruce awards him a certain number of "Master Class Points." Bruce tells Josh that if he earns enough of these points, he will receive a certificate declaring him a Grand Champion.

Soon, Josh begins entering and winning local tournaments. His trophy collection grows to an impressive size, and he becomes the number one ranked player in his age group. As the boy's ranking rises, the pressure that his father and teacher place on him intensifies. Gradually, Josh's desire to play chess has less to do with his love of the game and more to do with points, rankings, trophies, certificates, tournaments, and winning. Ultimately, Josh stops having fun with chess entirely and plays out of obligation to his father. In the end, his mother insists that certain changes be made in her son's life to restore his love of the game, and the movie concludes with Josh having a happier, more balanced childhood.

The finding that extrinsic motivation decreases intrinsic motivation has serious educational implications. Currently, many teachers are offering students rewards thinking that they increase interest in an activity when they actually decrease it. The most well-known examples of this phenomenon are those programs that offer students incentives for reading. Libraries, corporations, and other concerned groups organize these programs all over the country. When I taught first grade, the school distributed calendars to the kids each month. Every night they would enter the number of minutes they read. If, by the end of the month, the students read a designated number of total minutes, they would receive a prize.

The creators of these programs have the noblest of intentions. In criticizing the use of rewards, I'm not criticizing the well-meaning people who organize the programs. These individuals sincerely want children to choose to read more often. And, initially, that happens. Offered an incentive for reading, students, in the short run, will read more often. What happens, though, is that this level of reading activity doesn't last. Several months down the road, without the presence of the reward, the amount of reading declines significantly. In fact, a truly frightening research finding indicates that in the long run, students who were initially rewarded for reading not only choose to read less often than they did at the outset of the program but also choose to read less often than children who never participated in these programs in the first place. The problem, according to Kohn, is not that the effects of the rewards don't last, but that the effects are the opposite of what was intended. "What rewards do, and what they do with devastating effectiveness, is smother people's enthusiasm for activities they might otherwise enjoy."[17]

Kohn offers two reasons to explain why rewards decrease interest. First, he believes that "rewards are usually experienced as controlling, and we tend to recoil from situations where our autonomy has been diminished."[18] Second, he suggests that "anything presented as a prerequisite for something else—that is, as a means toward some other end—comes to be seen as less desirable. 'Do this and you'll get that' automatically devalues the 'this.'"[19]

Returning to our reading program example, students will figure out that if others are offering a reward for reading, then it must not be something they would want to do on their own.

It's just a stepping-stone to getting what they truly want: food, toys, and tickets to amusement parks. Educator A. S. Neill adds that rewarding students in this manner is "tantamount to declaring that the activity is not worth doing for its own sake."[20]

## COMING TO GRIPS WITH THESE FINDINGS

Kohn's identification of these problems comes at a time when the use of classroom rewards is at an all-time high. In fact, I would guess that over 90 percent of elementary school classrooms feature some type of extrinsic incentives. Rewarding has become so commonplace that when teachers discuss the issue, their conversations tend to focus on the what, when, and how of rewards rather than the why.

From the time we first begin our teacher training programs, we are led to believe that rewarding students to maintain control of the classroom is the way to go. Often, we are shown no alternative to this method. We learn about the theory of behaviorism and the idea of positive reinforcement in our courses, we work with master teachers who reward their students, and then we begin our first job in a school where our colleagues use rewards. We see no reason to question this approach because the professionals we respect offer incentives to their kids. It's all around us. We begin to reach a comfort level with this practice. After a few years of teaching, we become so comfortable with rewarding students that we cannot imagine managing a classroom without rewards (see Resource C).

Understandably, teachers who have reached this comfort level will find Kohn's work unsettling. Because it calls into question practices they hold so dear, many educators will initially resist or reject his conclusions. The most common response to Kohn's findings from teachers who have enjoyed success with the use of rewards is, "But they work!" I have heard this reply numerous times.

If by "work" they mean that rewards produce temporary obedience in students, then yes, they may work. If, however, they mean that rewards lead to the development and internalization of effective habits, then they do anything but work. Furthermore, bringing about this temporary obedience comes at a cost. It comes at the expense of autonomy, relationships, creativity, interest, meaning, challenge, and other valuable entities that lie at the core of a quality classroom.

Another common response to Kohn's work is, "But rewards motivate people!" There's truth in this statement, although not in the way most people interpret it. Rewards do not motivate individuals in any intrinsic sense. According to Kohn, "They motivate people to work for rewards."[21] They narrow our focus and reduce tasks to mere stepping-stones. Moreover, Deming remarks that when children are rewarded for doing well in school, "they learn to expect rewards for good performance."[22] They, in fact, become addicted to rewards. My first experience with this phenomenon came during my student-teaching. After school one day, I asked one boy if he could stay for a few minutes to help me clean up the room. His response: "What do you give me for it?"

Above all, rewards demonstrate a lack of confidence in our kids and sell them short. By relying on extrinsic incentives to control our students' behavior, it's almost as if we are announcing the following to our classes:

1. We don't think you are willing or able to behave and perform well on your own.

2. We need to use these tricks to manipulate you into doing the things you should be doing anyway.

3. These rewards benefit us, not you, but without them, we just don't think we're going to get very much done in here.

Of course, teachers who administer rewards don't think like that, but that's the subconscious message rewards send.

## A DIFFERENT APPROACH

In light of the considerable research on the effects of rewards, it becomes clear that neither rewarding nor punishing students offers teachers a management approach consistent with quality principles. The choice that so many educators face of whether to emphasize punishments or rewards in their classrooms, we now understand, is not really a choice at all. Both methods are extrinsic. Both seek to control the actions of students based on the promise that if you do this, this will happen to you, and, as a result, present a similar array of problems. Both rest on the assumptions of Theory X put forth by Douglas McGregor, and both exist because they are believed to be necessary to maintain order and effort.

If we step back and look at the bigger picture, we see then that the real choice is not between rewards and punishments, but between Theory X and Theory Y. If we believe in the assumptions of Theory X, our classroom management will center on the issue of control. We will "assume that people have to be tightly supervised if they're going to produce or perform well."[23] As teachers, if we believe our students will not put forth adequate effort on their own, then we will deem it necessary to incorporate rewards and punishments into our management plans. We will find ourselves offering stickers to improve spelling scores, distributing table points in exchange for smooth transitions, and giving marbles to straighten our lines.

However, if we embrace the ideas of Theory Y, then we will not rely on extrinsic motivators due to our belief that all students possess intrinsic motivation and due to our understanding of the dangers that extrinsic incentives present. A belief in Theory Y means that we hold very different assumptions about our kids and will manage them accordingly. Rather than emphasizing control, our paradigm, according to Covey, will be one of "release."[24] Under this paradigm, we assume "that, given the freedom, opportunity, and support, people will bring out the highest and best within them and accomplish great things."[25] We further assume that students can and will put forth substantial effort on their own in the service of objectives to which they are committed.

Teachers and students will only achieve quality in classrooms and schools managed according to Theory Y assumptions. In fact, it is impossible to implement the other seven Essentials for Empowered Teaching and Learning in the type of coercive and controlling environment necessitated by a belief in Theory X. How can you increase the enthusiasm of your students when rewards decrease interest? How can you build strong, trusting relationships among members of your classroom when rewards rupture relationships? How can you foster the development of self-directed, responsible learners when rewards control behavior and thwart the development of responsibility? How can you encourage kids to play with possibilities and follow hunches when rewards discourage risk taking? How can you foster a spirit of group problem solving and continuous improvement when rewards ignore reasons? Why would you spend one minute on training when you could always offer a reward to elicit desired behavior? The problems that rewards present only serve to undermine the worthwhile purposes set forth in a class mission statement.

Intrinsic motivation is the fuel that powers the quality engine. The pursuit of quality requires a tremendous amount of motivation, and the only true motivation comes from inside. "If our goal is quality, or lasting commitment to a value or behavior, no artificial incentive can match the power of intrinsic motivation."[26] Intrinsically motivated people "pursue optimal challenges, display greater innovativeness, and tend to perform better under challenging conditions."[27] Back when I discussed Essential 1, I shared the story of the Enterprise School District and mentioned Superintendent Jenkins' belief that student enthusiasm is the number one asset that any school possesses. I believe intrinsic motivation to be just as important a commodity, worthy of similar attention, emphasis, and protection.

The good news is that we, as teachers, have tremendous influence over our students' level of intrinsic motivation. There are certain practices that nurture it and others that destroy it. Our job is to eliminate the forces that destroy intrinsic motivation (e.g., fear, coercion, competition, blaming, ranking, and failure) and commit ourselves to promoting those that strengthen it. I describe these nurturing forces in the following section.

## NURTURING FORCES OF INTRINSIC MOTIVATION

In this section I describe several forces that nurture intrinsic motivation. In addition to promoting student desire to engage in specific tasks, these forces benefit a classroom more generally. Collectively, they build morale and enthusiasm for learning, enhance self-esteem, deepen the sense of connection individuals feel to the classroom and to one another, and increase student willingness to put forth sustained effort.

- **Purpose**

  The first Essential for Empowered Teaching and Learning, you will recall, involves establishing a sense of purpose with your students. The effort to establish purpose requires a number of steps, including the introduction of an aim, development of a class mission statement, application of the seven life roles, and creation of personal mission statements. Taking these steps helps students find meaning in their work and helps them understand how learning can improve their lives now and in the future. The connection between establishing purpose and intrinsic motivation is a simple one. Students who understand the purposes of their learning are more motivated to learn and more willing to commit themselves to academic pursuits than students who don't.

- **Contribution**

  Students will be more motivated to engage in a task when their work contributes to the well-being of others. One example of this phenomenon is cross-age-tutoring, where older students assist younger ones. I have heard many stories about struggling fifth or sixth grade students whose lives were turned around after having the opportunity to help struggling younger students. I have seen similar increases in motivation when classes stage performances for senior citizens' centers or become involved in environmental causes. Helping others brings out the best in us and offers a win-win situation for everyone involved. Take advantage of these benefits by seeking out opportunities for your kids to put their learning to use in the service of others.

- **Interest**

  Since intrinsic motivation is often defined in terms of the interest that individuals find in a task, it makes sense that to increase the motivation of our students, we should attempt to make tasks as interesting as possible. There's a direct relationship between the two concepts. Recall, from Chapter Five, the three primary ways I help my students find more interest and enjoyment in their academic work: promoting a hands-on approach, providing for as much student choice as possible, and encouraging the kids to determine their preferred learning style.

Interest can also be cultivated in nonacademic tasks, such as the ones included on the list of training routines in Figure 6.1. My students and I are always looking for ways to add interest to tasks that may otherwise be quite mundane. My favorite example deals with how I excuse the kids for recess. When I taught first grade, I excused one table at a time to walk to the yard. "Table A, you may go, Table D, you may go, etc." When I made the switch to third and fourth grade, I tried another approach.

Here's how it works. First, I select a student volunteer to pick a category, such as foods, animals, or sports. Next, I ask the kids to think of their favorite item in that category. Once the students have all done so, I start naming individual items. Students have permission to leave the room as soon as I name their item. My goal is to see if I can name the favorites of every student in the room without any clues from them. I always call the most obvious items first, such as baseball, football, and basketball, if the category is favorite sport. After I name the obvious items, most of the kids leave, but there are always a few remaining. (Oftentimes, the kids stay to watch even after their favorites have been called.) I then proceed to the lesser-known ones to see who else leaves. Inevitably, there are two or three kids left who experience great delight in knowing that I haven't yet called their favorite. The kids take great pride in their ability to stump me. At some point, I surrender and ask them to tell me their favorite. Because the category changes each day, every child has many chances to stump me.

This method of excusing students takes a little more time, but it's time well spent. It gives us the opportunity to bond, to learn more about one another, and to express different aspects of our personalities. It's also fun. Sometimes, depending on the category, it's even educational. Above all, though, it's a way for us to generate interest where none had existed before. Figure 7.2 lists many of the categories I have used with my students.

- **Challenge**

  Human beings will seek out challenging activities. The degree of challenge, however, must be appropriate. We have little desire to engage in tasks that are too simple because they offer no stimulation. We also have little desire to engage in tasks that are too difficult because we wish to avoid the discouragement. Situations of optimal challenge bring out the best in us; they motivate us to the fullest. If you think about the times in your life when your motivation to complete a task was at its highest, it was probably because the task was neither too difficult nor too easy for you, but appropriately challenging. This realization, however, can be daunting for teachers since our job involves providing optimal challenge for each of our students, of whom no two are alike. Because no teacher can hope to know his or her students better than they know themselves, this is yet another reason to allow students to make choices about what and how they learn.

- **Success**

  Closely related to the idea of challenge is that of success. Nothing motivates like success, and nothing demotivates like failure. Finding an optimal degree of challenge for each of our students increases the likelihood that they will be successful. As teachers, we must do everything in our power to find a way for every child to achieve some degree of academic success initially, no matter how far away they may be from mastering year-end standards.

  Initial success keeps intrinsic motivation alive and begins to build confidence. Once students realize their first success, they will develop an appetite for more. The key is getting

**Figure 7.2** Ways to Excuse Students

| Favorite: | National flag | Halloween costume |
|---|---|---|
| Fruit | Polygon | Charity |
| Color | Hockey team | Suggestion for this list |
| Day of the week | Movie | Clothing design |
| Subject | Movie character | Baseball team |
| Food | Action figure | Musical instrument |
| Sport | Myth | Singing group |
| Animal | Phone company | Part of the PDSA cycle |
| Basketball team | Topic to study | Song |
| Cartoon character | Candy | Store on 3rd Street Promenade (local shopping area) |
| Method of transportation | Season | |
| Football team | Eye color | Bone in the body |
| Month | Least favorite food | TV show |
| World capital | Thanksgiving food | TV station |
| Number | Read-a-loud book | Sesame Street |
| Web site | Battery | Character |
| Dog | Basketball shoe | Amusement park |
| Architectural structure | Restaurant | Ice cream flavor |
| Shoe | Market | Pizza topping |
| Baseball player | Zodiac sign | Author |
| Place to go on a pupil free day | Computer | Word in the dictionary |
| | Radio station | Place for a vacation |

that first one. Some of the kids that enter our rooms in September may have never experienced academic success before and may be on the verge of giving up. We can't let this happen. We must keep them in the game. For example, if an incoming fourth grader doesn't read well, then we can't start him with a fourth grade text; he would fail. Instead, we may choose to focus on the sounds of each letter of the alphabet. Let's assume the student knew these sounds. Now, rather than beginning the year experiencing immediate failure, he encounters success. We, by no means, stop at this point or lower standards for him. We simply select a different entry point because we understand that success builds on itself. Of course, a tremendously demanding road still awaits this child, but success is the key to ensuring that he decides to make the trip.

- **Inspiration**

  One of my favorite things about being a teacher is that I can read something in the newspaper or see something on television one day and share it with my kids the next. I'm always on the lookout for stories that I can use to inspire my students. A few years back, America learned about the life of baseball star Sammy Sosa. His rise from extreme poverty in his native Dominican Republic to fame and fortune as a member of the Chicago Cubs reminded us that anything is, indeed, possible with enough hard work, perseverance, and dedication. Students need to hear these stories. Hearing about people all over the world who overcome long odds to realize their dreams, make great lives for themselves, and contribute to society powerfully impacts their own motivation. Children will be better able to appreciate the value of perseverance and other important qualities when they see how others have benefited from them.

Inspiration doesn't have to come only from newspapers and television. It's all around us. There's inspiration in poetry, song lyrics, and the rich family histories students bring to school. Invite your kids to share examples of inspirational stories and writings with their classmates. In addition, encourage them to keep some of this material in their Student Handbooks (see Resource D) so they can look to it when they need a morale boost.

An effective way to incorporate examples of inspiration into your daily routine is to feature a "Quote of the Day." When the students come to the rug to begin our morning circle time, I choose a volunteer to read the quote that's written on the board. Sometimes I write the quote, other times the student leaders do. We take these quotes from a variety of sources; occasionally, we create our own. These quotes relate to, and reinforce, the important ideas we often discuss, such as character, self-discipline, and quality. After our volunteer reads the quote, I first give everyone a few moments to think about it. Next, I ask them to share their thoughts with a partner, and then I call on several students to offer an interpretation of its meaning to the group. We also talk

**Figure 7.3**   Quotes of the Day

---

"What lies before us and what lies behind us are small matters compared to what lies within us."—Henry David Thoreau

"A man who wants to lead the orchestra must turn his back to the crowd."—James Crook

"I am not afraid of storms, for I am learning how to sail my ship."—Louisa May Alcott

"There is no exercise better for the heart than reaching down and lifting people up."—John Andrew Holmes

"Nothing great was ever achieved without enthusiasm, and true enthusiasm comes from giving ourselves to a purpose."—Ralph Waldo Emerson

"We are the music makers. We are the dreamers of dreams."—Willie Wonka

"I get knocked down, but I get up again. You're never going to keep me down."—Taken from the song "Tubthumper" by the group Chumbawamba

"Best vitamin for making friends: B1"—Rudy Benton, PE teacher extraordinaire

"Victories that are easy are cheap. Those only are worth having which come as the result of hard work."—Henry Ward Beecher

"The future belongs to those who believe in the beauty of their dreams."—Eleanor Roosevelt

"We are what we repeatedly do. Excellence, then, is not an act, but a habit."—Aristotle

"7 days without exercise makes one weak."—Rudy Benton

"True enjoyment comes from activity of the mind and exercise of the body. The two are ever united."—Humboldt

"The game is never more important than the people you play it with."—Pat Vickroy, PE teacher extraordinaire about the significance of the quote as well as how we can apply it to our lives. This conversation only takes a few minutes, but it's a valuable exercise because it encourages the kids to think deeply, because there's a high tone to the dialogue that appeals to the best in us, and because it allows us to start our day on a positive note. Figure 7.3 shows several of the quotes that I have used in the past with my students.

- **Cooperation**

The type of classroom environment teachers create strongly affects student motivation and performance. Cooperation is one environmental component that research has "shown to have a positive effect on students' social and psychological well-being, which eventually leads to higher academic achievement."[28] Cooperation nurtures intrinsic motivation because it satisfies our students' need for belonging and because it usually makes activities more enjoyable. Furthermore, when kids work together, they are more likely to be successful at a given task than they would be alone.

- **Trust**

Trust is another vital component of classroom environments that nurture intrinsic motivation. In a low-trust culture, according to Covey, supervision is tight and takes the form of "snoopervising."[29] Managers manipulate behavior with carrots and sticks. Rules and regulations are numerous and cumbersome to prevent loose cannons from wreaking havoc. The emphasis is on control. Initiative is low.

Conversely, in high-trust cultures intrinsic motivation flourishes. People are internally driven by a sense of teamwork and purpose. The emphasis is on release, not control. People's energies are liberated. Workers are "fueled by the fire within,"[30] not by carrots and sticks. They are able to pursue organizational objectives, free from burdensome rules and regulations. Individuals experience joy.

- **Feedback**

Imagine for a moment that you are a student in my class. You have recently published a Writer's Workshop story, and you're waiting for me to assess it and hand it back to you. When I do, you notice that I've scored it to be a 2 on our 4-point Ideas rubric. You decide to continue working on the story to improve your score to a 3, the standard. But before you can begin to improve it, you need to know which specific areas to address. You look all over for my comments, but you don't find any. I have given you no feedback indicating what you did well, where you had difficulty, and how you can bring your work up to the standard. Understandably, you are demotivated because you don't know how to proceed.

On the other hand, imagine that I return your work with extensive comments about each of the story elements and quality writing traits. You now know exactly what you need to address to raise your score. This information guides you. It helps motivate you to put forth the effort required to improve the story. Feedback is motivating. It contributes to success and represents a vital part of building a culture of continuous improvement and quality.

I once heard someone remark, "Man knows everything about his work, except how to improve it. After all, if he knew how to improve it, he would be doing it already." This is where feedback helps us. When we are sincerely trying to improve in a given area but are unsure how to do so, we benefit from the expertise, experience, and wisdom of others. As Covey puts it, "Getting other perspectives will help us improve the quality of our own."[31]

In a quality classroom feedback takes many forms and flows in many directions. Most commonly, feedback flows from teacher to student. This type of feedback allows us to provide helpful information to kids about both their academic work and behavior. We offer our comments in writing and, when we have time, during one-on-one conversations. Feedback can also flow from student to student. As teachers, we facilitate this exchange of feedback among team members by encouraging them to work cooperatively as frequently as possible, such as during Writer's Workshop when it comes time to revise an initial story draft. Promoting student-to-student feedback sends the message that you consider all your kids to be resources, capable of contributing to the betterment of the classroom community.

Finally, feedback flows from student to teacher. I strongly believe that if I expect the kids to listen to my feedback, then I should listen to theirs. I see this partially as an issue of fairness, but more than that, I actively solicit feedback because I know that the class as a whole benefits from the ideas the students offer. The insights they provide are usually quite keen. In addition, kids appreciate teachers who are willing to listen to them. Feedback, then, benefits students not only when they receive it, but also when they have a chance to provide it. Such opportunities improve their morale, give them greater ownership of the classroom, and generally result in a more productive environment.

In February a few years back, for example, we conducted our first set of Student-Led Conferences, a variation of the traditional parent-teacher meetings that I described in Chapter 4. At the time, I was planning a second set for May or June. Although the conferences went very well and the attendance rate was high, I wanted to make the second round better than the first. (Another example of the spirit of continuous improvement.) I had some ideas of how we could improve these meetings, but I wanted feedback from the kids.

I used a simple quality tool called a "Plus/Delta Chart" to collect student feedback. A copy of our chart is shown in Figure 7.4. On the "Plus" side I wrote down everything that the kids liked about how we first conducted the conferences and that they wanted to hold constant for next time. On the "Delta" side I recorded all the ways they thought we could improve our format for the second set. (Delta is a Greek letter used in science to mean "change in.") A Plus/Delta Chart, then, tells us what to preserve and what to modify. I found myself agreeing with the group's recommendations and made a commitment to act on them the next time we conducted Student-Led Conferences.

- **Recognition**

  A recent survey by the Council of Communication Management sought to discover what single factor had the greatest effect on worker motivation. According to author Bob Nelson, it wasn't money. It was recognition. He reports, "While money is important to employees, what tends to motivate them to perform—and to perform at higher levels—is the thoughtful, personal kind of recognition that signifies true appreciation for a job well done."[32]

  The effects of recognition are just as powerful in the classroom as they are in the workplace. Acknowledging team members for noteworthy achievements makes them feel valued, boosts self-esteem, and builds confidence. When recognized, students realize that other people notice their hard work and care about the effort they put forth. They also feel a greater sense of connection to the classroom. As a result, intrinsic motivation thrives.

**Figure 7.4** Plus/Delta Chart for Student-Led Conferences

| + | △ |
|---|---|
| 1. Liked that they had the opportunity to lead the conference without help from the teacher | 1. Should conduct these meetings on more than one day in case any parents are unable to attend |
| 2. Thought the outline was helpful in getting organized for the conference | 2. Should include Web logs as part of the work students show to parents |
| 3. Appreciated the freedom to choose the order in which they presented all the work to their parents | 3. Should use technology even more during the conferences |
| 4. Believed we did a good job of decorating the room for the conferences, including displaying all the science projects throughout the class so that parents could observe them | 4. Should invite other school personnel, with whom the students work, to meet with parents |
| 5. Enjoyed using the computer to show their parents some of the work they had done recently | 5. Teachers should participate in these conferences with their own families |
| 6. Felt that the work they showed thoroughly covered all the major subject areas | |

Because the benefits of recognition are so numerous, it's important for members of a team to acknowledge one another's efforts frequently. Like feedback, recognition should take many forms and flow in all directions. The following list contains several ways, formal and informal, in which teachers and students can offer recognition on a regular basis. Try as many of these options as you can. You will notice an immediate change in your classroom environment.

○ *Statements of Recognition*—Whenever you have a few free moments before the end of a class period, ask your students to point out the special efforts of their classmates. The acknowledgements can focus on academic achievements, the habits of mind or character, or gestures of friendship. Make sure the students mention both whom they are recognizing and why they are recognizing that person. For instance, it's not enough for Alexis to say, "Henry." She would need to make a more specific statement, such as "Henry has really been working hard on his math lately." Also, encourage the kids to acknowledge as many different people as possible. This way, every child experiences the pride that comes from being recognized. If you notice that certain children do not receive recognition from classmates, make it a point to acknowledge them yourself. Every child must feel valued.

○ *"Way to Go" Notes*—These are notes that any team member can give to any other team member for a job well done (see Figure 7.5). "Way to Go" Notes truly bring out the best in kids, both those giving and those receiving the acknowledgements. In fact, a few of my kids enjoy giving these notes more than they do receiving them. I'll never forget the day Sara was so excited to hand out a "Way to Go" Note that she built a wall of books around her desk to hide her blushing face. These papers take almost no time to fill out and to present, but the positive feelings they produce are lasting.

## An Idea From a Teacher:
## Putting Essential 7 Into Practice

Viola Callanen

*Corpus Christi School*
*Pacific Palisades, CA*
*2nd Grade Teacher*

I had an exceptionally competitive class this year, and fostering intrinsic motivation was a challenge. What I learned was that by affording my students opportunities throughout the day to celebrate their own successes, they began to take ownership of their accomplishments. My favorite self-recognition by a student was, "I would like to recognize myself because one of my goals this year is to be a better sportsman on the playground. Today I noticed that I didn't have any complaints about my behavior all week. That makes me feel really happy!"

SOURCE: Viola Callanen and 2nd grade students at Corpus Christi School.

Kids develop very clever ways of delivering these sheets. Some will wait until after school and place a note in the recipient's desk so that he or she will discover it the following morning. Others will have me run interference for them as they transport the notes. For example, Chris once asked me if I could call Tiimo outside for a minute to discuss something so he could hide a "Way to Go " note in Tiimo's backpack. Most kids, however, will just walk over and deliver the notes face to face. Seeing the handshakes and smiles that accompany these exchanges is one of the highlights of my day.

o *Recognition Board*—On a bulletin board or wall area, create a space for every student to display his or her best, favorite, or most satisfying piece of work. Allow the kids to update their displays at any time. Giving this area a name such as "The Quality Wall" or "The Pride Zone" further distinguishes it as a special place.

o *Recognition Day*—A formal event held every few months, Recognition Day is a time to honor the noteworthy efforts of all team members. At the ceremony, each student receives a certificate stating an accomplishment for which he or she is being recognized. Again, these acknowledgements can pertain to academic work, habits of mind or character, or gestures of friendship. Every student is nominated either by a teacher, classmate, parent, or administrator.[33] To add a special feeling to the event, and to accommodate parents and other guests, arrange, if you can, to have Recognition Day in the school auditorium or cafeteria. Students can even give speeches at the outset of the ceremony, act as emcees, and present the certificates to one another. The more student-run the event, the better.

Before closing out discussion of this topic, I want to distinguish between recognitions and rewards. Many consider them to be one in the same. In fact, I vividly recall a course I taught to a group of teachers where I was pointing out the dangers of rewards and suggesting instead the nurturing of intrinsic motivation based on the ideas described in this section. One member of the group, however, drew the conclusion that, because some of the recognition ideas involve notes and certificates, now we are supposed to give students rewards but call them recognitions instead. He saw no clear difference between the two approaches.

**Figure 7.5**    "Way to Go" Note

Way to Go

Presented to

for

From,

My response was that recognitions are qualitatively different from rewards. The critical issue in separating the two is that of control. Rewards are used to control the behavior and effort of students. Recall Kohn's (1993) definition of a reward: "If you do this, you will get that." When children are offered a "goody" for completing a task, their energies are narrowly channeled in that direction. There's a controlling context when something is promised in advance. With recognitions, there's no effort to control students. Recognitions are meant to acknowledge a job well done and to express appreciation. Although recognitions often come in tangible form, they are never promised in advance and are not used to manipulate behavior. There's no "if you do this, you will get that" at work.

Confusion arises when we think of rewards as objects, rather than as situations. A "Way to Go" Note is not, in itself, a reward; it depends on the context in which the note is presented. For example, if I hold up a "Way to Go" Note at the beginning of the day and say, "Kids, I will present one of these sheets to every student who behaves well today," then that would be a reward because it fits Kohn's definition: if the kids behave well, they will get a "Way to Go" Note. However, if I approach a student at the end of the day and say, "Alice, you really did great work today, and I'd like you to have this," then that's a recognition because it's presented after the fact to acknowledge a job well done with no attempt to control behavior.

I don't mean to imply that recognitions have no potential downside. It's certainly possible for a student to receive acknowledgement for a job well done and then to continue behaving this way for the sole purpose of receiving further acknowledgement. Students can become addicted to recognition just as they do to rewards. The answer, however, is not to eliminate recognition. I don't know too many people who would want to work in a classroom where teachers and students didn't acknowledge one another's efforts. You'd need a jacket in that kind of cold atmosphere. Rather, any difficulties associated with recognition should be dealt with honestly and openly through class discussions. Be proactive. By identifying and discussing potential problems before they occur, we greatly decrease the likelihood that they ever will.

## INTRINSIC MOTIVATION: A SUMMARY

The list in Figure 7.6 summarizes the forces that nurture intrinsic motivation. These forces work synergistically to create an environment where quality can flourish. No extrinsic motivators, either alone or in combination, can come close to producing such results. No student has ever been rewarded or punished into excellence. True success comes only when we bring out the very best in our students. And for us to bring the best *out* of our students, we must appeal to the best *in* them. These forces do just that.

**Figure 7.6** Summary of Forces That Nurture Intrinsic Motivation

| | | |
|---|---|---|
| 1. Purpose | 5. Success | 9. Feedback |
| 2. Contribution | 6. Inspiration | 10. Recognition |
| 3. Interest | 7. Cooperation | |
| 4. Challenge | 8. Trust | |

## KEY POINTS FROM ESSENTIAL 7

- Managing by fear robs individuals of pride in workmanship, creates a stressful work environment, eliminates joy, and distracts from the pursuit of quality.
- How people manage employees depends largely on their assumptions of human behavior. Believers in Theory X will rely on a coercive, controlling approach while those advocating Theory Y will choose an approach that encourages workers to exercise self-direction and self-control in the pursuit of meaningful, shared objectives.
- Management systems consistent with Theory X assumptions currently dominate our classrooms. Rewards and punishments are seen as necessary to maintain order.
- Both rewards and punishments feature a variety of negative consequences that significantly undermine many worthwhile classroom goals and purposes.
- A classroom management approach consistent with Theory Y assumptions will yield the highest possible student learning gains. The other seven Essentials are only possible to achieve in an environment that nurtures intrinsic motivation.
- It is our job as educators to eliminate the forces that destroy intrinsic motivation and commit ourselves to promoting those that strengthen it.
- Collectively, the nurturing forces of intrinsic motivation increase student desire to engage in specific tasks, build morale and enthusiasm for learning, enhance self-esteem, deepen the sense of connection individuals feel to the classroom and to one another, and increase student willingness to put forth sustained effort.
- No student has ever been rewarded or punished into excellence. True success comes only when we bring out the very best in our students. And for us to bring the best *out* of our students, we must appeal to the best *in* them. These forces do just that.

## REFLECTION QUESTIONS

- What thoughts and feelings did you have about intrinsic and extrinsic motivation before reading this chapter?
- How, if any, have these views changed as a result of reading this chapter?
- In light of the information presented in this chapter, what changes might you consider making to your classroom management plan?
- Which of these changes might you be able to make right away and which may require a longer period of time to implement?
- How will you use the nurturing forces of intrinsic motivation to realize the greatest possible benefits?

Essential 8

EXERCISING
LEADERSHIP

xercising leadership isn't simply the eighth and final Essential for Empowered Teaching and Learning; it's the Essential that makes the other seven possible. Quality learning cannot occur without strong classroom leadership. If we view the first seven Essentials as individual pieces to the quality puzzle, then leadership is the Essential that gives shape to these pieces and connects them into a comprehensive whole.

## THE BIG PICTURE

The diagram presented in Figure 8.1 provides a "big picture" look at how the various Essentials fit together in a successful classroom. The map you see is an adaptation of one published by the Quality Academy of Florida's Pinellas County School System in August of 1997. It's no coincidence that leadership is at the top of this figure (Oval A). The exercise of leadership both begins the chain of events represented in the diagram and sustains it every step of the way.

Let's examine the leadership role that teachers play in bringing this big picture to life. The chain of events begins with the first important decision that classroom leaders make, determination of the overall aim (Oval B). The aim announces your highest priorities to the larger school community. You will recall that based on the work of Superintendent Jenkins and the Enterprise School District, I selected the aim, "Increasing learning while increasing enthusiasm" for my classroom. It is our responsibility as teacher-leaders to adopt an aim, introduce it to our students, and use it for guidance throughout the year. As Deming puts it, the task of leadership is to determine the aim of the organization and then direct the best efforts of everyone toward its achievement.[1]

The aim drives the creation of our year-end goals (Oval C). You will recall from Chapter 2 my decision to establish four major goals for my students: (1) increasing enthusiasm, (2) learning the content standards, (3) developing habits of mind, and (4) developing habits of character. Each of these goals stems directly from the aim. Translating the aim into measurable goals provides an objective way to assess student progress. As leaders, we must determine both what our primary goals will be and how we will measure progress toward their attainment. Without clear goals, there would be no reliable way of knowing whether students are making progress toward the ideas contained in the aim.

**Figure 8.1**    The Big Picture of Classroom Leadership

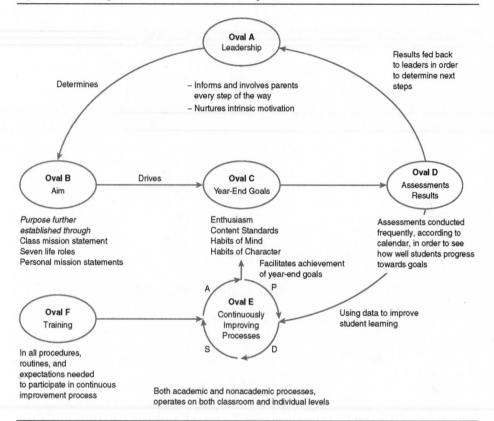

Leaders assess student progress toward each of the goals frequently (Oval D). As I discussed in Chapter 3, quality cannot be inspected into a product after it has been completed; quality must be built into the process from the beginning. For educators, this means that we can't wait until June to find out whether our kids have learned what we expect them to learn. By then, it's too late to do anything with the results. By assessing frequently and collecting relevant data, we give ourselves multiple opportunities to improve classroom instruction so that it addresses areas of identified need (Oval E). The PDSA Cycle plays a prominent role in this process. We, therefore, use the results of one round of assessment to help students perform better during the following round. In our quest for continuous improvement, we also actively solicit feedback from those who know the processes the best, the kids. When students and teachers work cooperatively to improve classroom processes and share freely what we have learned from our experiences, we give ourselves the greatest possible chance of reaching the year-end goals.

Training is featured in the bottom left corner of the diagram (Oval F). Leaders understand the importance of investing the time to train students thoroughly in all classroom routines, expectations, and procedures. Diligent training empowers team members to perform their roles effectively. It enables them to participate fully in the continuous improvement process that's so vital for successful attainment of the year-end goals.

Essential 4 (Involving Parents) and Essential 7 (Nurturing Intrinsic Motivation) are also included in the big picture of classroom leadership. Because of the powerful effect parents have on their children's academic performance, teacher-leaders willingly make the effort to build and maintain an open line of communication between the home and school. We welcome parents as partners, creating meaningful opportunities to involve them in their children's education. At the same time, however, we realize that no matter how involved parents become, their role remains a supporting one. The students themselves must assume primary responsibility for their own learning. We, therefore, strive to develop self-directed, self-motivated learners, capable of charting their own direction. As we carry out this endeavor, we protect the most important assets that children bring with them to school, their enthusiasm for learning and their intrinsic motivation to learn and to grow. As Deming puts it, "One inherits a right to enjoy his work. Good management helps us to nurture and preserve these positive innate attributes of people."[2]

## ROUNDING OUT THE LEADERSHIP SKELETON

The diagram shown in Figure 8.1 provides a view of what I call the "Leadership Skeleton." Just as a human skeleton contains the bones that form the foundation of a healthy body, the Leadership Skeleton shows how the various Essentials fit together to form the foundation of a successful classroom. By itself, however, a human skeleton is not enough to sustain life. It must be rounded out with tissues, organs, and fluids for life to exist. Similarly, the Leadership Skeleton cannot, on its own, produce quality. There are other important aspects of effective classroom leadership that go beyond implementation of the first seven Essentials, responsibilities that round out the Leadership Skeleton and give life to classroom quality. This section focuses on these critical aspects of effective leadership.

### Leading by Example

During my graduate training at UCLA, an instructor once remarked to our class that no matter what subject any of us went on to teach, we would all impact our students most powerfully with the examples that we set. He cautioned us not to lose sight of the fact that although we may teach science or English, more than anything else, we are teaching *ourselves;* we are teaching who and what we are. Years later, when students look back on the time spent in our rooms, they might not remember all the content. They will remember us.

Classroom teachers must pay very careful attention to the example we set for our students. This doesn't mean that we have to be perfect or that we should hold ourselves to some unrealistic standard. It does, however, mean that we make every effort to model for our students the qualities and behaviors that we promote. When leaders walk their talk, they accomplish a great deal more than they do with words alone. For example, in the beginning of every school year, one of my main objectives is to create an environment of trust in my classroom. What is the most effective way for me to do that? Is it to establish a rule that everybody must trust everybody else? No. It is to *be* trustworthy. I must make and keep promises to my students so their trust in me grows. I show them how to play the role of trusted team member by playing it myself. Talking at my students will not achieve the same results. Leaders understand the power of a strong example.

Constantly look for ways to model the principles and attitudes you hold dear. Let your actions do the talking. For instance, to show how much you value physical fitness, change into your tennis shoes occasionally and participate in a class PE activity. Say "please" and "thank you" every chance you get to encourage the development of proper manners. Demonstrate the high priority you place on literacy by bringing in a book during silent reading time and joining in with the group. Share stories about your golf game or some other hobby to show your students how you apply the spirit of continuous improvement to your own life. Kids remember examples.

## Building Credibility

As we make the commitment to lead by example, our students learn that we mean what we say. They take our words seriously because they know that we support these words with actions. We establish among our kids a reputation for integrity. As a result of our efforts, we develop the most valuable asset a classroom leader can have, credibility.

Credibility is an indispensable leadership ingredient. Instead of relying on extrinsic motivators to control students, as teachers in Theory X classrooms must, Theory Y leaders seek to bring out the best in their kids by developing a sense of shared mission and purpose. They preside over the creation of a class mission statement to help all students discover the compelling, deep-burning "Yes!" that guides future action. Furthermore, leaders want team members to invest themselves emotionally in that mission. Consequently, they make every attempt to enlist the heart, mind, and commitment of each child.

---

### An Idea From a Teacher: Putting Essential 8 Into Practice

#### Darlene Fish

*Corinne A. Seeds University Elementary School*

*Los Angeles, CA*

*Primary Demonstration Teacher (7–9-year-olds)*

From the second students walk into the classroom on the first day of school, they are watching. I know they're not only watching what I say, but also watching what I do. It is critical, therefore, that I lead by example. For example, if the water policy is to get drinks before school, at break, at lunch, and after school, the first time a student asks to get a drink during class time, all of the students are watching my response. It doesn't matter how many times I say the words, all it takes is once for the actions to contradict those words, and the students catch on. Before long, everyone starts interrupting class to get water. I have found that while I may seem strict in some students' eyes, they do know that I'm credible and that I mean what I say because I consistently demonstrate follow-through.

---

SOURCE: Darlene Fish, Corinne A. Seeds University Elementary School.

Credibility, then, becomes significant because enlisting from each child a commitment of this magnitude requires it. Students will only commit themselves to the class mission when they believe in the class leader. They will only invest themselves emotionally in actions that a credible leader has convinced them to be important. They will only trust a leader who has earned their trust and only volunteer their hearts and minds when they see that the leader has done so first. Teachers cannot lead without credibility.

In contrast, in a Theory X classroom the leader's credibility takes on less importance because less is demanded from the person in charge. The very presence of extrinsic incentives reassures teachers that no matter what happens, no matter how unruly the class becomes, they can always use these instruments to regain control. Rewards and punishments, not shared mission and purpose, hold the group together. Their consistent use keeps everything functioning smoothly—on the surface.

As teachers, we have a leadership choice to make. We can choose to draw power from our credibility or from our authority. If we choose to have credibility serve as the principal source of our power, then we lead by example. Our students will follow because they believe in us and because they want to go where we want to take them. They are willing to commit to the leader because the leader has committed to them. On the other hand, if we choose to draw power from our authority, the kids will follow either because they are afraid of what will happen to them if they don't (what Covey calls "Coercive Power") or because they have been promised tangible benefits if they do (what he calls "Utility Power").[3] One choice results in loyalty, the other in temporary obedience. Both options are available to teachers. Credibility, though, is the only authentic source of leadership.

## Cultivating a Spirit of "We"

One day after school, I was in the teacher's workroom checking my mailbox before heading home. As I opened the door to leave, one of my first graders came frantically running up to me. "Mr. Reifman," he gasped, "I left my jacket in your classroom. Could you please unlock the door so I can get it?" "Taylor," I replied, "I'm happy to open the door for you, but remember, it's not *my* classroom, it's *our* classroom."

Leaders speak in terms of "we" and "us." We use these words to build a sense of teamwork and to help children understand that we are all in this together. Look back at the 1996–1997 Team 1011 Mission Statement shown in Figure 1.3. It contains the word *we* 14 times. In fact, every sentence begins with it. As a literary work, our statement may suffer from a lack of variety in terms of its word choice and sentence structure. But as the document on which our class was founded, it sets the appropriate tone.

Many of us are lucky enough to have once been part of a special team, perhaps an athletic squad that earned a league championship or an orchestra that worked exceptionally well together. Whatever the activity, belonging to this cohesive group and contributing to a purpose larger than ourselves powerfully affected both our self-esteem and our performance. A classroom should provide students with this same type of positive team experience.

Successful teams are inclusive. They offer a seat at the table to everyone. No matter what interests, personalities, and backgrounds our students bring to the classroom, we find a way to make every child feel like an important part of the group. For example, on Friday afternoons we randomly select a student leader for the following week and set aside a bulletin board to allow that individual to display ribbons, certificates, and photographs of family and friends, treasures that give us a deeper look into that child's life and a deeper appreciation of his or her unique qualities. (See Figure 8.2 for a complete list

**Figure 8.2**   Student Leader Responsibilities

**Student Leader Responsibilities**

- Morning Greeter
- All-Purpose Monitor
- Clean-Up Supervisor
- Daily Schedule Writer
- Quote of the Day Chooser
- Conflict Mediator
- Line Leader

of responsibilities the student leader fulfills each week.) In addition, we make a consistent effort to ask our kids' opinions, recognize their accomplishments, and search for common bonds. We promote team unity however we can, through such gestures as hanging a class picture on the wall, including every student's name on the perimeter of class stationery, or designing a poster expressing the central ideas that establish the group's identity (see Figure 8.3).

A team, however, will develop and grow only as each individual within it develops and grows. Covey makes the point that total quality begins with total *personal* quality.[4] There's no conflict between individual needs and those of the group; one does not have to take precedence over the other. Unfortunately, many see this situation as an either/or proposition: "Either we emphasize the needs of each individual or we emphasize the importance of the group." This is a harmful way of thinking. There is harmony, not tension, between individual and group priorities. The team will only reach its goals and fulfill its potential when the individuals who comprise the team reach their own personal goals.

## Understanding the Classroom as a System

An important part of cultivating a spirit of "we" involves understanding the classroom as a system. Deming defines a system as "a network of interdependent components that work together to try to accomplish . . . (an overall) aim."[5] I share this definition not to dehumanize teachers and students by referring to us as "components," but to make the point that no member of a classroom operates in isolation. On a daily basis we all interact with others, influencing their actions and affecting their performance.

Sometimes the influence is a positive one. Students will share supplies, work cooperatively to solve a difficult math problem, or provide comfort to a sick friend. Occasionally,

**Figure 8.3**    Team 1011 Poster

QualiTy

Enthusiasm

CAring

Intrinsic Motivation


Continuous Improvement

RecOgnition

HIgh Expectations

PrIde

they'll go out of their way to offer assistance to a classmate. This brings to mind an example from my first year of teaching. It occurred early one morning a few weeks into the school year. The children had just entered the room and were working at their desks. As part of my training efforts, I was helping the kids get into the routine of putting their belongings away in the closet and starting on the first activity as soon as possible.

A few minutes after the bell rang I scanned the room to see how everyone was doing. All the kids were hard at work except for one young boy, Kevin. I had seen Kevin earlier that morning, but he wasn't at his desk now. I turned around and noticed that he seemed to be loitering by the front door. Just as I was about to ask him what he was doing over there, I saw Michelle standing behind him, coming through the door. Michelle had cerebral palsy and walked with some difficulty. Kevin had met Michelle at the door to help carry her backpack and lunch box. He took her by the hand, walked her to the closet, and put everything away for her. Nobody asked him to do it; he did it on his own. Kevin helped make Michelle's day (and mine) much brighter. To this day, it remains one of the greatest things I've ever seen in a classroom.

Leaders understand the interdependent nature of learning and encourage the cooperation of everyone. They help students see that they are part of a larger system and that their actions affect others.

An enjoyable way to introduce your kids to the concept of a system is to conduct the Tennis Ball Experiment.[6] For this exercise you will need one can of tennis balls and six volunteers. Have the volunteers remain seated at their desks to begin the activity. Designate one student as the first thrower. That student must throw the ball softly to one of the other volunteers. Emphasize that the throws must be catchable: this is not a time for major league fastballs. After catching the ball, the second volunteer then tosses the ball to a third. The ball continues around the room until it reaches the last of the six volunteers. Once established, the order does not change. Have the volunteers practice throwing the ball in this order until they can do so smoothly.

Then, hand all three tennis balls to the first thrower, and give the empty can to the final person in the order. Begin the process again. This time, the volunteers will use all three balls. After the first ball begins to make its way around the room, the first thrower starts the second ball on its way and then the third. The activity ends when the last volunteer has all three balls safely back in the can. Give the group some time to practice with all three balls.

Once the volunteers are able to move all three balls, in order, from the first person to the last, time the process. After an initial time has been established, challenge the group to cut it in half. Encourage the participants to stand up, rearrange themselves, or try any other ideas that they think will help them achieve this goal. Allow the students who are watching the experiment to share suggestions as well. As long as the kids preserve the same order for all three balls, they can attempt any strategy they wish. Keep encouraging the volunteers to halve their time until you feel they have cut it as much as they can.

If the kids have trouble generating improvement ideas, suggest the following possibilities. The group's time should steadily decrease as it progresses through this list. By the end, the volunteers may very well lower their time to less than a second.

1. Have the participants stand in a line and pass the balls down, one at a time, from the first person to the last.

2. Staying in line, have the kids pass all three balls down at once from the first person to the last.

3. Have the first person hold all three balls steady and have everybody, in order, touch them all.

4. Have the students stand back in their line. Have the first person hold all three balls and walk down the line, making sure to touch them to everybody's hands.

5. Put the balls in the can and pass the can down the line.

6. Have the first person quickly run the can through everybody's hands.

From the Tennis Ball Experiment, students learn, first hand, what makes a system successful. Specifically, they come to appreciate that in a system

1. Everyone works together with a sense of purpose toward a common goal.

2. The group needs the contributions and suggestions of everyone if it is to maximize its potential.

3. Continuous improvement leads to success.

4. Improvement comes from paying careful attention to the process.

5. The actions of one team member impact the performance of the entire group.

A second way to introduce students, especially younger ones, to the idea of a system is to read them the story of *The Old Ladies Who Liked Cats*, by Carol Greene (1991). This picture book is about a group of ladies who live on an island that is protected by a strong navy. The navy stays strong by drinking plenty of fresh milk. Cows give good milk because they eat sweet red clover. The clover grows thick because bees carry pollen from blossom to blossom.

The bees can carry the pollen because there are no mice around to eat their honeycombs. There are no mice around because the old ladies' cats chase them into the forest each night.

All this changes one evening when the mayor trips over one of the cats and hastily makes a law forbidding the ladies to let their cats out at night. The mayor's new law sets off a whole chain of events that results in the navy's being unable to defend the island from invaders. Ultimately, the ladies, who fully understand the principles of systems thinking, convince the mayor to change the law back to the way it was, and the island becomes safe again. This book helps students understand that the components of a system must work together cooperatively for the system, as a whole, to prosper.

Finally, we can look to the animal kingdom for an example of systems thinking. Geese travel through the air by flying in a "V" formation. Doing so enables the flock to cover more distance with less effort. Teamwork makes everyone's job easier. When the goose leading the formation becomes tired, another one willingly takes over. Along the journey everybody has the opportunity to contribute. By performing cooperatively, the entire formation reaches its destination together.

## Removing Barriers

In every class, no matter how well-intentioned team members may be, no matter how deeply they commit themselves to fulfilling their shared mission, conditions will inevitably arise that interfere with the pursuit of quality. Sometimes, these barriers relate to physical features of the classroom system: a wobbly chair, a distracting bulletin board display, a crashed computer. Other times, improvement efforts are thwarted by less tangible factors: an unnecessary rule, a policy with unintended consequences, an ineffective procedure. Leaders pay careful attention to both the tangible and intangible aspects of the overall system to ensure that they facilitate, not stifle, the group's progress.

Barriers to quality aren't always easy to detect. For example, imagine that I'm organizing a class soccer game for PE, and I have to find a way to group the kids into two teams. Without much thought, I decide, like I always do, to select two captains whom I ask to take turns picking players for their squads. Within a few minutes the sides are formed, and the game begins. As the action unfolds, I notice two students across the field who show no interest in participating. As I approach the pair, one of the kids tells me that they both dread PE because they're always the last ones chosen by the captains. The other adds that they're tired of the humiliation that this public selection process brings. Their words convince me that what I thought was a quick, harmless method of selecting teams was, in fact, a serious roadblock, undermining my sincere efforts to increase the enthusiasm of the kids and weakening my attempts to help every child feel valued and appreciated. Although this method of team selection may take less than a minute, the resulting harm is enduring.

When faced with a situation such as this, leaders must change course so that policies and procedures are better aligned with the class aim and mission. Returning to the soccer example, there are a number of other ways we could have formed our teams. I could have divided the kids alphabetically, or I could have put the kids in a line and counted off, numbering each student a "1" or a "2." Had I chosen either of these options, we still would have formed two sides, but we would have avoided the emotional damage. The latter approaches are, thus, more consistent with our larger purposes. Policies and procedures may often appear to be nothing more than a bunch of small details, but details matter.

Removing barriers can be done in a few different ways. First, our own, ongoing reflection and self-analysis of daily classroom life will lead us, unilaterally, to discover and change parts of the system that are inconsistent with our aim. Second, we can involve the kids and periodically brainstorm a list of factors that may be impeding our pursuit of quality. Should issues arise that deserve to be addressed, we can take steps to improve the situation. Finally, removing barriers will occur naturally as part of the PDSA Cycle during the process of creating an improvement plan that responds directly to the ideas that students contributed to the Fishbone Diagram.

## Finding the Time to Communicate

Each school day is so packed with activity that there rarely seems time to stop and talk with our students about all the things that are happening in class. When I coach basketball after school, however, I don't face this problem. Time for me to communicate with my players has been built into the structure of every game. There's a short break between each quarter, a longer one between the first and second half, and several timeouts for me to use at my disposal. These breaks in the action give us the opportunity to discuss strategy, talk over any problems, and reestablish who we are and what we are trying to accomplish together. Successful team play requires constant communication.

The need for ongoing communication is even greater in the classroom than it is on the basketball court. As a coach, I'm responsible for directing the actions of only five players at any given time. As a teacher, I oversee the efforts of two or three dozen people. To keep everyone moving in the right direction, I need regular opportunities to meet with my kids, sometimes as a group, sometimes one-on-one.

The Friday Circle and the Five Minute Chat provide teachers with two effective ways of communicating with students on a consistent basis. The Friday Circle is a weekly class meeting, conducted during the last hour of the school week. During this time the kids sit in a circle so they can all see and hear one another easily. These gatherings are held on Friday afternoons for three reasons. First, concluding the week with a class meeting allows you and your students to review the previous week and look ahead to the next. Second, Friday afternoon is a strategic time for these meetings because the last hour of the day before the weekend is generally when kids have the greatest difficulty focusing on academic work. Third, ending with a team-building activity gives me the opportunity to wrap up the week in a positive fashion and send everyone home happy.

The Friday Circle agenda consists of nine items. Proceeding through every item usually takes between 30 and 45 minutes. When our schedule doesn't allow us this much time, we do what we can. Agenda items follow, along with brief descriptions of each:

1. *Recognitions*–Students are invited to acknowledge the noteworthy efforts of their classmates. These comments help the kids feel appreciated and valued, positively affecting their intrinsic motivation and sense of connection to the group. Recognitions can be shared either orally or in the form of "Way to Go" Notes.

2. *Accomplishments*–This is a time for the kids to share what they accomplished during the week, either in the academic subjects, the habits of mind or character, or even something outside of school. Celebrating their achievements helps children build confidence and makes them feel successful.

3. *Contributions*–Students describe what they did during the week to make the class a better place, such as donate supplies or help clean the room. Such a discussion reinforces the importance of service.

4. *Next week . . .* –In this part of the meeting, the kids express what they hope to accomplish or contribute during the week ahead. Looking to the immediate future in this manner whets their appetite for what's to come and strengthens their commitment and ability to plan ahead.

5. *Learning Connections*–Students discuss something they learned during the week and explain how it relates to their everyday lives or how it may relate to their future lives. For example, Aline may say, "This week I learned about the human body, and that helps me because I want to be a doctor when I grow up." Thinking about these connections reinforces the purposes of classroom learning.

6. *Numbers*–We begin our daily morning routine with a brief team-building activity adapted from Jeanne Gibbs' book *Tribes*.[7] Using a 1–10 scale, each student states a number expressing how he or she is doing that day. A "10" means that life couldn't be better. The student is happy, energetic, and ready for a great day. On the other hand, a "1" means that something serious is wrong. Either the child is sick, upset, or troubled by something outside of school. The kids pick any number between 1 and 10, fractions and decimals included, to share with the group. Students who do not wish to participate have the freedom to pass. Going around the circle takes only a minute or two because the kids are only saying numbers; they aren't revealing the reasons behind their numbers, thus preserving everyone's right to privacy.

   I'm always on the lookout for low numbers so that, as the day unfolds, I can offer these students comfort and cheer to boost their spirits. I encourage the kids to do the same. This activity builds a sense of inclusion and mutual caring; it also strengthens the bonds among team members. In addition, whenever possible, we try to find time at the end of the day to go around the circle again so that we can determine whether there have been any changes from the morning. Building this activity into the Friday Circle agenda ensures that even if there isn't time to compare numbers on any other afternoon during the week, there will always be a chance to do so on Fridays.

7. *Problems*–We openly and honestly discuss any problems we may be having and try to solve them together in a positive way. This part of the meeting enables us to continue the dialogue we began during our training period. We use this time to practice problem-solving strategies and talk about how to prevent similar problems from occurring in the future. The constructive tone that underlies these conversations helps me reinforce the point that the proper response to problems is not anger and blame, but thoughtful action.

8. *Suggestions*–This is an opportunity for team members to suggest any ideas that they believe will improve the performance, appearance, or morale of the class. Every individual has valuable ideas and should have the chance to express them to a teacher who's willing to listen. Implement as many suggestions as possible so the kids realize you take their proposals seriously. As a matter of fact, a few of the ideas found in this book originated from student suggestions. Keep and post a running list of all the suggestions your kids offer so that they take pride in the contributions they are making to the class.

9. *Sharing* (otherwise known as *Show and Tell*)–Another way to build a sense of inclusion, this final segment of the Friday Circle allows students to share objects and possessions from home.

Training your students to lead these meetings allows you to participate as a fellow team member. Begin the year by presiding over the first few Friday Circles; your modeling will help the kids learn the specific requirements of the various agenda items. Then, recruit nine volunteers each week, one per section. (Of course, you may also choose to have the student leader conduct the entire meeting.) Use a chart like the one shown in Figure 8.4 to record the names of the students who will alternate as leaders. Whenever a new part of the meeting begins, the individual designated to lead that agenda item moves to the front of the room. After introducing the new section, the leader calls on everyone who requests a turn to speak. Let the leaders lead. The kids should not be looking to you to keep things moving. Only intervene when you absolutely must. The leaders are responsible for making decisions and keeping order.

The Friday Circle is only one type of class meeting. Its purpose is to ensure that you and your students have a regularly scheduled time to communicate about the items described earlier. Apart from these weekly, nine-part gatherings, you may also choose to call team meetings to address specific topics or issues. You may, for example, want to discuss the results of a recent Enthusiasm Survey, solicit feedback using a Plus/Delta Chart, or take a specific process through the steps of the PDSA Cycle. The Friday Circle is not the time for these endeavors. Class meetings dedicated to a singular topic or issue should be scheduled for other times.

The Five Minute Chat provides another way for you to communicate with your kids on a regular basis. Unlike the Friday Circle, however, which includes the entire class, a Five Minute Chat is a one-on-one conversation. It's important to schedule these talks during independent work time so that you're able to focus your full attention on the matter at hand. We conduct our chats during silent reading. Every team member has the authority to initiate a Five Minute Chat. When I have something to discuss with a student, I call him or her over to my chair. When the kids wish to discuss something with me, they sign up on the board for a Five Minute Chat, with the understanding that I may not be able to meet with them right away. Students, however, don't usually have to wait very long for an appointment. Because I believe one-on-one time with the kids to be so beneficial, I conduct as many chats as I possibly can.

Conduct a Five Minute Chat to discuss the following:

- Students' progress toward their Habits of Character goals
- Strategies to help students learn or behave better
- Factors that increase or decrease student enthusiasm for learning
- Student suggestions for improving the class
- Any material students have difficulty understanding
- Ongoing problems or troubles
- Recurring behavioral issues
- Individual pieces of student work
- Assessment results
- Long-term projects
- Recent successes or accomplishments

For teachers to recognize the intrinsic worth of each individual, we must find the time to talk with each individual. Five Minute Chats enable us to do that. They offer a private setting where students are able to speak freely, without worrying about what their classmates are going to say and think, and where we are able to get to know our kids on a deeper level. These conversations increase our capacity as educators because, as reform leader Ted Sizer puts it, "one cannot teach a student well if one does not know that student well."[7] Trust grows, bonds strengthen, and performance improves as a result of these chats.

**Figure 8.4**   Friday Circle Leadership Chart

| Agenda Item | Leader |
|---|---|
| 1. Recognitions | 1. |
| 2. Accomplishments | 2. |
| 3. Contributions | 3. |
| 4. Next Week . . . | 4. |
| 5. Learning Connections | 5. |
| 6. Numbers | 6. |
| 7. Problems | 7. |
| 8. Suggestions | 8. |
| 9. Sharing | 9. |

## CONCLUSION

There's an old sports adage claiming that a team will gradually take on the personality of its coach. If, for example, the coach remains calm and poised during pressure situations, then, the saying predicts, players will come to do so as well. I believe the same adage applies to teaching, and this belief gives me hope. It tells me that if I take my leadership responsibilities seriously and if I consistently model the habits and attitudes that I hold dear, then sooner or later my students will come to value these priorities as well.

Although I can't force my kids to care about learning, I trust that if I communicate frequently enough with each one of them, set a credible enough example, and paint a compelling enough picture of what their futures will be like should they decide to commit themselves to academic pursuits, then ultimately my students will enthusiastically invest their hearts and minds in the class mission. They will work hard and work together, not out of a desire to avoid punishment or earn rewards, but because they choose to work this way. They will make this choice because they understand the many benefits of learning and because they know that there are places they want to go where only a quality education can take them. Doing everything in our power to prepare students for this journey is the essence of effective leadership.

To an outsider visiting your room for the first time, nothing may appear out of the ordinary. The classroom may look the same as many others, but after implementing the eight Essentials, it won't be. You and your students will have built a quality culture, unique in its intangible features. Well-established purpose, highly developed teamwork, nurtured intrinsic motivation and other foundational concepts can't be seen, but they govern student action and interaction far more effectively than any external-control-based model ever devised. Such an environment, however, is not achieved with shortcuts. As Covey puts it, a "quality culture (is) nourished over time" and is "*always* home-grown."[8] Others can borrow your materials or copy your methods, but they can't copy your culture. It is the "one competitive advantage that cannot be duplicated."[9]

## KEY POINTS FROM ESSENTIAL 8

- Exercising Leadership is the Essential that gives life to the other seven Essentials and brings them together into a cohesive whole.
- Teachers, first and foremost, lead by example and should strive to model the qualities and behaviors we promote to our students. Leading by example enables teachers to develop credibility.
- Cultivating a spirit of "we" means that teachers strive to create inclusive teams, in which every student feels welcomed and valued.
- Teacher-leaders encourage students to adopt a "big picture" outlook to understand that all parts of the system must work together for the classroom, as a whole, to prosper.
- Inevitably, barriers to quality arise in all classrooms. Teacher-leaders work together with students to remove these barriers so that the classroom consistently functions as efficiently and effectively as possible.
- Teachers must find time to communicate with students, both individually and as a group, on a regular basis.

## REFLECTION QUESTIONS

- What are some steps you can take to "walk your talk" to model the qualities and behaviors you promote to your students?
- What are some ways in which you can lead by example to build credibility with your students?
- How will you cultivate a spirit of "we" so that all students feel as though they are welcomed and valued as important members of the class?
- Might there be any policies or procedures that are inconsistent with your larger purposes and that may need to be changed to be better aligned with your classroom aim and mission?
- How will you find time on a regular basis to communicate with your students, both individually and as a group?

# Resource A

## *The Seven Life Roles*

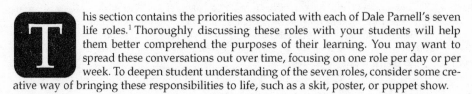his section contains the priorities associated with each of Dale Parnell's seven life roles.[1] Thoroughly discussing these roles with your students will help them better comprehend the purposes of their learning. You may want to spread these conversations out over time, focusing on one role per day or per week. To deepen student understanding of the seven roles, consider some creative way of bringing these responsibilities to life, such as a skit, poster, or puppet show.

**Lifelong Learner**—writing, reading, listening, speaking, arithmetic and math, solving problems, thinking creatively, seeing things in the mind's eye, critical thinking

**Citizen**—understanding responsibilities of a citizen, understanding local and state operations, coping with bureaucracies, understanding basic principles of taxes and the economy, locating community resources, understanding principles in the conservation of natural resources, understanding human diversity

**Consumer**—understanding principles of goods and services; evaluating quantity and quality of goods and services; understanding basic legal documents; computing interest rates and understanding credit; understanding insurance, annuities, savings principles; understanding the basic economic system, understanding business organization

**Producer**—understanding of careers; developing saleable skills; managing money, time, and materials; using information; using computers; acquiring and evaluating data; understanding systems; understanding organizations; using technology

**Individual**—understand and practice physical health principles, understand and practice mental health principles, understand and practice principles for making moral choices, responsibility, self-management, integrity, self-esteem, developing interpersonal and intergroup skills

**Family Member**—understanding social and legal responsibilities for parenting; understanding family planning; understanding the principles for managing family finances; learning to deal with family crisis, i.e., death, divorce, illness, family problems

**Aesthetic/Leisure Participant**—developing an appreciation for the good, true, and beautiful; developing avocational skills; developing creative abilities; understanding the role of recreation; understanding and protecting the natural environment

---

SOURCE: Figure excerpted from Dale Parnell's *Why Do I Have to Learn This?* (1995), CORD Communications. Used with permission.

# *Guiding Approaches*

## MULTIPLE INTELLIGENCES

### Characteristics of the Eight Multiple Intelligences [1]

With each intelligence listed here, you will find characteristics associated with that intelligence, ways that students who exhibit strength or interest in that intelligence learn best, and games and activities that can help develop that intelligence further.

#### *Bodily-Kinesthetic*

- Processes information using bodily sensations
- Likes to touch or be touched when talking
- Uses hand gestures when speaking to convey ideas and emotions
- Likes working with hands on crafts and hobbies, such as clay, finger painting, and papier-mâché
- Touches things to learn more about them
- Thinks of self as well-coordinated
- Prefers to move around rather than sit still
- Learns by doing rather than by watching
- Is good at using hands or body to make or do things
- Spends time exercising, playing sports, or participating in dance, ballet, gymnastics, plays, puppet shows, or other performances

<u>Learns best by</u> Touching, moving, interacting with space, or processing knowledge through bodily sensations

<u>Some games and activities to foster your child's development:</u> Skits, Charades, Mime, Dance, Construction, Sign Language, Sports, Models, Toss Across, Jenga, Twister, Perfection, Pick-Up-Sticks

#### *Linguistic*

- Likes to tell jokes, stories, or tales
- Likes to read
- Listens often to radio or tapes
- Writes easily and enjoys it
- Quotes passages from texts
- Easily memorizes spoken or written information
- Speaks comfortably in public

- Likes crosswords, word games, and playing with language and words
- Possesses advanced vocabulary
- Spends time writing poems, stories, or journal entries

<u>Learns best by</u> Listening, reading, writing, or speaking

<u>Some Games and Activities to foster your child's development:</u> Scrabble, Hang-Man, Up-Words, Password, Balderdash, Boggle, Wheel of Fortune

### Logical-Mathematical

- Computes math problems easily
- Enjoys math and using computers
- Likes strategy games
- Prefers to take objects apart and figure out how they work
- Likes using logic and reason to solve problems
- Easily figures out number and sequence patterns
- Easily solves logic puzzles and brain teasers
- Likes to use data to measure, calculate, and analyze
- Is good at constructing things, pulling them apart, or asking "why?"
- Spends time working with computers, models, or science projects

<u>Learns best by</u> Analyzing, explaining, categorizing, classifying, working with abstract patterns and relationships, and understanding "why?"

<u>Some games and activities to foster your child's development:</u> Othello, Sorry, Trouble, Mastermind, Uno, Parcheesi, Dominoes, Tri-Ominoes

### Spatial

- Visualizes clear pictures
- Thinks in pictures and images
- Is sensitive to color
- Can navigate through unfamiliar areas
- Likes illustrated books
- Easily reads maps and charts
- Enjoys jigsaw puzzles and mazes
- Likes comics, slides, movies, and photographs
- Is good at looking at things, drawing, and using maps
- Spends time drawing, doodling, or painting

<u>Learns best by</u> Visualizing, using the minds eye, making a picture, map, or diagram of an idea

<u>Some games and activities to foster your child's development:</u> Connect Four, Chinese Checkers, Chess, Backgammon, Checkers, Legos, Simon, Pictionary, Jigsaw Puzzles, Memory, Tangrams

### Musical

- Likes to listen to music
- Is sensitive to music and sounds in the environment

- Recognizes off-key recordings
- Can remember melodies
- Remembers television jingles and lyrics of many different songs
- Enjoys singing or humming
- Creates own songs or raps
- Keeps time to music
- Is good at recognizing, remembering, humming, or singing tunes
- Spends time playing an instrument

**Learns best by** Turning things into a song or tuning into rhythm or melody

**Some games and activities to foster your child's development:** Name That Tune, Playing Instruments, Rhythmic Clapping, Singing, Humming, Rapping

### Interpersonal

- Teaches or counsels others
- Prefers team sports
- Prefers to join and/or lead groups, clubs and social activities
- Makes friends easily and has many close friends
- Resolves conflicts among peers
- Enjoys and works well with others
- Is comfortable in a crowd
- Notices and has empathy for the goals, motivation, and intentions of others
- Is good at understanding, knowing, and appreciating people
- Spends time with others

**Learns best by** Working with others (e.g., sharing, comparing, relating, cooperating, interviewing)

**Some games and activities to foster your child's development:** Any cooperative activity that your child enjoys

### Intrapersonal

- Is aware of and analyzes own inner feelings, strengths, and weaknesses
- Enjoys individual hobbies and activities
- Sets personal goals
- Understands own emotions, goals, and intentions
- Keeps private diaries or journals
- Functions well independently and confidently
- Is motivated by independent study
- Is good at doing things by own initiative
- Spends time doing things alone
- Has a strong sense of right and wrong

**Learns best by** Taking time to understand things alone

**Some games and activities to foster your child's development:** Goal Setting, Personal Journals, Visualization (plus any individual activity that your child enjoys)

*Naturalist*

- Likes to know classification of species
- Can hear animal and bird sounds clearly
- Sees detailed or specifics in flora and fauna
- Is happiest outdoors exploring the world
- Likes tending to plants and animals
- Knows the names of trees, plants, birds, and animals
- Enjoys watching videos or television shows with nature themes
- Enjoys camping, canoeing, and hiking
- Is good at grasping the specific details of nature
- Spends time in nature

<u>Learns best by</u> Connecting subject matter to some aspect of nature

<u>Some games and activities to foster your child's development:</u> Observing Life in Nature, Classifying Plants and Animals, Investigating Natural Phenomena, Identifying and Analyzing Patterns in Nature, Nature Walks, Hiking, Camping, Canoeing

## CONSTRUCTIVISM

Taken from Glatthorn (2000), these are the nine basic principles of constructivism:[2]

1. Learning is not a passive receptive process but is instead an active meaning-making process. It is the ability to perform complex cognitive tasks that require the active use and application of knowledge in solving meaningful problems.

2. Thus, learning at its best involves conceptual change—modifying one's previous understandings of concepts so that they are more complex and more valid. Typically, the learner begins with a naive or inaccurate concept; the learning process enables the learner to develop a deeper or truer understanding of the concept.

3. In this sense, learning is always subjective and personal. The learner best learns when (s)he can internalize what is being learned, representing it through learner-generated symbols, metaphors, images, graphics, and models.

4. Learning is also situated or contextualized. Students carry out tasks and solve problems that resemble the nature of those tasks in the real world. Rather than doing "exercises" out of context, the students learn to solve contextualized problems.

5. Learning is social. Learning at its best develops from interaction with others as perceptions are shared, information is exchanged, and problems are solved collaboratively.

6. Learning is affective. Cognition and affect are closely related. The extent and nature of learning are influenced by the following affective elements: self-awareness and beliefs about one's abilities, clarity and strength of learning goals, personal expectations, general states of mind, and motivation to learn.

7. The nature of the learning task is crucial. The best learning tasks are characterized by these features: optimal difficulty in relation to the learner's development, relevancy to the learner's needs, authenticity with respect to the real world, and challenge and novelty for the learner.

8. Learning is strongly influenced by the learner's development. Learners move through identifiable stages of physical, intellectual, emotional, and social growth that affect what can be learned and in what depth of understanding. Learners seem to do best when the learning is at their proximal stage of development, challenging enough to require them to stretch but attainable with effort.

9. Learning at its best involves metacognition, reflecting about one's learning throughout the entire learning process.

SOURCE: *The Principal as Curriculum Leader* (Glatthorn, 2000), Corwin Press.

# DISCIPLINARY UNDERSTANDING[3]

- The disciplines can be seen as different lenses, as different kinds of glasses, as different ways of approaching the world, and as fundamental ways of knowing. For elementary schools, relevant disciplines include science, mathematics, history, and art.
- Disciplines are the ways in which experts construe the phenomena of their world. They serve as entry points for considering the deepest questions about the world.
- Disciplines are ways of thinking that allow us to make sense of the world; they are the most sophisticated means for addressing the questions that preoccupy human beings, the major questions of human life.
- The disciplines offer practiced methods for dealing with issues and questions. The disciplines offer enhanced access to full participation in the world of ideas.
- Disciplines all deal with impressions, observations, facts, theories, and competing explanatory models. Each has its own means, its own moves for making sense of initial data. Among the disciplines, there are fundamental differences in subject matter, rules of evidence, approach, expression, interpretation, aesthetic, and how problems and explanations are framed. For example, how scientists use evidence differs from how historians use evidence.
- According to Howard Gardner, (1) the purpose of education is to master the fundamental ways of knowing, (2) these forms of knowledge must be constructed (they won't arise on their own), and (3) more sophisticated understandings that reflect the contours of each discipline must replace students' initial, and often incorrect, understandings.
- Disciplinary understanding is necessary, according to Howard Gardner, for students to make sense of various claims made about individuals, events, and ideas from the past and present. To gain this understanding, he asserts that students need not memorize technical details. They should understand how those working within a discipline approach questions, and they should gain familiarity with a few evocative examples.

## Characteristics of the Disciplines

### Mathematics

- Mathematics represents a search for truth.
- The simplicity, elegance, and form in which one presents the truth is important.
- Mathematics represents the efforts of human beings to discover and lay out with precision the abstract relationships among idealized quantities and forms in the world.

- Mathematicians crave patterns in numbers and forms.
- Mathematicians seek to demonstrate, preserve, and explain the reasons for these patterns.
- Mathematical truths, once verified, remain true.

## Art

- Artists include musicians, writers, and performers as well as those who are usually considered artists, such as painters and sculptors.
- Artists are inspired by imaginative thoughts and feelings.
- Artists help us discover common properties as well as differentiating features of the various arts.
- Artists constantly move between two worlds, and the realities of these worlds are quite different. The first contains the artist's thoughts, feelings, beliefs, visions, imagination, and experiences. The second contains the artist's media, materials, and techniques. Success requires mastery of both.
- Notions of beauty are not regularly supplanted.

## Science

- Science represents a search for truth, an attempt to explain the regularities of the world.
- Science deals with facts, not opinions.
- Science relies on systematic, impartial, and skeptical thinking.
- Scientists make observations and place them within a systematic framework, the most developed form of which is a theory.
- Scientific theories are falsifiable (i.e., they can be proven wrong).
- "Cycle of Progress": as methods become more refined, and more evidence is gathered, existing theories are replaced by more sophisticated ones that are more firmly supported by the evidence

## History

- Historians begin with an event and create (construct) an account of what happened using primary and secondary sources.
- History involves piecing many pieces of data together into a puzzle. The analysis is messy because key facts are often uncertain, primary and secondary sources are often biased, and information is often conflicting.
- Historians do not merely record data or tell a simple story; they must offer explanations and make interpretations.
- Historians must think their way into a situation to understand why people did what they did and how they interpreted or misinterpreted events.
- Historians must always ask if their discoveries and information are consistent with what they know about the time period.

# Classroom Management Plan

D iscovering the negative effects of extrinsic motivation can be quite unsettling to teachers accustomed to using rewards and punishments to manage students. For many, it is difficult even imagining any other way to preserve order and sustain effort on a daily basis. Removing extrinsic motivators from your repertoire may seem like a devastating loss, tantamount to unilateral disarmament. But this is really a case of addition by subtraction.

Classroom management is not about punishing kids when they misbehave or rewarding them when they obey. It is about the three P's: (1) **preventing** discipline problems from occurring in the first place, (2) **promoting** the development of positive habits, and (3) **providing** opportunities for reflection and improvement. A classroom management plan consistent with the eight Essentials does not rely on rewards or punishments. Instead, effective management is based on successful implementation of the ideas described throughout this book. Such a plan includes the following components, each of which has been discussed in a previous chapter.

*A Strong Sense of Purpose*—Teachers establish purpose with an aim, a class mission statement, the seven life roles, and personal mission statements. Then, throughout the year we connect the purpose of daily lessons to these larger ambitions. When students find meaning in their work and believe that what they are doing is important, they are less likely to disrupt, act out, or cause problems.

*Clear Year-End Goals*—Discipline problems often originate when students have no clear goals to pursue. Ambitious goals provide a sense of direction, helping kids understand exactly what's expected of them by the end of the year. Specific expectations channel student energy in a positive way.

*Student Self-Evaluation of Behavior*—Students hold *themselves* accountable for their behavior by completing the Weekly Evaluation Sheet at the end of each school day. They also set weekly goals, in which they commit to improving their behavior. Reflecting on how well they have behaved, combined with consistent goal-setting, gives students their best chance to affect genuine behavioral change.

*Thorough Training in All Routines, Procedures, and Expectations*—Training students during the first four to six weeks of each new school year in the routines, procedures, and expectations we've established for them is an important priority. Training efforts do require a substantial investment of time and energy, but this investment will pay off, resulting in better use of class time, smoother functioning, fewer problems, and higher-quality learning throughout the year.

*Frequent Communication With Each Child*—Five Minute Chats allow us to develop deep bonds with our kids. As we come to know our students well, we can discuss issues openly and customize our approach to the unique needs of each child. We attempt to arrive at mutually agreeable, long-term solutions to behavioral difficulties. Our interactions with the kids are characterized by a problem-solving orientation, a lens through which troubling situations are viewed as learning opportunities; mistakes, as teachable moments. Working effectively with students who consistently exhibit behavioral problems is one of the most difficult challenges teachers face. It requires time, patience, flexibility, and a sincere desire to help children improve.

*Close Working Relationships With Parents*—Guided by a sense of trust and mutual support, teachers and parents communicate frequently to address any ongoing behavior problems. These efforts also require time, patience, and flexibility.

*High Levels of Intrinsic Motivation*—Nurtured by the forces described in Chapter 7.

*Shared Ownership of What Occurs in the Classroom*—Alienated students who feel like nobody notices or cares about them are prime candidates to cause problems. In a quality classroom, however, feelings of this sort have no chance to develop because we, as teachers, won't let them. We spend a great deal of time recognizing the importance of each student. We treat every child as a co-owner of the classroom whose contributions are recognized and valued. When teachers cultivate a spirit of "we" so that everyone feels a sense of belonging, kids are unlikely to rock the boat.

# Using Student Handbooks

**S**tudent Handbooks are folders or three-ring binders that provide kids with easy access to important quality-related papers. Here is a list of items you may want students to store in their handbooks. The numbers in parentheses refer to the figures where examples of these pieces can be found. Although I have organized the items by Essential, there is no strict order in which handbook papers must be kept.

### Essential 1

Overall Aim

Class Mission Statement (1.3, 1.4)

The Seven Life Roles

Personal Mission Statements

### Essential 2

Quality Work Rubric (2.1)

Habits of Mind Definitions (2.3)

### Essential 4

Portfolio Organization Form (4.7)

Student-Led Conference Outline (4.8)

### Essential 5

Habits of Character Definitions (5.1)

Weekly Evaluation Sheet (5.2)

Habits of Character Progress Sheet (5.3)

Individual Improvement Projects (5.10 and 5.11)

**Essential 6**

List of Training Routines (6.1)

**Essential 7**

"Quotes of the Day" List (7.3)

"Way to Go" Notes (7.5)

Student-selected examples of inspirational stories, writings, and poems

Photographs of class events and other commemorative materials

# Notes

## INTRODUCTION

1. C. S. Kilian, *The World of W. Edwards Deming* (Knoxville, TN: SPC Press, Inc., 1992), 25.
2. C. S. Kilian, *The World of W. Edwards Deming* (Knoxville, TN: SPC Press, Inc., 1992), 10.
3. C. S. Kilian, *The World of W. Edwards Deming* (Knoxville, TN: SPC Press, Inc., 1992), 10.

## ESSENTIAL 1

1. L. Jenkins, *Improving Student Learning: Applying Deming's Quality Principles in Classrooms* (Milwaukee, WI: ASQC Quality Press, 1997), 114.
2. L. Jenkins, *Improving Student Learning: Applying Deming's Quality Principles in Classrooms* (Milwaukee, WI: ASQC Quality Press, 1997), 115.
3. L. Jenkins, *Improving Student Learning: Applying Deming's Quality Principles in Classrooms* (Milwaukee, WI: ASQC Quality Press, 1997), 115.
4. L. Jenkins, *Improving Student Learning: Applying Deming's Quality Principles in Classrooms* (Milwaukee, WI: ASQC Quality Press, 1997), 4.
5. L. Jenkins, *Improving Student Learning: Applying Deming's Quality Principles in Classrooms* (Milwaukee, WI: ASQC Quality Press, 1997), 115.
6. L. Jenkins, *Improving Student Learning: Applying Deming's Quality Principles in Classrooms* (Milwaukee, WI: ASQC Quality Press, 1997), 4.
7. S. Covey, *First Things First* (New York: Fireside, 1994), 79.
8. S. Covey, *First Things First* (New York: Fireside, 1994), 221.
9. S. Covey, *First Things First* (New York: Fireside, 1994), 221.
10. S. Covey, *First Things First* (New York: Fireside, 1994); S. Covey, *The Seven Habits of Highly Effective People* (New York: Fireside, 1989). I created this list of criteria by synthesizing ideas from these two books.
11. S. Covey, *First Things First* (New York: Fireside, 1994), 222.
12. S. Covey, *First Things First* (New York: Fireside, 1994), 219.
13. The name "Team 1011" describes the multi-age class of third and fourth graders that my partner and I taught in Rooms 10 and 11.
14. S. Covey, *First Things First* (New York: Fireside, 1994), 219.
15. S. Covey, *First Things First* (New York: Fireside, 1994), 78.
16. S. Covey, *First Things First* (New York: Fireside, 1994), 103.
17. S. Covey, *First Things First* (New York: Fireside, 1994), 221.
18. D. Parnell, *Why Do I Have to Learn This?* (Waco, TX: CORD Communications, 1995), 2.
19. D. Parnell, *Why Do I Have to Learn This?* (Waco, TX: CORD Communications, 1995), 44.
20. D. Parnell, *Why Do I Have to Learn This?* (Waco, TX: CORD Communications, 1995), 44, 45.
21. This example is adapted from one offered by Newmann, Secada, and Wehlage in *A Guide to Authentic Instruction and Assessment: Vision, Standards, and Scoring* (Wisconsin Center for Educational Research, 1995).

22. G. Wiggins, *Assessing Student Performance* (San Francisco: Jossey-Bass, 1993), 223, 224.
23. There are more than nine events in the Winter Olympics, but I limited the number for the purposes of the project.
24. S. Covey, *First Things First* (New York: Fireside, 1994), 61.
25. S. Covey, *First Things First* (New York: Fireside, 1994), 169.
26. S. Covey, *First Things First* (New York: Fireside, 1994), 103, 104.
27. S. Covey, *First Things First* (New York: Fireside, 1994), 110.
28. S. Covey, *First Things First* (New York: Fireside, 1994), 107–109.

## ESSENTIAL 2

1. W. Glasser, *The Quality School* (New York: Harper & Row, 1990), 59–61.
2. P. Crosby, *Quality Without Tears* (New York: McGraw-Hill, 1984), 60.
3. M. Walton, *The Deming Management Method* (New York: Perigee Books, 1986), 32.
4. T. Sizer, *Horace's Hope* (New York: Houghton Mifflin Company, 1996), 45.
5. Students feel a strong sense of ownership when the class regularly uses ideas that they themselves generate. Thus, it makes sense to have your students create a new list every year. On the other hand, once you find something you like that works well, it makes sense not to want to start from scratch the following year. There are advantages and disadvantages to both approaches. When a list is simply presented to students at the beginning of the year, they may not feel the same sense of ownership. On the other hand, when students are starting from scratch, we run the risk of creating something less effective than what we had the year before. In addition, when students are generating something and we already have an idea of how we would like it to turn out, the tendency exists for teachers to steer students in certain directions and decrease their autonomy. If we decide to let students generate their own habits of character list, we should give them the freedom to do so without our preconceived notions about how it should look in the end.

## ESSENTIAL 3

1. I provide detailed information about a variety of guiding approaches in Resource B.
2. H. Gardner, *The Disciplined Mind* (New York: Penguin Books, 1999).
3. C. A. Tomlinson, *The Differentiated Classroom: Responding to the Needs of All Learners* (Alexandria, VA: Association for Supervision and Curriculum Development, 1999), 11.
4. "Should the need arise" is a phrase I use frequently when discussing differentiated instruction because I believe differentiation should only occur when there is an important reason to do so, such as to provide students with more choices, extra support, or extra challenge. Differentiating for the sake of differentiating should be avoided.
5. On p. 72 of *The Disciplined Mind*, Gardner shares his belief in the possibility of a ninth intelligence, the existential, which refers to the ability of humans to ponder issues of life and death. Because this intelligence doesn't seem to have the same relevance to classroom instruction as do the others, I only refer to the first eight.
6. H. Gardner, *Multiple Intelligences: The Theory in Practice* (Alexandria, VA: Basic Books, 1993).
7. C. Hannaford, *Smart Moves: Why Learning Is Not All in Your Head* (Marshall, NC: Great Ocean Publishers, 1995). For additional information regarding Brain Gym please consult the following: D. E. Wilson, *Minute Moves for the Classroom*, or any of the Brain Gym instructional materials developed by Paul Dennison.

## ESSENTIAL 4

1. "Think Win/Win" is the fourth habit Covey describes in his well-known *The Seven Habits of Highly Effective People* (New York: Fireside, 1989).
2. S. Covey, *The Seven Habits of Highly Effective People* (New York: Fireside, 1989), 188–190.
3. "UVF" stands for Unit Visual Framework and comes from a terrific book by Christine Allen Ewy entitled *Teaching With Visual Frameworks: Focused Learning and Achievement Through Instructional Graphics Co-Created by Students and Teachers* (2003). I have provided more information about this book in the References section.

## ESSENTIAL 5

1. This list of competencies is part of a larger document known as the SCANS Report, produced in 1991 by a national panel assembled by the Secretary of Labor. SCANS stands for the Secretary's Commission on Achieving Necessary Skills. For more information please see *What Work Requires of Schools: A SCANS Report for America 2000* (Washington, DC: U.S. Department of Labor, 1991).
2. S. Covey, *First Things First* (New York: Fireside, 1994), 189.
3. W. Glasser, *The Quality School Teacher* (New York: Harper Perennial, 1993), 106.
4. W. Glasser, *The Quality School Teacher* (New York: Harper Perennial, 1993), 106.
5. B. Cleary and S. Duncan, *Tools and Techniques to Inspire Classroom Learning* (Milwaukee, WI: ASQC Quality Press, 1997), 57.
6. The Pareto Chart shown in Figure 5.4 is not a "textbook" Pareto Chart. For the sake of simplicity, I have omitted the numerical information that most Pareto Charts include.
7. The year I created this Pareto Chart, our school had not yet begun using the Six Traits writing program. Thus, the traits to which I refer on the chart are different from those featured in the Six Traits program.
8. Beyond these three ways to increase enthusiasm, another fact needs to be mentioned at this point. A tight connection exists between how students feel about a subject and how strong they believe themselves to be in that subject. Whenever a student puts a sad face for a given subject, it is usually because that student struggles with that subject. Thus, over the long term, as students improve their skills in a subject and develop more confidence, an increase in enthusiasm for that subject should inevitably occur.
9. I first started focusing on high frequency words with regard to spelling instruction after attending a workshop by spelling expert Rebecca Sitton.
10. If a flowchart doesn't seem to work in your situation, it's perfectly acceptable to define the system in some other clear written or graphic manner.
11. W. E. Deming, *The New Economics for Business, Education, and Government* (Cambridge, MA: MIT Center for Advanced Engineering Study, 1986), 30.

## ESSENTIAL 6

1. M. Walton, *The Deming Management Method* (New York: Perigee Books, 1986), 32.
2. T. Cocheu, *Training and Development Journal* (January 1989).
3. T. Cocheu, *Training and Development Journal* (January 1989).
4. P. Crosby, *Quality Without Tears* (New York: McGraw-Hill, 1984), 61.

## ESSENTIAL 7

1. M. Walton, *The Deming Management Method* (New York: Perigee Books, 1986), 72.
2. M. Walton, *The Deming Management Method* (New York: Perigee Books, 1986), 35.
3. D. McGregor, *The Human Side of Organizations* (New York: McGraw-Hill, 1960), 33–34, 47–48.
4. A. Kohn, *Punished by Rewards* (New York: Houghton Mifflin, 1993), 50.
5. A. Kohn, *Punished by Rewards* (New York: Houghton Mifflin, 1993), 52.
6. A. Kohn, *Punished by Rewards* (New York: Houghton Mifflin, 1993), 55.
7. A. Kohn, *Punished by Rewards* (New York: Houghton Mifflin, 1993), 56.
8. A. Kohn, *Punished by Rewards* (New York: Houghton Mifflin, 1993), 55.
9. A. Kohn, *Punished by Rewards* (New York: Houghton Mifflin, 1993), 56.
10. A. Kohn, *Punished by Rewards* (New York: Houghton Mifflin, 1993), 57.
11. A. Kohn, *Punished by Rewards* (New York: Houghton Mifflin, 1993), 58.
12. A. Kohn, *Punished by Rewards* (New York: Houghton Mifflin, 1993), 60.
13. A. Kohn, *Punished by Rewards* (New York: Houghton Mifflin, 1993), 63.
14. A. Kohn, *Punished by Rewards* (New York: Houghton Mifflin, 1993), 63.
15. A. Kohn, *Punished by Rewards* (New York: Houghton Mifflin, 1993), 63.
16. A. Kohn, *Punished by Rewards* (New York: Houghton Mifflin, 1993), 71.
17. A. Kohn, *Punished by Reward.* (New York: Houghton Mifflin, 1993), 74.
18. A. Kohn, *Punished by Rewards* (New York: Houghton Mifflin, 1993), 78.
19. A. Kohn, *Punished by Rewards* (New York: Houghton Mifflin, 1993), 76.
20. This quote is found in A. Kohn, *Punished by Rewards* (New York: Houghton Mifflin, 1993), 76. Neill, the author of *Summerhill*, was quoted in M. Morgan, "Reward-Induced Decrements and Increments in Intrinsic Motivation," *Review of Educational Research* 54 (1984): 5.
21. A. Kohn, *Punished by Rewards* (New York: Houghton Mifflin, 1993), 67.
22. W. E. Deming, *The New Economics for Business, Education, and Government.* (Cambridge, MA: MIT Center for Advanced Engineering Study, 1986), 110.
23. S. Covey, *First Things First* (New York: Fireside, 1994), 143.
24. S. Covey, *First Things First* (New York: Fireside, 1994), 143.
25. S. Covey, *First Things First* (New York: Fireside, 1994), 143.
26. A. Kohn, *Punished by Rewards* (New York: Houghton Mifflin, 1993), 68.
27. This quote is found in A. Kohn, *Punished by Rewards* (New York: Houghton Mifflin, 1993), 69. Kohn found the quote in R. Koestner, M. Zuckerman, and J. Koestner, "Praise, Involvement, and Intrinsic Motivation," *Journal of Personality and Social Psychology* 53 (1987): 389.
28. H. Gardner, *Multiple Intelligences: The Theory in Practice* (Alexandria, VA: Basic Books, 1993), 244.
29. S. Covey, *First Things First* (New York: Fireside, 1994), 236.
30. S. Covey, *First Things First* (New York: Fireside, 1994), 236.
31. S. Covey, *First Things First* (New York: Fireside, 1994), 247.
32. B. Nelson, *1001 Ways to Reward Employees* (New York: Workman Publishing, 1994), xv.
33. I like to place a box (one resembling a ballot box) in the classroom a few weeks prior to the event so everyone can make their nominations privately. Then, a few days before the event, I read all the nominations and write the accomplishments on the certificates. If there are students who receive more than one nomination, I decide which one to use. If there are students who don't receive any nominations, I make a nomination on their behalf.

## ESSENTIAL 8

1. W. E. Deming, *The New Economics for Business, Education, and Government.* (Cambridge, MA: MIT Center for Advanced Engineering Study, 1986), 52.
2. W. E. Deming, *The New Economics for Business, Education, and Government.* (Cambridge, MA: MIT Center for Advanced Engineering Study, 1986), 108.

3. S. Covey, *Principle-Centered Leadership* (New York: Fireside, 1990), 101–102.
4. S. Covey, *Principle-Centered Leadership* (New York: Fireside, 1990), 265.
5. W. E. Deming, *The New Economics for Business, Education, and Government.* (Cambridge, MA: MIT Center for Advanced Engineering Study, 1986), 50.
6. I learned of the Tennis Ball Experiment from a UCLA Extension course taught by Steve Keleman that offered an introduction to the principles of Total Quality Management.
7. J. Gibbs, Tribes (Sausalito, CA: CenterSource Systems, LLC,1995), 249.
8. T. Sizer, *Horace's Hope* (New York: Houghton Mifflin Company, 1996), xiii.
9. Both quotations in this sentence are taken from S. Covey, *First Things First* (New York: Fireside, 1994), 266.
10. S. Covey, *First Things First* (New York: Fireside, 1994), 265.

# RESOURCE A

1. D. Parnell, *Why Do I Have to Learn This?* (Waco, TX: CORD Communications, 1995), 46.

# RESOURCE B

1. Adapted from "Getting Started with Differentiated Instruction," by Amy O'Keefe and Jill Matthews.
2. A. Glatthorn, *The Principal as Curriculum Leader* (Thousand Oaks, CA: Corwin Press, 2000), 113–114.
3. The items in this section about Disciplinary Understanding are drawn from the work of Howard Gardner's *The Disciplined Mind* (New York: Penguin Books, 1999).

# References

Cleary, B., & Duncan, S. (1997). *Tools and techniques to inspire classroom learning.* Milwaukee, WI: ASQC Quality Press.

Cocheu, T. (1989, January). *Training and Development Journal.*

Covey, S. (1989). *The seven habits of highly effective people.* New York: Fireside.

Covey, S. (1990). *Principle-centered leadership.* New York: Fireside.

Covey, S. (1994). *First things first.* New York: Fireside.

Crosby, P. (1984). *Quality without tears.* New York: McGraw-Hill.

Deming, W. E. (1982). *Out of the crisis.* Cambridge, MA: MIT Center for Advanced Engineering Study.

Deming, W. E. (1986). *The new economics for business, education, and government.* Cambridge, MA: MIT Center for Advanced Engineering Study.

Ewy, C. A. (2003). *Teaching with visual frameworks: Focused learning and achievement through instructional graphics co-created by students and teachers.* Thousand Oaks, CA: Corwin Press.

Gardner, H. (1993). *Multiple intelligences: The theory in practice.* Alexandria, VA: Basic Books.

Gardner, H. (1999). *The disciplined mind.* New York: Penguin Books.

Gibbs, J. (1995). *Tribes: A new way of learning and being together.* Sausalito, CA: Center Source Systems, LLC.

Glasser, W. (1990). *The quality school.* New York: Harper & Row.

Glasser, W. (1993). *The quality school teacher.* New York: Harper Perennial.

Glatthorn, A. (2000). *The principal as curriculum leader.* Thousand Oaks, CA: Corwin Press.

Gonzales, N., Moll, L., & Amanti, C. (Eds.) (2005). *Funds of knowledge: Theorizing practices in households, communities, and classrooms.* Mahwah, NJ: Erlbaum.

Greene, C. (1991). *The old ladies who liked cats.* New York: HarperCollins.

Hannaford, C. (1995). *Smart moves: Why learning is not all in your head.* Marshall, NC: Great Ocean Publishers.

Jenkins, L. (1997). *Improving student learning: Applying Deming's quality principles in classrooms.* Milwaukee, WI: ASQC Quality Press.

Kilian, C. S. (1992). *The world of W. Edwards Deming.* Knoxville, TN: SPC Press, Inc.

Koestner, R., Zuckerman, M., & Koestner, J. (1987) Praise, involvement, and intrinsic motivation. *Journal of Personality and Social Psychology, 53,* 389.

Kohn, A. (1993). *Punished by rewards.* New York: Houghton Mifflin.

McGregor, D. (1960). *The human side of enterprise.* New York: McGraw-Hill.

Morgan, M. (1984). Reward-induced decrements and increments in intrinsic motivation. *Review of Educational Research, 54,* 5.

Nelson, B. (1994). *1001 ways to reward employees.* New York: Workman Publishing.

Newmann, F., Secada, W., & Wehlage, G. (1995). *A guide to authentic instruction and assessment: Vision, standards, and scoring.* Madison: Wisconsin Center for Educational Research.

Parnell, D. (1995). *Why do I have to learn this?* Waco, TX: CORD Communications.

Sizer, T. (1996). *Horace's Hope.* New York: Houghton Mifflin Company.

Tomlinson, C. A. (1999). *The differentiated classroom: Responding to the needs of all learners.* Alexandria, VA: Association for Supervision and Curriculum Development.

U.S. Department of Labor. (1991). *What work requires of schools: A SCANS report for America 2000.* Washington, DC: Author.

Walton, M. (1986). *The Deming management method.* New York: Perigee Books.

Wiggins, G. (1993). *Assessing student performance.* San Francisco: Jossey-Bass.

# INDEX